COMTE DE GABALIS

BY THE

ABBÉ N. DE MONTFAUCON DE VILLARS.

RENDERED OUT OF FRENCH INTO ENGLISH

WITH A

COMMENTARY.

"When a thing is hidden away with so much pains, merely to repeal it is to destroy it."

TERTULLIAN.

This ancient monument of the Mysteries portrays the action of the Solar Flame in and about the God-enlightened man. When governed and directed upward this Flame becomes the instrument which the soul uses to build up its deathless Solar or Spiritual Body.

INVOCATION TO THE FLAME.

I CALL UPON THEE, O LIVING GOD, RADIANT WITH ILLUMINATING FIRE. O UNSEEN PARENT OF THE SUN! POUR FORTH THY LIGHT GIVING POWER AND ENERGISE THY DIVINE SPARK. ENTER INTO THIS FLAME AND LET IT BE AGITATED BY THE BREATHS OF THY HOLY SPIRIT. MANIFEST THY POWER AND OPEN FOR ME THE TEMPLE OF ALMIGHTY GOD WHICH IS WITHIN THIS FIRE! MANIFEST THY LIGHT FOR MY REGENERATION, AND LET THE BREADTH, HEIGHT, FULLNESS AND CROWN OF THE SOLAR RADIANCE APPEAR, AND MAY THE GOD WITHIN SHINE FORTH

WARNING.

This book is for the student who seeks to illuminate his intelligence by the Torch of his own divinity. Let him whose quest is the gratification of a selfish intellectualism beware its pages, for this is a book of hidden mystery and power. Therefore let the mind be pure that it may invite the approach of the Pilgrim Soul and come into a new realisation of God's Omnipotence and Justice.

The Polish Rider, by courtesy of the Berlin Photographic Company, London and New York.

"A nobleman of high rank and a great Cabalist, whose lands lie towards the frontiers of Poland."

PAINTED BY

Rembrandt,

1606 A.D.--1669 A.D.

THE BOOK.

Across the title page of the first edition of Comte de Gabalis, published at Paris in the year 1670, runs the cryptic phrase from Tertullian "Quod tanto impendio absconditur etiam solummodo demonstrare destruere est," [1]suggesting to the mind that there is a concealed mystery. Hungry souls, heeding these words, have sought and found beneath the esprit and sparkle of its pages a clue to that truth which all the world is seeking.

Many readers will recall Sir Edward Lytton's citation of Comte de Gabalis in his strange novel Zanoni, certain portions of which were based upon this source. And others will remember the high esteem in which the wit and wisdom of the Abbé de Villars' masterpiece were held by litterateurs, as well as occultists, in the early years of the 18th century. Alexander Pope, in his dedication to the Rape of the Lock, the first draft of which was written in 1711, says "The Rosicrucians are a people I must bring you acquainted with. The best account I know of them is in a French book call'd *Le Comte de Gabalis*, which both in its title and size is so like a Novel, that many of the Fair Sex have read it for one by mistake. According to these Gentlemen, the four Elements are inhabited by Spirits, which they call Sylphs, Gnomes, Nymphs, and Salamanders. The Gnomes or Demons of Earth delight in mischief; but the Sylphs, whose habitation is in the Air, are the best-condition'd

---

[1] When a thing is hidden away with so much pains merely to reveal it is to destroy it

11

Creatures imaginable. For they say, any mortals may enjoy the most intimate familiarities with these gentle Spirits, upon a condition very easy to all true Adepts, an inviolate preservation of Chastity."

Alexander Pope's poem bears the same relation to its inspiration Comte de Gabalis, that a dancing mote does to the sunbeam whose brilliance it reflects. For the reader of to-day this light shines, as it were, through a window fashioned in an alien age, and mullioned with a frankness of speech almost unknown in this century of conventional circumlocutions. To throw a stone at the window were ungrateful. Rather let the reader view these Discourses with sympathetic understanding of the thought of the period in which they were written. Let him regard not their letter but their word, and so justify our belief that years are past in which to point out spiritual worth wherever found is to compass its destruction, and that the day has come when we should seek to unlock the treasure of this ancient volume with a key fashioned from the Philosopher's Stone.

ABBÉ N. DE MONTFAUCON DE VILLARS.

Before the Abbé de Villars met the Comte, he had been prepared for a work which has insured him the gratitude and reverence of those seekers for truth who have followed in his footsteps. May we, to-day, be as humble servants of that great ideal to which he dedicated himself, and which he set forth in a life of action and noble endurance. N. de Montfaucon de Villars was born in the diocese of Alet, near Toulouse, in the year 1635. He was a member of the very ancient family of the Canillac-Villars, being a grandson of Jean François de Montfaucon de Roquetaillade Canillac-Villars, and a nephew of the celebrated and learned Benedictine father, Bernard de Montfaucon of Saint Maur.

Having taken orders, he came to Paris in the year 1667 with the intention of advancing himself through preaching, and fired with that enthusiasm which the country brings to the city, hoped for a brilliant career. The Abbé's wit, eloquence, and quiet demeanour charmed all with whom he was brought into contact, and he soon gained many illustrious friends, entré into the most exclusive circles, won the esteem of Madame de Sévigné, and became the centre of a *coterie* of *beaux esprits* who were in the habit of meeting at the Porte Richelieu. He awakened a desire for truth in the jaded though brilliant minds of that effete period, and sought to turn them from their chief consideration, the degradation of the times, by pointing out the possibility of regeneration, doing much to elevate the thoughts of all who came under the sway of his gentle and persuasive influence.

The Abbé de Villars was an earnest worker for the cause of liberty and religious tolerance, and the author of several books and pamphlets, some of which remain to be discovered. One of these, on the origin of species, inspired Jean-Baptiste Lamarck, whose writings stimulated Darwin in his quest, and who was the real father of the modern doctrine of biological evolution. Few of the works to-day attributed to the Abbé were written by him. They are forgeries contrived, as are the sequels and interpolations in the later editions of Comte de Gabalis itself, by those who feared and sought to nullify the profound influence which this book exercised over the minds and imaginations of its readers. For there were those who regarded the truth which it embodies as unorthodox and harmful to the temporal authority of the church.

To a politico-religious source may therefore be ascribed the ingenious fiction that Comte de Gabalis is a direct translation of an Italian book La Chiave del Gabinetto, by Gioseppe Borri, published in 1681, eleven years after the appearance of the first edition of these Discourses. Thoughtful comparison of La Chiave del Gabinetto, with the contemporary French and English editions of Comte de Gabalis reveals the fact that the Italian book is but a faulty translation and expansion of the former, masquerading under the guise of letters dated from Copenhagen in 1666, which imaginary date was employed to lend colour to its pretension to priority, and to cast discredit upon the Abbé's book.

The pleasure loving spirit of this brilliant preacher was latterly beclouded by the loss of his friends, consequent upon the persecutions of the church which forbade him the pulpit and forced him to withdraw his publications. The Abbé de Villars is supposed to have been assassinated while on a journey to Lyons in the year 1673. Like many of his Craft, however, his true place of burial is unknown. "Perhaps he only pretended to die, as is the way of Philosophers who feign death in one place only to transplant themselves to another." May the soul of this great disciple of a great Master be now in the presence of God.

CONTENTS

DISCOURSE II.

THE PEOPLE OF THE ELEMENTS.

COMMENTARY.
Pass the entire night in Prayer.
Excursion.
I Worship Thee, O Mighty God.
Chastity.
Philosophic Balance.
When your Eyes have been Strengthened.
The People of the Elements.
Alliance.
Cause of the Evolution of Consciousness.
Wisdom of the Serpent.
Circumlocutions.
The Universal Fire or Solar Force.
Globe of Crystal.
Exalt the Element of Fire.
Compressed Air, Water, or Earth.
Philosophic Procedures.
Seats and Religions, their Cause.
The Second Death.
The Philosophy of Nutrition.
To Prepare the Earth.
Hermes, Messenger of the Gods.

EVOLUTION OF THE DIVINE PRINCIPLE IN MAN.

DISCOURSE III.

THE ORACLES.

COMMENTARY.
Ancient Religion of his Fathers
the Philosophers.
The Gardens of Ruel and the
Cardinal.
Muhammedan Embassy.
Engastrimyths.
Maidens of Gaul.
Master of Israel.
Divine Names.
Agla.
Sacred Books of the Sibyls.
Maxim of the Poet of the
Synagogue.
The Principle of All Things.
The Delphic Oracle's Prophecy
regarding Christ.   MAN'S PLACE IN NATURE.
Aristotle on Exhalation.
Cicero on Exhalation.
Plutarch on Exhalation.
Gradations of His Spiritual
Creatures.
The Generation of Animals
(cited)
Ethics (cited)
Aristotle.
Plutarch an Initiate.
Priestesses of Apollo.
Plutarch on the Oracles.
Micah.
Michal and David.
Rachel, Jacob and Laban.
Teraphim.
Dual Aspect of Solar Force.
Interior Stars.
Angel of the Grand Council.

18

DISCOURSE IV.

CHILDREN OF THE PHILOSOPHERS

COMMENTARY.
Satan Cabalistically Defined.
Plato on the People of the Elements.
St. Antony.
St. Antony and the Elementary Being.
Temptation of St. Antony.
Divorce.
Allegory of Eve and the Serpent.
Mighty and Famous Men.
Marriages of the Gods.
Numa.
Jabamiah.
The Greek Myth.
Oromasis.
Alexander the Great.
Greatest of the Sylphs.
Plato a Son of the Sun.
Melchizedek and Shem.
The Man who Thinks, Wills to know.
Birth of Apollonius of Tyana.
St. Jerome on Apollonius of Tyana.
Justin Martyr on Apollonius of Tyana.
Merlin.
Melusina a Nymph.
Children of the Philosophers.
Ancient Persian Monument.

CHILDREN OF THE SUN.

DISCOURSE V.

CHARITY OF THE PHILOSOPHERS

COMMENTARY.
Sanhedrin of the New Law.
Geomancy.
St. Benedict and the Salamander
The Holy Kings.
Prayer.
Nehmahmihah.
Soul.
Prince of the World.
Non-Existence.
Enchanted Isles.
Hymn to Sabazius.
Storm Wizards.
The Four Ambassadors of the Sylphs.
Marriage in the Reign of Wisdom.
For Man even in this Life can, and is created to enjoy God.
Another Volume.

THE LIFE OF THE TRUE LIGHT IS RADIATION.

COMMENTARY CONTINUED. DISCOURSE I.

Map of the Horoscope.
Harmony of the World.
Numbers of Pythagoras.
Jerome Cardan.
The Sylphs of Cardan.
Averroes.

DISCOURSE II.

St. Paul an Initiate.
Plato, His Place as a Philosopher.
Plato meets his Master Socrates.
Benvenuto Cellini sees a Salamander.
Book of Enoch.
The History of the Watchmen.
The Egg and Serpent Symbol.
Those Reserved for Greater Things.
Moses meets his Master Melchizedek.
Panic Terrors, Origin of Term.
The Great Pan is Dead.
Jansenists.
Jean Bodin.
Moses and Elias fasted Forty Days.
Bacchus and Osiris the Same.

COMMENTARY CONTINUED. DISCOURSE III.

Muhammed, Prophet of God and Bringer of Light to Islam.
King Saul.
Pausanias on the Oracle of Dodona.
Divine Power of Letters.
Celius Rhodiginus and his Oracle.
Sambethe, Daughter of Noah.
Justin Martyr's Statement.
Justin Martyr meets a Master.
Temple of Hercules in Armenia.
Plato on Man's Place in Nature.
Sir Thomas Browne on Man's Place in Nature.
That Roman in Asia was Curtius Rufus.
King Rodriguez' Warning.
The Inmates of the Cave or the Story of the Seven Sleepers.
Sleep.

DISCOURSE IV.

Behemoth and Leviathan.
The Holy Language described by Emmanuel Swedenborg.
Samson.
Moses an Initiate.
The Brazen Serpent.
Book of the Wars of the Lord.
Sacred Fire.
Noah, Vesta, and Egeria.
Prince de Mirande and the Cabala.

COMMENTARY CONTINUED. DISCOURSE IV.

Japhet.
Zoroaster.
Nymph of Stauffenberg.
Magdalen of the Cross.
Cassiodorus Renius.
Gertrude, Nun of the Monastery of Nazareth.
Romulus. Servius Tullius.
Hercules.
Master Defined.
Roman Worship of a Supreme Deity without Image or Statue.
Recent Tidings of the Elementary Peoples?
Tyresias.
Merlin's Prophecy of the Conquest of the Air and of Aerial and Submarine Warfare.
The Birth of Jesus as related in the Koran.

DISCOURSE V.

Cherubim.
Proclus on Prayer.
Lord of Bavaria.
The Sabbat.
Zedekias.
Capitularies, Karoli Magni et Ludovici Pii Christioniss:--
Capitula.
Magicians sent by Grimaldus, Duke of Beneventum.
Agobard, Bishop of Lyons.

COMMENTARY CONCLUDED.

SEVEN ANCIENT PROPHECIES OF WORLD PEACE.
The Magi's Prophecy of World Peace and a Universal Language.
The Sibylline Prophecy of World Peace and the Reign of Justice.
Enoch's Prophecy of World Peace and the Giving Forth of Books.
Micah's Prophecy of World Peace and Freedom of Religion.
Elder Edda Prophecy of World Peace and Return of the Ancient Wisdom.
Bible Prophecy of World Peace declaring the Manner of its Accomplishment.
Merlin's Prophecy of World Peace and Enlightenment.
TRUTH.
Muhammed's Prophecy of Truth.
JUSTICE.
Israels' Prophecy of Justice.
THE MESSENGER.
Ancient Prophecy of the Messenger and of the Stone that shall be set up in Egypt.
"My Port Paternal in the Courts of Light."

THE COMTE DE GABALIS

DISCOURSE I

AY the soul of the Comte de GABALIS[2] be now in the presence of God, for they have just written me that he has died of apoplexy. The Amateurs will not fail to say that this manner of death usually befalls those who deal incautiously with the secrets of the Sages, and that since the Blessed Raymond Lully[3] so decreed in his

---

[2] COMTE DE GABAIS.--Paracelsus says of the practice of Philosophy, "this Art is taught by Gabalis (the spiritual perception of man)." These words inspired the title Comte de Gabalis which veils the identity of a great Teacher from whom the instruction embodied in these Discourses was received. The Comte's true name will be widely recognised.

[3] 1235, A.D.--RAYMOND LULLY--1315, A.D.--Spanish Initiate and alchemist, known during his life time as the "Illuminated One." His greatest work, "Ars Magna," was written to prove that the doctrines of Christianity are truths which have been demonstrated and are capable of scientific, though supersensible, demonstration. He was the first to place the chemistry of his day upon a sound basis, and

testament, an avenging angel has never failed promptly to wring the necks of all who have indiscreetly revealed the Philosophic Mysteries.

But let them not condemn this learned man thus hastily, without having received an explanation of his conduct. He revealed all to me, it is true, but he did so only with the utmost cabalistic circumspection. It is necessary to pay his memory the tribute of stating that he was a great zealot for the Religion of his Fathers the Philosophers, and that he would rather have gone through fire than have profaned its sanctity by taking into his confidence any unworthy prince, or ambitious or immoral man, three types of persons excommunicated for all time by the Sages. Happily I am not a prince, I have but little ambition, and you will presently see that I have even a trifle more chastity than is requisite for a Philosopher.

He found me to be of a tractable, inquiring, and fearless disposition. A dash of melancholy is

introduced into Western Europe the use of chemical symbols, which he had learned from an arabian Adept subsequent to his Initiation into the Mysteries in Arabia. His system, consisting of an arrangement of hieroglyphs, is in use to-day. Raymond Lully is said to have been the first christian student of the Cabala.

HIS TESTAMENT.--"Nevertheless, declaring these truths to you, as I do, upon behalf of the Supreme Architect of the Universe, I warn you to guard them, when imparted, with all possible secrecy; lest you squander this treasure upon the unworthy and God require an accounting from you."-- TRANSLATED FROM. RAYMOND LULLY'S "TESTAMENTUM NOVISSIMUM." BOOK I.

lacking in me, else I would make all, who are inclined to blame the Comte de GABALIS for having concealed nothing from me, confess that I was a not unfit subject for the Occult Sciences. One cannot make great progress in them, it is true, without melancholy; but the little that I possess in no wise disheartened him. You have, he told me a hundred times, Saturn in an angle, in his own house, and retrograde; some day you cannot. fail to be as melancholy as a Sage ought to be; for the wisest of all men, as we learn in the Cabala[4], had like you Jupiter in the Ascendant, nevertheless so powerful was the influence of his Saturn, though far weaker than yours, that one cannot find proof of his having laughed a single time in all his life.

The Amateurs must, therefore, find fault with my Saturn and not with the Comte de GABALIS, if I prefer to divulge their secrets rather than to practise them. If the stars do not do their duty the Comte is not to blame for it; and if I have not sufficient greatness of soul to strive to become the Master of Nature, overthrow the Elements, hold communion with Supreme Intelligences, command

---

[4] THE CABALA.--Sacred book of the Jews, is an occult interpretation or key to their Scriptures, and contains explicit revelation of the art of communing with spirits. Tradition states that it has been transmitted from Adam and Abraham by a continuous chain of Initiates to the spiritual heads of the Hebrew race to-day. The Cabala can be read in seven different ways. Its inner mystery has never be written, but is imparted orally by hierophant to disciple. In its original form the system of esoteric Masonry was identical with that of the Cabala.

demons, become the father of giants, create new worlds, speak with God upon His formidable Throne, and compel the Cherubim who guards the gate of terrestial Paradise to let me stroll now and then in its alleys, it is I, and I alone, who am to blame or to be pitied. One must not, on this account, insult the memory of that rare man by saying that he met his death because he taught me all these things. Since the fortunes of war are uncertain, is it not possible that the Comte may have been overcome in an encounter with some unruly hobgoblin? Peradventure while talking with God upon His flaming Throne, he could not keep his glance from straying to His face, now it is written that man may not behold God and live[5]. Perhaps he merely pretended to die, as is the way of Philosophers, who feign death[6] in one place, only

---

[5] IT IS WRITTEN THAT MAN MAY NOT BEHOLD GOD AND LIVE.--And Moses said, I beseech thee, shew me Thy glory. And He said, "Thou canst not see my face; for there shall no man see me and live."--EXODUS xxxiii., 18, 20.

[6] PRETENDED DEATH.--When a Philosopher has passed a certain number of years in service for the uplift-ment of humanity, having fulfilled the purpose of his soul upon incarnation, he earns the right to retire from the world and to enjoy the freedom demanded for his own spiritual evolution. In the Order of the Philosophers are enrolled the names of many Brothers who have feigned death in one place or who have mysteriously disappeared, only to transplant themselves to another. The burial place of Francis St. Alban has never been divulged by those who know. Lord Bacon's death at the age of 65 is said to have occurred in the year 1626. It is significant that a rare print of John Valentine Andrea, author of certain mystical tracts of of profound influence in Germany, appears to be a portrait of Lord Bacon at 80 years of age and bears a helmet, four roses, and the St. Andrew's cross, the arms of St. Alban's town.(See Frontispiece Volume 1. 'A

to transplant themselves to another. Be that as it may, I cannot believe that the manner in which he entrusted his treasures to me merits punishment. This is what took place.

As common sense has always made me suspect the existence of much claptrap in all the so-called Occult Sciences, I have never been tempted to waste time in perusing books which treat of them nevertheless it does not seem quite rational to condemn, without knowing why, all those who are addicted to these Sciences, persons often perfectly sane otherwise, and for the most part scholars, distinguished at the law and in society. Hence to avoid being unjust, and in order not to fatigue myself with tedious reading, I determined to

---

Catalog ue Raisonné,' F. L. Gardner.) Within the past hundred years a notable feigned death has been that of Marshall Ney, a Brother and 'the bravest of the brave,' (HISTORIC DOUBTS AS TO THE EXECUTION OF MARSHALL NEY. By J. A. WESTON. Published New York, Thomas Whittaker, 1895.) who lived for many years after his supposed execution in France as a respected citizen of Rowan County, North Carolina. Another Brother, 'the friend of humanity,' Count Cagliostro, supposedly died in prison only to pass the remainder of his life in the East.
In the higher degrees of the Order, a Philosopher has power to abandon one physical body no longer suited to his purpose, and to occupy another previously prepared for his use. This transition is called an Avesa, and accounts for the fact that many Masters known to history seemingly never die. The Comte de Gabalis is himself a noteworthy example of this temporal immortality. "To every thing there is a season, and a time to every purpose under the heaven: A time to be born, and a time to die; a time to plant, and a time to pluck up that which is planted." Eccle. III., v., 1, 2. These times and seasons are known to the true Philosopher.

pretend to all whom I could learn were interested in Occultism, that I was infatuated with it.

From the outset I had greater success than I had even dared hope. Since all these gentlemen, however mysterious and reserved they may pride themselves upon being, ask nothing better than to parade their theories and the new discoveries they pretend to have made in Nature, it was not long before I became the confidant of the most important among them, and I had always some one or another of them in my study, which I had purposely furnished forth with the works of their most fantastic authors. Without exception there was no foreign scholar upon whom I did not have an opinion, in short, as regards the Science in question, I soon found myself a personage of importance. I had as companions, princes, men of lofty rank, lawyers, beautiful ladies, (and ugly ones as well), doctors, prelates, monks, nuns, in fact people from every walk in life. Some were seeking Angels, others the Devil, some their guardian spirit, others evil spirits, some a panacea for every ill, others knowledge of the stars, some the secrets of Divinity, and almost all the Philosopher's Stone. [7]

---

[7] THE PHILOSOPHER'S STONE IS a term used by Cabalists to denote the Supreme Wisdom, the union of the divine consciousness or omniscient Solar Principle in man with the lower consciousness or personality, which union has been the goal of .Initiates in all ages. Exoterically the Philosopher's Stone is the secret of the transmutation of the baser metals into gold.

They were to a man agreed that these mighty secrets, and especially the Philosopher's Stone, are hard to find and that few people possess them, but all entertained a sufficiently good opinion of themselves to fancy that they were of the number of the Elect.

Happily, the most advanced were at that time expecting with impatience the arrival of a German, a nobleman of high rank and a great Cabalist, whose lands lie toward the frontiers of Poland. He had written to the Children of the Philosophers at Paris, promising to pay them a visit when passing through France on his way to England. I was commissioned to answer this great man's letter. I sent him the map of my horoscope that he might judge whether I[8] should aspire to the Supreme Wisdom. Fortunately my map and letter caused him to do me the honour of replying that I should be one of the first persons whom he would see in Paris, and that Heaven willing, it would not be his fault if I did not enter the Society of the Sages.

To my joy, I kept up a regular correspondence with the illustrious German. From time to time, I propounded to him weighty, and so far as in me lay, well reasoned problems concerning the Harmony of the World[9], the Numbers of Pythagoras[10], the

---

[8] MAP OF THE HOROSCOPE, see Note A Commentary Continued. Many notes relevant to the Discourses but non-essential to an understanding of their meaning have been placed at the end of the book.
[9] HARMONY OF THE WORLD. Note B Commentary Continued.

Visions of St. John [11] and the first Chapter of Genesis[12]. The profundity of these subjects enraptured him, he wrote me unheard of wonders, and I soon recognised that I was dealing with a man of very vigorous and very vast imagination. I have three or four score of his letters written in so extraordinary a style that I could never bring myself to read anything else the moment I was alone in my study.

One day as I was marvelling at one of the most sublime of these letters, a very good looking man came in and bowing gravely to me, said in French but with a foreign accent, "Adore, oh my Son, adore the very good and the very great God of the Sages, and never allow yourself to become puffed up with

----

[10] NUMBERS OF PYTHAGORAS. Note C Commentary Continued.

[11] VISIONS OF ST. JOHN.--"Now, in plain words, what does this very occult book, the Apocalypse, contain? It gives the esoteric interpretation of the Christosmyth; it tells what 'Iêsous the Christos' really is; it explains the nature of 'the old serpent, who is the Devil and Satan; ' it repudiates the profane conception of an anthropomorphic God; and with sublime imagery it points out the true and only path to Life Eternal. It gives the key to that divine Gnôsis which is the same in all ages, and superior to all faiths and philosophies-- that secret science which is in reality secret only because it is hidden and locked in the inner nature of every man, however ignorant and humble, and none but himself can turn the key."--JAMES M. PRYSE. "THE APOCALYPSE UNSEALED."

[12] FIRST CHAPTER OF GENESIS.--"When I find learned men believing Genesis literally, which the ancients with all their failings had too much sense to receive except allegorically, I am tempted to doubt the reality of the improvement of the human mind."-GODFREY HIGGINS.

pride because He sends one of the Children of Wisdom to initiate you into their Order[13], and to make you a sharer in the wonders of His Omnipotence."

The novelty of the salutation startled me, and for the first time in my life, I began to question whether people may not sometimes see apparitions; nevertheless, collecting myself as best I could, and looking at him as politely as my slight fear permitted, I said, "Who ever you may be whose

---

[13] ORDER OF THE PHILOSOPHERS.--Deep down in the human soul is implanted that divine instinct which reveals to man his oneness with God and his fellows. And any wilful segregation of a soul, or group of souls, for the purpose of syndicating God's benefits to His children, is rightly esteemed unnatural, and is sooner or later disintegrated either by force, opinion, or the trend of human evolution which is in accord with the divine Law of Nature willing obedience from all things. The Order of the Philosophers, if not in accord with this Law, could not have endured through every age of which records exist. This organisation is is composed of those souls who have reached the crest of evolution on this planet, and who have passed beyond intellectualism into spiritual realisation. The aim of all souls who have attained to this level of consciousness is an entirely disinterested one--the stimulation of human evolution and the benefit of mankind. They have renounced self (the personality.) Renunciation is the word of power compelling admission to this Brotherhood of the Servants of God, and inevitably bringing association with its members through the attainment of that consciousness which transcends the barriers of time and space. There are no oaths, no vows of secrecy, and nothing is required of a member which is contrary to the dictates of his own soul. Yet no true Initiate has ever been known to sell divine knowledge for money, nor to exercise his spiritual gifts for personal gain.

greeting is not of this world, your visit does me great honour; but, before I adore the God of the Sages, may it please you to let me know to what Sages and to what God you refer, and if agreeable to you pray take this armchair and have the kindness to enlighten me as to this God, these Sages, this Order, and, before or after all this, as to the manner of being to whom I have the honour of speaking."

"You receive me very sagely sir," he replied with a smile, taking the profferred armchair; "You ask me to explain to you in the beginning certain things, which with your permission, I shall not touch upon to-day. The words of the compliment I have paid you the Sages address, at the outset, to those to whom they have determined to open their hearts and reveal their Mysteries. From your letters I adjudged you so advanced that this salutation would not be unknown to you, and that you would esteem it the most gratifying compliment the Comte de Gabalis could pay you."

"Ah Sir," I exclaimed, recollecting that I had a great rôle to play, "How shall I render myself worthy of such kindness? Is it possible that the greatest of all men is in my study, and that the renowned GABALIS honours me with a visit?"

"I am the least of the Sages, "he answered gravely, "and God, who dispenses the Light of his Wisdom together with its responsibilities in that measure which His Sovereignty deems best, has bestowed upon me but a very small portion of the Light, in comparison to that at which I marvel in my fellow

Initiates[14]. I expect you to equal them some day, if I dare judge from the map of your horoscope with which you have honoured me. But why Sir," he added mirthfully, "Are you doing your utmost to get into my bad graces by mistaking me at first sight for a phantom?"

"Ah, not for a phantom," I said, "But I confess, Sir, that I suddenly recalled that story of Cardan's. He says his father was one day visited in his study by seven unknown beings, clothed in different colours, who[15] made rather strange statements to him as to their nature and occupation--"

---

[14] INITIATION, OR SPIRITUAL REBIRTH, results from the quickening in man of that Divine Spark which evolves, through upward direction of the Solar Force, (*Solar Force defined.*) into the deathless Solar Body. (*The Solar Body is the Spiritual Body.*) The degrees of Initiation are but the degrees of the evolution of the God in man; Illumination being that degree in which the Divine Self masters and enkindles its manifestation, the personality, which is henceforward subservient to its evolution. At the moment of Illumination man becomes, in truth, a "Son of God," having claimed and made his own his divine and natural birthright. Initiation and Illumination are the destiny of the race. " For all creation, gazing eagerly as if with outstretched neck, is waiting and longing to see the manifestation of the Sons of God. For those whom He has known beforehand He has also predestined to bear the likeness of His Son, that He might be the Eldest in a vast family of brothers."--ROMANS viii., 19, 29; "NEW TESTAMENT IN MODERN SPEECH." R. F. WEYMOUTH, D.LIT.

[15] CARDAN AND THE SYLPHS OF CARDAN. SEE NOTE D, COMMENTARY CONTINUED.

"I am familiar with the incident to which you refer," interrupted the Comte, "They were Sylphs; I will tell you about them some day. They are a kind of etherial being, and now and then they come to consult the Sages about the books of Averroes [16] which they do not understand very well. Cardan is a rattlepate to have published that in his 'Subtilties.' He found the reminiscence among his father's papers. His father was one of Us. Realising that his son was a born babbler, he did not wish to teach him anything of moment, and let him amuse himself with ordinary astrology whereof he knew only enough to forecast that his son would be hanged. So that rascal is to blame for your having insulted me by taking me for a Sylph?"

"Insulted you!" I exclaimed, "What have I done that I should be so unfortunate--?"

"I am not angry with you," he interposed, "You are under no obligation to know that all these Elementary Spirits are our disciples; that they are only too happy when we condescend to instruI them; and that the least of our Sages is more learned and more powerful than all those little fellows. We will speak of these matters, however, at another time; it is enough to-day that I have had the satisfaction of seeing you. Strive to render yourself worthy to receive the Cabalistic Light, my Son, the hour of your regeneration is at hand; it rests solely with you to become a new being. Pray ardently to Him, who alone has the power to create

---

[16] AVERROES. SEE NOTE E, COMMENTARY CONTINUED.

new hearts, that He may give you one capable of the great things which I am to teach you, and that He may inspire me to withhold from you none of our Mysteries."

Then he arose, kissed me solemnly, and without giving me a chance to reply said, "Adieu, my Son, I must see the members of our Order who are in Paris, afterward I shall give you my news. Meanwhile, WATCH, PRAY, HOPE AND BE SILENT." [17]

With these words he left my study. On the way oi to the door I expressed my regret at the shortness of his visit, and at his cruelty in forsaking me so soon after he had shown me a Spark of his Light[18]. But

---

[17]

WATCH	The lower nature and mind.
PRAY	Demand and realise power to govern them.
HOPE	Aspire to the highest.
BE SILENT	Let the personality listen that it may hear the voice of the Divine Self.

[18] SPARK OF HIS LIGHT.--Light is used as a synonym for spiritual knowledge and evolution since, to the seer, the spirit or Solar Principle of man is at certain times actually visible as a light that " true Light which lighteth every man that cometh into the world."(St. John, I., 9;) The spirit of the average man or woman exists, as it were, in embryo only, and appears as a dim and tiny light at some distance above the head. In the Master this light, developed, is visible as an elongated cleft flame extending upward from the centre of the forehead. This flame ever the distinctive mark of all highly evolved beings who are able to manifest and to keep in touch with their divine consciousness while in the physical body. Such were the flames, those "cloven tongues like as of fire,"(

assuring me, with very great kindness, that I would lose nothing by waiting, he entered his coach and left me in a state of amazement which beggars description.

I coûld believe neither my eyes nor my ears. "I am sure," I kept saying to myself "that this is a man of exalted rank, that he has inherited a yearly income of fifty thousand pounds; moreover he appears to be a person of great accomplishment; can it be that he has lost his head over these occult follies? He talked to me about those Sylphs in an exceedingly cavalier fashion. Is it not possible that he may be a sorcerer, and may I not have been altogether mistaken in believing, as I hitherto have, that sorcerers no longer exist? On the other hand, if he is a sorcerer, are they all as devout as he seems to he?"

Acts, ii., 3;) which descended at Pentecost upon the heads of the twelve Apostles, who went out from that degree of Initiation qualified to do Master works.

The Christ, Melchizedek, and other high priests of humanity, in whom the Divine Principle has evolved to the supreme point manifestable on earth, are abl to make visible to their disciples the spiritual or Solar Body, and to appear when they so desire, "clothed with the sun." We read that Christ led Peter, James and John" up into an high mountain apart, and was transfigured before them: and his face did shine as the sun, and his raiment was white as the light." (St. Matthew, xvii., 1, 2;) The words "For the Lord thy God is a consuming fire,"(Deuteronomy, iv., 24;) and "He maketh the spirits His angels, His ministers a flaming fire"(Psalms, 4) are literally true.

I could not solve this riddle, nevertheless, I
determined
to see the matter through to the
end, although I fully realised that I
should have to put up with not
a few sermons, and that the
demon tormenting him
was of a highly
moral and pious
character.

HE Comte wished me to pass the entire night in prayer[19], and the next morning at daybreak sent a note to say that he would be at my house at eight o'clock, and that, if agreeable to me, we would make an excursion together. I awaited [20] him, he came, and after we had exchanged

---

[19] PASS THE ENTIRE NIGHT IN PRAYER.--It is a tradition that the aspirant should pass the night before Initiation in prayer. Hence the Knight of the Grail prayed and kept vigil over his armour (his lower nature and mind) prior to receiving the golden spurs, symbols of the Sun and Divine Illumination.

[20] EXCURSION.--When the disciple leaves his physical body in full consciousness for the first time, he is usually accompanied by his Master. Thus Swedenborg, in a passage which prefaced his work on the astral regions, says that "his first astral flight was guided by, an angel." The emphasis laid upon solitude and freedom from interruption would indicate

greetings, he said, "Let us go to some place where we may be alone, and where our interview cannot be interrupted."

I told him I thought Ruel a pleasant place and rather unfrequented. "Let us go there then," he replied. We got into the coach, and during the drive I kept studying my new Master. I have never in my life remarked in anyone so great a depth of contentment as was apparent in all that he said and did. His mind was more open and tranquil than it seemed possible for that of a sorcerer to be. His entire air was in nowise that of a man whose conscience reproaches him with black deeds; and I felt a marvellous impatience to have him enter upon the subject of our interview, for I could not comprehend how a man, seemingly so judicious and so perfect in every other way, could have let his mind become unbalanced by the visions to which I

---

that this event is about to take place, and the solemnity and mantric value of the Comte's charge to the Abbé on reaching the spot chosen for their interview as well as the character of the instruction given tends to confirm this statement. For this experience in a disciple's training is made the occasion for teaching him through observation many truths regarding superphysical beings and states of consciousness. Henceforward he is able to leave and to enter his body at will and with an ever increasing freedom, until gradually the experiences while out of the body become as real and continuous as those in the flesh. Thus the great Initiate St. Paul says, "And I knew such a man, (whether in the body, or out of the . body, I cannot tell: God knoweth)."--II. CORINTHIANS, CHAPTER xii., 3. *Proof that St. Paul was an Initiate and a Cabalist is found in I. Corinthians, chapter ii., 6--8. Authority for this Statement. Note F, Commentary Continued.*

had perceived him to be subject on the preceding day. He discoursed divinely on political economy, and was enchanted to hear that I had read what Plato has written on this subject[21]. "Someday you will have greater need of all that than you imagine," he said, "And if we come to an agreement to-day, it is not impossible that you may in time put these sage maxims into practice."

We were just entering Ruel and went to the garden; but the Comte disdained to admire its beauties and made straight for the labyrinth.

Perceiving that we were as much alone as he could desire, he raised his hands and eyes to Heaven and cried aloud, "I praise the Eternal Wisdom for inspiring me to conceal from you none of her Ineffable Truths. How happy you will be, my Son, if she is gracious enough to put into your soul the resolutions which these High Mysteries require of you. Soon you will learn to command all Nature, God alone will be your Master, and only the Sages your equals. The Supreme Intelligences will glory in obeying your desires, the demons will not dare to be found where you are, your voice will make them tremble in the depths of the abyss, and all the Invisible Peoples who dwell in the four Elements will deem themselves happy to be the ministers of your pleasure. I worship Thee, oh mighty God[22],

---

[21] PLATO. HIS PLACE AS A PHILOSOPHER, PLATO MEETS HIS MASTER. NOTE G, COMMENTARY CONTINUED.

[22] I WORSHIP THEE, O MIGHTY GOD.

"God" is the rendering in the English versions of the Hebrew "El," "Eloah," and "Elohim." (THE JEWISH

because Thou hast crowned man with such great glory, and hast created him Sovereign Monarch of all the works of Thine hands. My Son," he added turning towards me, "do you feel within yourself that heroic ambition which is the infallible characteristic of the Children of Wisdom? Do you dare seek to serve God alone, and to master all that is not of God? Do you understand what it means to be a Man? And are you not weary of being a slave when you were born to a Sovereign? And if you have these noble thoughts which the map of your horoscope does not permit me to doubt, consider

---

ENCYCLOPEDIA.) "El" does not signify Deus (God) but Sol (Sun)." (SIR W. DRUMMOND. OEDIPUS JUDAICUS, PAGE 270.) "The word El ought to be written Al. In the original it is AL and this word means the God Mithra, the Sun, as the Preserver and Saviour." (GODFREY HIGGINS. THE ANACALYPSIS, VOL. I, PAGE 71.) Since the word translated God in the first chapter of Genesis is 'Elohim', the majestic plural form of El, the Sun, translatable as 'MIGHTY SUN' (GENSENIUS' HEBREW GRAMMAR, PAGE 398. NOTE 2.) and since we read that "Elohim made two great lights, the greater light to rule the day, and the lesser light to rule the night, he made the stars also." GENESIS, I, 16. ELOHIM (GOD) IS SEEN TO BE THE PARENT OF THE SUN OF OUR SOLAR SYSTEM, KNOWN TO OCCULTISTS AS THE SUN BEHIND THE SUN. AS MAN IS INFORMED BY AN INVISIBLE SOLAR OR SPIRITUAL PRINCIPLE, IN LIKE MANNER THE MANIFESTED UNIVERSE IN ANIMATED BY AN INVISIBLE OR SPIRITUAL LIGHT.
The identity of the God of the .Mohammedans with the God of the Hebrews and Christians, and of the inner truth of these religions, is indicated by the fact that the word Elohim or MIGHTY SUN written in Arabic with the article means Allah, God Manifesting in Nature, the Undefinable, the Beginning, and the End. "He is the Lord of Sirus." (The Dog Star), Koran Sura, liii, The Star.

seriously whether you will have the courage and strength to renounce everything which might prove an obstacle to your attaining that eminence for which you were born."

He paused and looked at me fixedly, as if either awaiting my reply or seeking to read my heart.

From the beginning of his discourse I had greatly hoped that we should soon enter upon the subject of our interview, but at these last words I gave up all anticipation of doing so. The word 'renounce' frightened me, and I no longer doubted he was about to propose that I should renounce either Baptism or Paradise. So not knowing how to get out of the difficult situa- tion in which I found myself I said, "Renounce, Sir, is it necessary to renounce anything."

"It is absolutely necessary," he answered, "and truly, so vitally essential that it is the first thing required of one. I do not know whether you can make up your mind to it, but I know only too well that Wis- dom never dwells in a body subject to sin, even as she never enters a soul prepossessed by error or malice. The Sages will never admit you to their Order if you do not from this moment renounce one thing which can never go hand in hand with Wisdom. It is necessary," he added in a whisper bending close to my ear, "It is necessary to renounce all sensual relationships with women."

I burst out laughing at this absurd proposal. "Sir," I exclaimed, "You have let me off easily. I was expecting you to propose some extraordinary renunciation, but since you merely desire me to renounce women[23], that was done long ago. I am chaste enough, thank God! Nevertheless Sir, since Solomon was more of a Sage than I may ever be, and since all his Wisdom could not prevent his becoming corrupted, pray tell me how you gentlemen manage to do without the other sex[24]? And why would it be inconvenient if, in the Philosopher's Paradise, every Adam should have his Eve?"

"You are asking me something very important," he replied, as if reflecting whether or not he should answer my question. " Since I see, however, that you disengage yourself without difficulty from the society of the fair sex, I will tell you one of the reasons which have compelled the Sages to exact this condition from their disciples. Forthwith you will perceive in what ignorance all men live who are not of our number."

When you have been enrolled among the Children of the Philosophers, and when your eyes have been strengthened[25] by the use of the very Holy

---

[23] "CHASTITY is the obedience of the body to the the desire of the soul subservient to the Divine Will."

[24] PHILOSOPHIC BALANCE.--A Philosopher is able to balance the sex nature autodynamically through knowledge of the Law governing Solar Force.

[25] WHEN YOUR EYES HAVE BEEN STRENGTHENED.--A ganglion of the sympathetic nervous system, known as the pineal gland, is situated in the brain directly posterior to the extremity of the third ventricle. " From its broad anterior end two white bands pass forward, one on the inner side of each optic thalamus." When through the use of the Holy Catholic

Medecine, you will straightway discover that the Elements are inhabited by most perfect beings. Unhappy Adam's sin has deprived his unfortunate posterity of all knowledge of these beings and of all intercourse with them. The immense space which lies between Earth and Heaven has inhabitants far nobler than the birds and insects. These vast seas have far other hosts than those of the dolphins and whales; the depths of the earth are not for the moles alone; and the Element of Fire, nobler than the other three, was not created to remain useless and empty.

The air is full of an innumerable multitude of Peoples[26],whose faces are human, seemingly rather

---

Medecine (government of Solar Force) the pineal gland is regenerated, it endows man with superphysical or seer vision.

[26] THE PEOPLE OF THE ELEMENTS.--Man's consciousness is limited in direct proportion to the development of his senses of perception. Man has within himself, in the sympathetic and cerebro spinal nervous systems, minor brain centres. When, by purity of life and thought and the right use of Solar Force, man awakens and energises these centres, he is able to penetrate into other states of being and discovers himself to be living in a world teeming with intelligences and entities existing in certain well defined realms of consciousness hitherto unknown and unperceived by him.

Paracelsus sheds light upon the method whereby man may make acquaintance with the Peoples of the Elements when he says, "We come to the conclusion then that all the Elements are not joined together, but that they are altogether aerial, or igneous, or terrestial, or aqueous solely and without admixture. This also is settled that every Element nourishes itself, or does that which is in it, or its world." For when those centres in man which are intimately related to the distribution of the essences which nourish the Earth, Air, Water and Fire bodies, or vestures of man's spirit, have been

haughty, yet in reality tractable, great lovers of the sciences, cunning, obliging to the Sages, and enemies of fools and the ignorant. Their wives and daughters have a masculine beauty like that of the Amazons.

"Why, Sir," I ejaculated, "Do you mean to tell me that these hobgoblins are married?"

"Don't be upset by such a trifle, my Son," he rejoined, "Believe me, everything that I am telling you is sound and true. These are but the Elements of the ancient Cabala, and it only rests with you to verify my statements with your own eyes. Receive with a submissive spirit the Light which God sends

---

regenerated, man is enabled to attain ranges of consciousness co-extensive with those of the four races of beings inhabiting the essences of these four Elements, since the Peoples of the Air, "the Dwellers in the Earth, the Nymphs, the Undines, and the Salamanders, receive their long life in an alien essence." Their bodies are built up of those finer materials which interpenetrate gross matter and its interspaces, even as man's own finer bodies are thus built up.

When speaking of the four Elements, their range of vibration in matter is meant. Obviously visible and transitory flame cannot be the habitat of a long lived race. Yet the Element of Fire, or its rate of vibration, interpenetrates every manifestation of Nature, even the grossest, as the finding of radium in pitchblend evidences, and in this clearly defined range of vibration a race of intelligences highly differentiated and evolved has its being. The essences of the Earth, Air and Water are also filled with conscious and appropriate life. If man will purify his body, emotions and mind he may, through knowledge of the Law governing Solar Force and the regeneration of certain minor brain centres, enter into a harmonious relationship with these People of the Elements.

you through my mediation. Forget all you may have heard on this subject in the schools of the ignorant, or later, when convinced by experience, you will have the sorrow of being compelled to own that you persisted stubbornly is in the wrong."

"Hear me to the end and know that the seas and rivers are inhabited as well as the air. The ancient Sages called this race of people Undines or Nymphs. There are very few males among them but a great '" number of females; their beauty is extreme, and the daughters of men are not to be compared to them.

The earth is filled well-nigh to its centre with Gnomes, people of slight stature, who are the guardians of treasures, minerals and precious stones. They are ingenious, friends of man and easy to govern. They furnish the Children of the Sages with all the money they require, and as the price of their service ask naught save the glory of being commanded. The Gnomides, their wives, are small but very amiable, and their dress is exceedingly curious.

As for the Salamanders, flaming dwellers of the Region[27] of Fire, they serve the Philosophers, but do not seek their company eagerly, and their daughters and wives rarely show themselves."

"They do right," I interrupted, "And I had rather have their room than their company."

---

[27] BENVENUTO CELLINI SEES A SALAMANDER. NOTE H, COMMENTARY CONTINUED.

"Why so?" inquired the Comte.

"Why so, Sir?" I replied, "Who would care to converse with such an ugly beast as a Salamander, male or female?"

"You are mistaken," he rejoined, "that is merely the idea which ignorant painters and sculptors have of them. The Salamander women are beautiful, more beautiful even than any of the others, since they are of a purer Element. I had not intended to speak about them, and was passing briefly over the description of these Peoples since you will see them yourself at your leisure, and with ease if you have the curiosity to do so. You will see their dresses, their food, their manners, their customs and their admirable laws. The beauty of their intellects will charm you even more than that of their bodies, yet one cannot help pitying these unfortunates when they tell one that their souls are mortal, and that they have no hope whatever of eternal enjoyment of the Supreme Being, of Whom they have knowledge and Whom they worship reverently. They will tell you that they are composed of the purest portions of the Element in which they dwell, and that they have in them no impurities whatever, since they are made of but one Element. Therefore they die only after several centuries; but what is time in comparison with eternity? They must return for ever into nothingness. This thought grieves them deeply, and we have utmost difficulty in consoling them.

Our Fathers the Philosophers, when speaking with God face to face, complained to Him of the unhappiness of these Peoples, and God, whose mercy is boundless, revealed to them that it was not impossible to find a remedy for this evil. He inspired them to the realization that just as man, by the alliance which he has contracted with God, has been made a participant in Divinity, so the Sylphs, Gnomes, Nymphs, and Salamanders, by the alliance which they have it in their[28] power to

---

[28] ALLIANCE.--Although the author multiplies instances of marriages which have actually taken place between human and Elemental or superphysical beings, yet the reader will perceive the discrepancy between such relationships and the philosophic tenet of chastity upon which so much emphasis is laid. Nevertheless a real, though pure, relationship exists between every true Philosopher and the People of the Elements and is the mystical marriage to which the Comte refers.

As a general has lieutenants and armies at his command, so the Philosopher, a general 'in the liberation war of humanity,' has many helpers among the People of the Elements. Their duties are various. Some are messengers going to great distances to secure and deliver information, others are protesfive powers keeping at bay disturbing forces operative upon their own planes of consciousness.

All consciousness is matter played upon by force, the higher the level of consciousness the more subtle the matter and the more refined the vibration. As on the physical plane, so on the superphysical planes, when two centres each vibrating at a different rate meet, a balance is struck and a mean vibration results. The true Philosopher or Initiate is a highly dynamic centre of divine consciousness, and all less evolved entities and souls contasfing this centre have their own level of consciousness raised in consequence. Thus a Gnome or Sylph, Nymph or Salamander, by alliance with a Philosopher for the service of God and man, evolves through the stimulation of this constant associationship into immortality. The Law is that REALISATION OF IMMORTALITY (PERMANENCE OF CONSCIOUSNESS) IS IN DIRECT PROPORTION TO

contract with man, can become participants in immortality. Thus a Nymph or a Sylphid becomes immortal and capable of the Beatitude to which we aspire when she is so happy as to marry a Sage; and a Gnome or a Sylph ceases to be mortal the moment he espouses one of our daughters.

Thence sprang the error of the first centuries, of Tertullian, Justin Martyr, Lactantius, Cyprian, Clement of Alexandria, Athenagoras the Christian Philosopher, and of most writers of that period. They had learned that these Elementary Half-men sought the love of mortal maidens, and therefore imagined that the fall of the Angels had come about solely through their suffering themselves to be smitten with love for mortal women. Some Gnomes, desirous of becoming immortal, had sought to win the favour of our daughters by bringing them precious stones of which they are the natural guardians, and these authors believed, basing their conclusions upon the Book of Enoch[29] which they did not understand, that these precious stones were snares laid by the enamoured Angels for the chastity of our women.

THE RATE OF VIBRATION AND IN INVERSE PROPORTION TO THE DENSITY OF THE MEDIUM.
CAUSE OF THE EVOLUTION OF CONSCIOUSNESS:--The solar force, or life giving principle interpenetrates all matter and playing perpetually upon it causes different rates of vibration in its different densities. The more subtle the matter, the less the resistance to this force and the higher the vibration and resultant conscibusness. The evolution of consciousness is caused by the play of the life giving force or universal mind in matter.
[29] BOOK OF ENOCH. NOTE I, COMMENTARY CONTINUED.

In the beginning these Sons of Heaven, being beloved by the daughters of men, engendered famous giants; and those indifferent Cabalists, Joseph and Philo, (of which almost all Jews are ignorant,[30]) and subsequently all the authors I have just mentioned, as well as Origen and Macrobius, said that they were Angels, not knowing that they were Sylphs and other Elementary Peoples, who under the name of the Children of Elohim are distinguished from the Children of Men. Likewise that point which the Sage Augustine modestly refrained from deciding as to the pursuit of the African women of his time by so called Fauns or Satyrs[31]; that also is cleared up by what I have just said concerning the desire to ally themselves with man which all Inhabitants of the Elements have, since such an alliance offers the only means whereby they may achieve the immortality to which they are not heirs.

Ah! Our Sages take care not to ascribete fall of the first Angels to their love for women, nor do they accord the Devil such power over man as would enable them to attribute to him all the amorous intrigues of the Nymphs and Sylphs wherewith the writings of historians abound. There was never anything criminal in it at all. They were Sylphs who were striving to become immortal. Far from scandalizing the Philosophers, their innocent pursuits appeared so justifiable to us that we have, with one accord, resolved altogether to renounce

---

30 *Of the Cabalistic Wisdom.*
31 ST. AUGUSTINE ON FAUNS AND SATYRS. DE CIVITATE DEI BOOK XV, CHAPTER XXIII.

women and to apply ourselves solely to the immortalisation of the Nymphs and Sylphids."

"Oh God!" I protested, "What do I hear? To what extent does the f------"

"Yes, my Son," the Comte interrupted, "Marvel at the extent of the philosophical felicity. Instead of women, whose feeble allurements fade in a few days and are succeeded by horrible wrinkles, the Sages possess beauties who never grow old and whom they have the glory of rendering immortal. Imagine the love and gratitude of these invisible mistresses and the ardour wherewith they strive to please the charitable Philosopher who applies himself to their immortalisation."

"Ah! Sir," I once more exclaimed, "I renounce------"

"Yes, my Son," he continued as before without giving me an opportunity to finish, "renounce all futile and insipid pleasures such as one finds in the society of women; the fairest of them all is horrible beside the most insignificant Sylphid. No revulsion ever follows our wise love making. Wretched ignoramuses! How greatly you are to be pitied for your inability to taste the pleasures of the Philosophers!"

"Wretched Comte de GABALIS! " I exclaimed with mingled wrath and compassion, "Will you let me tell you, once for all, that I renounce this insane

Wisdom[32], that I find this visionary Philosophy absurd, that I abhor these abominable embracings of phantoms, and that I tremble for you lest one of your pretended Sylphids should suddenly carry you off to Hell in the midst of your transports, fearing that so good a man as you might at length perceive the madness of this chimerical ardour, and repent so great a crime."

---

[32] WISDOM OF THE SERPENT.--The Wisdom which the Comte hints at and which the Abbé here renounces is the Wisdom of the Serpent, the knowledge resulting from government of the Serpent Fire or Solar Force.

"The Earth derives from the Sun not merely light and heat, but, by transformation of these, almost every form of energy manifest upon it; the energy of the growth of plants, the vital energy of animals, are only the energy received from the Sun changed in its expression." (E. WALTER MAUNDER, F.R.A.S., THE SCIENCE OF THE STARS. PAGE 75. THE PEOPLE'S BOOKS. 42) A supreme manifestation of this vital or solar energy upon the physical plane is found in the sympathetic and cerebro spinal nervous systems of man and its voltage can there be raised into that Super-Sensible Energy, the instrument which the soul of man uses to built up its deathless Solar or Spiritual Body.

The unfoldment of the supersensible or spiritual nature of man is but the progressive manifestation in him of that vital energy derived from the Sun and its Divine Source, known throughout the ages as the Solar Force or Serpent and proceeding from the Creator of the Sun and Worlds, the Great Architect of the Universe. " By His spirit He hath garnished the heavens; His hand hath formed the crooked serpent. Lo, these are parts of His ways: but how little a portion is heard of Him? but the thunder of His power who can understand?" Job xxvi, 13, 14. THE SOLAR FORCE IS THE SERPENT IN THE ANCIENT SYMBOL OF THE EGG AND THE SERPENT. NOTE J, COMMENTARY CONTINUED.

"Oh! ho!" he answered, recoiling three steps and looking at me with wrathful eyes, "Woe to you intractable spirit that you are!"

His behaviour frightened me I confess, but what was infinitely worse, as he went away from me, I saw him take a paper from his pocket. I caught a glimpse of it from a distance and perceived it to be covered with characters which I could not quite make out. He read it attentively, seemed vexed, and kept muttering to himself. I believed that he was evoking spirits to compass my ruin, and I somewhat repented my rash zeal. "If I escape from this adventure," I kept saying to myself, "No more Cabalists for me!" I was keeping my eyes fixed upon him as on a judge about to condemn me to death, when I saw his countenance regain its serenity.

"It is hard for you to kick against the pricks," he said, smiling and rejoining me. "You are a chosen vessel, Heaven has destined you to be the greatest Cabalist of your time. Here is the map of your horoscope which cannot be at fault. If it does not come to pass now and through my mediation, it will at the good pleasure of your retrograde Saturn."

"Ah! If I am to become a Sage," said I, "It will never be save through the mediation of the Great GABALIS; but to be plain with you, I sadly fear that you will find it hard to bend me to this philosophic love making."

"Can it be," he replied, "that you are such a poor Natural Philosopher as not to be persuaded of the existence of these Peoples?"

"I hardly know," I answered, "But I think that I should always fancy them to be merely hobgoblins in disguise."

"And will you ever believe more implicitly in the nurse of your childhood than in your native reason, than in Plato, Pythagoras, Celsus, Psellus, Proclus, Porphyry, Iamblichus, Plotinus, Trismegistus, Nollius, Dornée, Fludd; than in Great Philip Aureolus, Theophrastus Bombast, Paracelsus of Hohenheim, and all the members of our Order!"

"I would believe you Sir," I responded, "As much and more than all of them; but, my dear Sir, could you not arrange with your Fellow Initiates that I should not be compelled to devote myself to these young ladies of the Elements?"

"Alas!" he answered, "You are undoubtedly a free agent, and one does not love unless one wishes to do so. Few Sages, however, have been able to resist their charms. Nevertheless, there have been some who have reserved themselves wholly for greater things[33], (as you will in time know), and who have not been willing to do the Nymphs this honour."

---

[33] THOSE RESERVED FOR GREATER THINGS. NOTE K, COMMENTARY CONTINUED.

"Then I will be of their number," I replied, "As I should never be willing to waste time in the ceremonies which, I have heard a certain prelate say, one must practise in order to hold communion with such spirits."

"That prelate did not know what he was talking about," said the Comte, "For you will one day see that these are not spirits, and furthermore no Sage ever makes use either of ceremonies or of superstitious rites to get into touch with spirits, any more than he does in order to commune with the Peoples of whom we are speaking."

"The Cabalist acts solely according to the principles of Nature; and if strange words, symbols and circumlocutions[34] are sometimes found in our books, they are only used to conceal the principles of Natural Philosophy from the ignorant. Admire the simplicity of Nature in all her marvellous works! And in this simplicity a harmony and concert so great, so exact, and so essential that it will compel you, in spite of yourself, to relinquish your idle fancies. What I am about to tell you, we teach those, of our disciples whom we are not willing unreservedly to admit into the Sanctuary of Nature; yet whom we in no wise wish to deprive of the society of the Elementary Peoples because of

---

[34] CIRCUMLOCUTIONS.--"Every time you find in our books a tale, the reality of which seems impossible, a story which repugnant both to reason and common sense, then be sure that tale contains a profound allegory veiling a deeply mysterious truth; and the greater the absurdity of the letter the deeper the wisdom of the spirit." RABBI MOSES MAIMONIDES.

the compassion which we have for these same Peoples."

"As you may perhaps already have grasped, the Salamanders are composed of the most subtile portions of the Sphere of Fire, fused together and organised by! the action of the Universal Fire, of which I will discourse to you some day. It is called the Universal Fire[35] because it is the inherent cause of every movement in Nature."

"Likewise the Sylphs are composed of the purest atoms of the Air, the Nymphs of the most subtile essences of the Water, and the Gnomes of the finest particles of the Earth. Adam was closely related to these perfect creatures, for being created out of all that was purest in the four Elements, he combined in himself the perfections of these four races of Peoples and was their natural King. As you will

---

[35] THE UNIVERSAL FIRE OR SOLAR FORCE.--"IS the Paraklete, the light of the Logos, which in energizing becomes what may be described as living, conscious electricity, of incredible voltage and hardly comparable to the form of electricity known to the physicist." THIS FORCE CAN BE GOVERNED BY MAN, AND WHEN GOVERNED IS THE INSTRUMENT WHICH THE SOUL USES TO BUILD UP MAN'S SOLAR OR SPIRITUAL BODY.
The Paraclete or Super Solar Force (The Force of the Sun behind the Sun), Solar Force (the Force of the Sun), and Lunar Force (the Force of the Moon) are all termed Solar Force in this book.
"The material of the Philosopher's Stone is nothing else but Sun and Moon." PARACELSUS.
"The Sun and the Moon are the roots of this Art." HERMES TRISMEGISTUS.

learn later, however, the moment his sin had precipitated him into the dregs of the Elements, the harmony was disturbed and there could no longer be any relation between him, gross and impure as he had become, and these pure and subtile beings. How remedy this evil? How restring the lute and recover that lost sovereignty? Oh Nature! Why art thou so little studied? Do you not understand, my Son, how easy Nature finds it to restore to man the estate which he has lost?"

"Alas! Sir," I answered, "I am very ignorant concerning all these facilities of Nature to which you refer."

"Nevertheless it is exceedingly easy to become well informed about them," he rejoined. "If we wish to recover empire over the Salamanders, we must purify and exalt the Element of Fire which is in us, and raise the pitch of that relaxed string. We have only to concentrate the Fire of the World in a globe of crystal[36], by means of concave mirrors; and this is the art which all the ancients religiously concealed, and which the divine Theophrastus discovered. A Solar Powder is formed in this globe, which being purified in itself and freed from any admixture of the other Elements, and being

---

[36] GLOBE OF CRYSTAL.--TO the Seer, man appears surrounded by an oviform luminous mist or globe of crystal. This luminosity of the finer bodies is the manifestation of the emotions and thoughts of the individual. It is termed the aura and interpenetrates the physical body, being present during life and withdrawn at death. Dr. W. J. Kilner in his book "The Human Atmosphere" describes a method whereby persons having ordinary vision are enabled to see this aura.

prepared according to the Art, becomes in a very short time supremely fitted to exalt the Fire[37]

---

[37] EXALT THE ELEMENT OF FIRE.--Constant aspiration, and desire to know God's Law liberates in man that Force which is a Living Flame, and which acts under the direction of the God in man, and with or without the conscious effort of the finite mind. This Fire, once liberated, begins immediately to displace the sluggish nervous force and to open and perfect those nerve centres or minor brains, atrophied from disuse, and which when regenerated reveal to man superphysical states of consciousness and knowledge of his lost Sovereignty over Nature.

The Solar Force manifests on the physical plane by passing through the ganglia of the sympathetic nervous system and thence up the spine to the brain where its currents unite to build up the deathless Solar or Spiritual Body. In its passage from one ganglion to another its voltage is raised, and it awakens and is augmented by the power peculiar to each ganglion which it dominates. These ganglia or centres are the "concave mirrors whose property it is to concentrate the Fire of the World or Solar Force. In the cerebro spinal system there are many centres awaiting regeneration. Hence the spinal cord is the relaxed string whose pitch must be raised by the exaltation of the Element of Fire which is in us.

Knowledge as to the development of this Force has been sacredly guarded in all ages lest man, through ignorance, should employ it to his destruction. That soul who will renounce all personal ambition, and will seek by selfless service of his fellow beings to obey the Divine Spirit within may, without external teaching or assistance, evoke this Flame and achieve unaided a knowledge of Nature's secrets and mysteries. But unless governed by the God within, and with selfless purpose this Fire will intensify the lower passions and make the man a destructive force working contrary to the Law of Nature.

He who seeks divine knowledge will surely find it for the Divinity in man ever strives to render unto him his lost birthright. No sincere effort to solve God's Mystery passes unheeded by the Silent Watcher within.

which is in us, and to make us become, as it were, of an igneous nature. Thereafter the Inhabitants of the Sphere of Fire are our inferiors, and enraptured to see our mutual harmony re-established, and that we are again drawing near to them, they have as much-friendship for us as for their own kindred, and all the respect which they owe to the image and lieutenant of their Creator. They pay us every attention they can bethink themselves of, through their desire to obtain from us the immortality which they do not possess."

"It is true that they live a very long time, since they are more subtile than the people of the other Elements; hence they are in no hurry to exact immortality from the Sages. If the aversion you have evinced should prove lasting, my Son, you might be able to adapt yourself to a Salamander, perhaps it would never speak to you of that which you so greatly fear. It would not be thus with the Sylphs, Gnomes, and Nymphs. As they live for less time, they have more to do with us, so their familiarity is easier to obtain."

"One has only to seal a goblet full of compressed Air,[38] Water, or Earth and to leave it exposed to the

---

[38] COMPRESSED AIR, WATER, OR EARTH .--The Philosophers hold that man is four fold in nature, having four bodies corresponding to the four Elements. The physical or Earth body is interpenetrated by a body of finer matter vibrating at a higher rate, in which emotions and passions register, called the Water body. The Earth and Water bodies are interpenetrated by a body composed of still finer matter vibrating at a still higher rate, the mental body in which thoughts register, called the Air body. And informing these

Sun for a month. Then separate the Elements scientifically, which is particularly easy to do with Water and Earth. It is marvellous what a magnet for attracting Nymphs, Sylphs, and Gnomes, each one of these purified Elements is. After taking the smallest possible quantity every day for some months, one sees in the air the flying Commonwealth of the Sylphs, the Nymphs come in crowds to the shores, the Guardians of the Treasures parade their riches. Thus, without symbols, without ceremonies, without barbaric words, one becomes ruler over these Peoples. They exact no worship whatever from the Sage, whose superiority to themselves they fully recognise. Thus venerable Nature teaches her children to repair the elements by means of the Elements. Thus harmony is re-established. Thus man recovers his natural empire, and can do all things in the Elements without the Devil, and without Black Art. Thus you

---

three bodies and engendering them is the Divine Spark, the potential Solar Body or God in man, existing as it were in embryo awaiting the evolution of the Earth, Water and Air bodies to sustain the flow of the Solar Force which shall stimulate and perfect its divine unfoldment.

To seal a goblet of compressed Air, Water, or Earth, means to master the body, emotions and mind, and to differentiate appetites from emotions, and emotions from thoughts, for the purpose of gaining absolute control over the personal self. It is true, as the Comte de Gabalis here points out, that it is far easier to govern the body and emotions than to gain the mastery of the mind. This mastery should be striven for, and may be achieved through concentration in meditation, and by persistent effort at all times to impress the mind to reject falsehood and accept only Truth that it may purely reflect the God within.

see my Son, the Sages are more innocent than you imagined. Have you no answer to make me?"

"I marvel at you, Sir," said I, "And I am beginning to fear lest you should make me into a distiller."[39]

"Ah! God forbid, my child," he exclaimed, "Your horoscope does not destine you for such nonsense as that. On the contrary, I forbid you to trifle away your time over it. I have told you that the Sages only teach such things to those whom they have no wish to admit to their company. You will have all these, and infinitely more glorious and more desirable advantages, through Philosophic Procedures[40] which are quite different in character.

---

[39] *Alchemist.*

[40] PHILOSOPHIC PROCEDURES. -- By concentration in medtation upon a given subject, and by the EFFORT of regular breathing, the inhalation and exhalation occupying the same space of time, the mind may be held so that it is not subjeé to other thought than that pertaining to the object or symbol of expression about which man desires knowledge. And if man will persist in this practice he can enter into an harmonious relationship with the Divinity within and from that source can gain knowledge which is the result of the soul's own experience while passing through the higher and lower states of matter. At the same time, if man will concentrate upon the highest he can evoke from within self that Solar Force and Power which if directed upward will awaken and revitalise those ganglia or organs of perception hitherto withheld from his use. If it be true " From God we came, to God we return," life is but the attainment of that consciousness which is of God. And man is therefore shut out from the knowledge of his true being and estate until he seeks at-onement with his own Divine Life-Principle, and its evolution and manifestation in him. Thus concentration in meditation, holding the mind receptive to the Divinity within

I have only described these methods to make you see the innocence of this Philosophy and to allay your panic terrors[41]."

"Thanks be to God, Sir," I answered, "I no longer have so much fear as I had this afternoon. And although I have not yet made up my mind to this arrangement with the Salamanders which you propose, I cannot help being curious to learn how you have discovered that the Nymphs and Sylphs die."

"Verily," he replied, "They tell us so, and moreover we actually see them die."

"How is it possible you can see them die," I questioned, "when your alliance renders them immortal?

"That would be a point well made," said he, "if the number of Sages equalled the number of these Peoples; besides, there are many among them who prefer to die rather than run the risk of becoming immortal, and of being as unhappy as they see the demons to be. It is the Devil who inspires these

---

and in a positive attitude of repression to all outside thought, is seen to be an exalted form of prayer or communion with God, Nature, whereby man may become a sharer in the wonders of God's Omnipotence and recover his lost Sovereignty.
"For the mind shepherdeth Thy Word, O Spirit bearing Creator!" HERMES TRISMEGISTUS, "SECRET HYMNODY."
[41] PANIC TERRORS, ORIGIN OF TERM. NOTE L, COMMENTARY CONTINUED.

sentiments in them, for he leaves no stone unturned to prevent these poor creatures from becoming immortal through alliance with us. So that I regard this aversion of yours, my Son, as a very pernicious temptation and a most uncharitable impulse, and you ought so to regard it. Furthermore, as to the death of the Nymphs and Sylphs, of which you speak; who compelled the Oracle of Apollo to say, as Porphyry reports, that all those who used to speak through the Oracles were mortal like himself? And what,. think you, was the significance of that cry, which was heard throughout the coasts of Italy, and which struck such terror into the hearts of all who chanced to be upon the sea? 'THE GREAT PAN IS DEAD.' It was the People of the Air who were announcing to the People of the Waters that the chief and oldest of the Sylphs had just died."

"It seems to me," I remarked," that at the time that cry was heard the world was worshipping Pan and the Nymphs. Were then these gentlemen, whose fellowship you extol to me, the false gods of the Pagans?"

"That is true, my Son," he answered. "The Sages are far from believing that the Devil ever had power to make himself worshipped. He is too wretched and too weak ever to have had such pleasure and authority. But he has had power to persuade these Hosts of the Elements to show themselves to men, and to cause temples to be erected in their honour; and by virtue of the natural dominion which each one of these Peoples has over the Element in which it dwells, they kept troubling the air and the sea, shaking the earth and scattering the fire of heaven at their own good pleasure. Thus they had little difficulty in causing themselves to be mistaken for divinities so long as the Sovereign Being neglected the salvation of the nations. Yet the Devil did not derive from his mischief all the advantage he had hoped. For from that time it chanced that as Pan[42], the Nymphs, and other Elementary Peoples had found a means of exchanging this traffic in worship for a traffic in love, (you must needs remember that, among the ancients, Pan was held to be the king of the so-called incubus gods who ardently courted maidens), many of the Pagans escaped from the Devil, and will not burn in Hell."

"1 do not understand you, Sir," I replied.

"You take pains not to understand me," he continued mirthfully and in a mocking tone. "This is beyond your comprehension and would likewise be beyond that of all your doctors, for they have no idea. as to what glorious Natural Philosophy is. Here is the great mystery of all that part of Philosophy which has to do with the Elements, and which, if you have any self esteem, will surely remove the very unphilosophic repugnance which you have been evincing all day long."

"Know then, my Son, and be in no hurry to divulge this great Arcane to any unworthy ignoramus--

---

[42] THE GREAT PAN IS DEAD.' NOTE M, COMMENTARY CONTINUED.

know, that even as the Sylphs acquire an immortal soul through the alliance which they contract with men who are predestined: so men who have no right whatever to eternal glory, those unfortunates for whom immortality is but a fatal advantage, for whom the Messiah was not sent."

"You gentlemen of the Cabala are Jansenists[43] then?" I interposed.

"We do not know what Jansenism is my child," he answered brusquely, "and we scorn to inform ourselves as to wherein consist the differences in the various sects [44] and religions wherewith the

---

[43] JANSENISTS. NOTE N. COMMENTARY CONTINUED.
[44] SECTS AND RELIGIONS, THEIR CAUSE.--As soon, therefore, as the soul gravitates towards body in this first production of herself she begins to experience a material tumult, that is matter flowing into her essence. And this is what Plato remarks in the Phædo, that the soul is drawn into body staggering with recent intoxication, signifying by this, the new drink of matter's impetuous flood, through which the soul, becoming defiled and heavy, is drawn into a terrene situation. But the starry cup placed between Cancer and the Lion is a symbol of this mystic truth, signifying that descending souls first experience intoxication in that part of the heavens through the influx of matter. Hence oblivion, the companion of intoxication, there, begins silently to creep into the recesses of the soul. FOR IF SOULS RETAINED IN THEIR DESCENT TO BODIES THE MEMORY OF DIVINE CONCERNS, OF WHICH THEY WERE CONSCIOUS IN THE HEAVENS, THERE WOULD BE NO DISSENSION AMONG MEN ABOUT DIVINITY. But all, indeed, in descending, drink of oblivion; though some more, and others less. On this account though truth is not apparent to all men on the earth, yet all exercise their opinions about it; because A DEFECT OF MEMORY IS THE ORIGIN OF OPINION. But those discover most who have drank least of oblivion,

ignorant are infatuated. We ourselves hold to the ancient religion of our Fathers the Philosophers, concerning which I must one day instruct you. But to resume the thread of our discourse, those men whose melancholy immortality would be but an eternal misfortune, those unhappy children whom the Sovereign Father has neglected, have still the resource of becoming mortal by allying themselves with the Elementary Peoples. Thus you see the Sages run no hazard as to Eternity; if predestined they have the pleasure on quitting the prison of this body, of leading to Heaven the Sylphid or Nymph whom they have immortalised. On the other hand, if not predestined, marriage with the Sylphid renders their soul mortal and delivers them from the horror of the second death[45]. Thus the Devil beheld all those Pagans who had allied themselves with Nymphs escaping his clutches. Thus the Sages, or the friends of the Sages, to whom God inspires us to communicate any one of the four Elementary Secrets, which I have well

---

because they easily remember what they had known before in the heavens. MACROBIUS. COMMENTARY ON SCIPIO'S DREAM. CHAPTER XII.

[45] THE SECOND DEATH.--"That which Nature binds, Nature also dissolves: and that which the soul binds, the soul likewise dissolves. Nature, indeed, bound the body to the soul; but the soul binds herself to the body: Nature, therefore, liberates the body from the soul; but the soul liberates herself from the body. Hence there is a twofold death; the one, indeed, universally known, in which the body is liberated from the soul; but the other peculiar to Philosophers, in which the soul is liberated from the body. Nor does the one entirely follow the other." PORPHRY "AUXILIARIES TO THE PERCEPTION OF THE INTELLIGIBLES."

nigh taught you, may be set free from the peril of damnation."

"Truth to tell," I exclaimed, not daring to put him into a bad humour again, and deeming it expedient to postpone fully telling him my sentiments until he should have revealed to me all the secrets of his Cabala which, from this sample, I judged to be exceedingly odd and recreative; " truth to tell, you carry wisdom to very great lengths, and you were right in saying that this would be beyond the comprehension of all our doctors. I even believe that it would be beyond the comprehension of all our magistrates as well, and that if they could discover who these people are who escape the Devil by this method, as ignorance is ever unjust, they would take sides with the Devil against these fugitives and would use them ill."

"For that reason," said the Comte, "I have enjoined secrecy upon you, and I solemnly adjure you to maintain it. Your Judges are strange folk! They condemn a most innocent action as being the basest of crimes. What barbarism it was to condemn those two priests, whom the Prince de la Mirande knew, to be burned, each of whom had had his Sylphid for the space of forty years. What inhumanity it was to condemn to death Jeanne Hervillier, who had laboured to immortalise a Gnome for thirty six years. And what ignorance on the part of Bodin[46] to call her a sorceress, and to make her amorous intrigues a justification of the popular

---

[46] BODIN. NOTE O, COMMENTARY CONTINUED.

misconception regarding the so called sorcerers, In a book as extravagant as his Republic is rational."

"But it is late, and I am unmindful of the fact that you have not yet dined."

"You are speaking for yourself, Sir," said I, "for my part I could listen to you until to morrow without inconvenience."

"Ah! as for myself," he rejoined, smiling and walking towards the gate, "evidently you do not in the least know what Philosophy is. The Sages only eat for pleasure[47] and never from necessity."

---

[47] THE PHILOSOPHY OF NUTRITION.--"Nutrition is but little understood in the world to-day, for it is controlled by a Force outside of thought or will. THERE IS AN INDESTRUCTIBLE FORCE INHERENT IN ALL MATTER. Its mode of action is unchanging and it plays unceasingly upon humanity, acts simultaneously in all spheres of being, yet does not express itself in concrete form. THIS FORCE HAS THE PROPERTY OF STIMULATING THE ATOMS TO ASSUME NEW RELATIONSHIPS, AND GALVANISES THE ENERGY LATENT IN DORMANT CELLS INTO A HIGHER STATE OF ACTION. Food is the medium through which this Force acts in the human body. During metabolism that atomic energy is liberated which stimulates into conscious action those cells whose activity it required to carry forward cell evolution. Food, therefore, gives to the body only stimulation to atomic action. During the process it loses none of its properties, but is merely changed into other states or conditions. At his present stage of evolution man depends upon food solely because he has not become conscious of the Law governing the Force which gives atomic action to all parts of his organism. FOR THERE IS A LAW WHICH GOVERNS THE ACTION OF THIS EVER FLOWING

"I had quite the opposite idea of Sageness," I replied, I supposed that the Sage should only eat to satisfy necessity."

"You are mistaken," said the Comte, "How long do you think we Sages can go without eating?"

"How should I know?" said I, Moses and Elias[48] fasted forty days, no doubt you Sages fast for some days less."

"What a mighty endeavour that would be! " he answered, "The most learned man who ever lived, the divine, the almost to be worshipped Paracelsus affirms that he has seen many Sages who have fasted for twenty years without eating anything whatsoever. He himself, before being acknowledged Monarch of the Empire of Wisdom, whose sceptre we have justly accorded him, was pleased to essay living for several years by taking only one half scrupule of Solar Quintessence. And if you wish to have the pleasure of making any one live without eating, you have only to prepare the earth[49] as I

STREAM OR REGENERATING CURRENT DIRECTED UPON MATTER. When man, in time, becomes conscious of this Law he will be able to assimilate this Force and will no longer be dependent upon matter for the support of his physical organism."

[48] MOSES AND ELIAS FASTED FORTY DAYS. NOTE P, COMMENTARY CONTINUED.

[49] TO PREPARE THE EARTH--means to purify and to gain complete control over the earthly or physical body. To renew the earth when too dry means to recharge self with the Solar Force or Catholic Cabalistic Medicine.

The fact that man, at a certain period of evolution, will exist without taking nourishment is foretold in an ancient prophecy

have indicated that it may be prepared for the purpose of securing the partnership of the Gnomes. This Earth applied to the navel, and renewed when it is too dry, makes it possible for one to dispense with eating and drinking without the slightest inconvenience whatever, even as the veracious Paracelsus relates that he himself demonstrated during six months." "But the use of the Catholic Cabalistic Medicine liberates us in the very best way from the importunate necessities to which Nature subjects the ignorant. We eat only when it pleases us to do

so, and every superfluity
of food vanishes by unconscious transpiration,
we are never ashamed of being men. Then
he fell silent, perceiving that we were
within hearing of our servants,
and we went to the village to
take a slender repast, as
is the custom of
the Heroes of
Philosophy".

---

of the Magi, "that men shall be blessed, no longer needing food."

PLUTARCH, ISIS AND OSIRIS, CHAPTER xlvii.
PROPHECY OF THE MAGI OR MOST
ANCIENT SAGES FORETELLING
WORLD PEACE AND A
UNIVERSAL LANGUAGE.
NOTE I, COMMENTARY
CONCLUDED.

HERMES, the messenger of the gods, was said by the Greeks to typify and preside over the powers of the mind and to be the patron of gymnastic games. He is represented as bearing a caduceus or staff, gift of Apollo the Sun God, and emblem of the God's message to mankind. This staff represents the spine containing the cerebro spinal nervous system which is the wand of the magician, while the two intertwining serpents which ascend symbolise the positive and negative currents of Solar Force directed upward for the stimulation and evolution of the Solar Principle in man. Upon his left arm Hermes bears the Infant Bacchus, the Redeemer.

COMPARE BACCHUS AND OSIRIS,
NOTE Q, COMMENTARY
CONTINUED, FOR IDENTITY OF
THE INNER TRUTH OF
THE GREEK AND
EGYPTIAN
RELIGIONS.

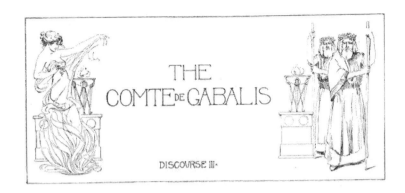

FTER dinner we returned to the labyrinth. I was pensive and my pity for the Comte's madness, which I fully realised would be hard to cure, prevented my being as much amused at all that he had told me as I should have been, could I have had any hope of restoring him to reason. I kept searching antiquity for some counter arguments which he would be unable to refute for, on my adducing the opinions of the church, he had declared that he cared for naught save the ancient religion of his Fathers the Philosophers [50]; and to seek to convince a Cabalist by reason would be a long winded

---

[50] ANCIENT RELIGION OF HIS FATHERS THE PHILOSOPHERS. The Philosophers hold that the relation of the Creator to His Creation has been the same in all ages; that all creeds evolved by man are but man's concept of this relation and in no wise alter it; that the Truth regarding the Fatherhood of God, Sonship of His Messengers, the great Teachers of humanity, and Brotherhood of all His creatures, is superior to creeds and religions, and will unify them when once apprehended.

undertaking, besides I vâas not anxious to get into a dispute with a man whose motives I did not as yet altogether understand.

It crossed my mind that what he had said concerning the false gods, for whom he had substituted the Sylphs and other Elementary Peoples, might be refuted by the Pagan Oracles whom Scripture everywhere calls devils, and not Sylphs. But not knowing whether the Comte might not in the tenets of his Cabala attribute the answer of the Oracles to some natural cause, I believed that it would be to the point to make him explain what he thought about them.

He gave me an opportunity to broach the subject when, before entering the labyrinth, he .turned towards the garden. "This is very fine," he said, "and these statues are rather effective."

"The Cardinal who had them brought here [51] " I replied, "had a fancy little worthy of his great

---

[51] THE GARDENS OF RUEL AND THE CARDINAL.--RUel, in the department of Seine et Oise, is fourteen kilometres distant from Paris, and "is situated at the base of those heights on which stood, in olden days, the magnificent villa of Cardinal Richelieu with its two chapels, hundred fountains, and lofty and balustraded cascade." In the years 1621-42 the cardinal minister established and maintained there a château and estate which eclipsed those of the King of France. Nowhere was there to be found so vast a collection of curiosities of every discription, such extensive gardens, so superb an orangery, nor such grottoes, fountains and cascades surpassing indeed anything previously known. These celebrated gardens, extolled by contempory authors, and even envied by the great King Louis XIV who sent Le Nôtre to Ruel

genius. He believed the majority of these figures to have given forth Oracles in bygone days, and paid exceedingly dear for them on that account."

"That is a failing of many people," the Comte reoined. "Every day ignorance causes a very criminal kind of idolatry to be committed, since people preserve with such great care and consider so precious those very idols which they believe the Devil formerly employed to make himself worshipped. O God, will people never in this world know that Thou hast precipitated Thine enemies beneath Thy footstool from the birth of time, and that Thou dost hold the demons prisoners under the earth in the vortex of darkness? This unpraiseworthy desire to conect these counterfeit instruments of the demons might become innocent, my Son, if people would let themselves be persuaded that the angels of darkness have never been allowed to speak through the Oracles."

"I do not believe," I interrupted, "that it would be easy to establish that hypothesis amongst the antiquarians, but possibly it might be amongst the free thinkers. For not long ago it was decided by the leading minds of the day, in a conference called for the purpose, that all these pretended Oracles were either a fraud due to the avarice of the Gentile priests, or but a political trick of the Sovereigns."

---

to study and reproduce them on a larger scale at Versailles, are a sad example of the transitoriness of the handiwork of man. A gradual deterioration culminating in their destruction during the Revolution has left almost no trace of them extant.

"Was this conference held and this question thus de-cided by the members of the Muhammedan Embassy [52] sent to your King?"

"No Sir," I answered.

"Then of what religion are these gentlemen," he retorted "since they set at naught the Holy Scriptures which make mention in so many instances of so many different Oracles, especially of the Pythian Oracles who made their abode and gave forth their replies in places destined for the multiplication of the image of God?"

"I mentioned all those ventriloquists," I answered, "and I reminded the company that King Saul [53] had banished them from his kingdom where, notwithstanding, he found one of them on the evening ofthe day before his death, whose voice had the wondrous power ofraising Samuel from the dead in answer to his prayer, and to his ruin. But

---

[52] MOHAMMEDAN EMBASSY.--The subtle irony of this allusion to the strained relations existing between Louis xiv and the Porte at this period is made plain by the following statement of the historian, E. Lavisse when summarising the foreign policy of France from 1661-1685. "During the second half of the 16th century the alliance 'of the lily and the crescent' was lost. In 1661 France, after several ambassadors had been ill treated, was represented at the Porte solely by a merchant whom 'the nation' had chosen. There was therefore in that direction a lost position for french diplomacy to regain." E. LAVISSE, HISTOIRE DE FRANCE. VOL. 7[II] PAGE 203. COMPARE MUHAMMED AND THE MUHAMMEDANS. NOTE R, COMMENTARY CONTINUED.
[53] KING SAUL. NOTE S, COMMENTARY CONTINUED.

these learned men did not alter their decision that there never had been any Oracles."

"If the Scripture made no impression upon them," a said the Comte, "you should have convinced them by all antiquity, wherein it would have been easy to point out a thousand marvellous proofs. There were so many virgins pregnant with the destiny of mortals, who brought forth the good and bad fortunes of those who consulted them. What do you allege as to Chrysostom, Origen and Oecumenius, who make mention of those divine men whom the Greeks called 'Engastrimyths,' [54] whose prophetic abdomens articulated such famous Oracles? And if your gentlemen did not care for the Scriptures and the Fathers, you should have reminded them of those miraculous maidens of whom the Greek Pausanias speaks, who changed themselves into doves and in that form delivered the celebrated Oracles of the Doves of Dodona[55]. Or else you might have said, to the glory of your nation, that there

---

[54] ENGASTRIMYTHS.--For it would be too absurd and puerile to conclude that God Himself, in the guise of Engastrimyths, that is to say tutelary deities speaking from within the abdomen, such as were of old called Eurycles and to-day Pythons, should the bodies of Prophets and make use of their mouths and voices as instruments for speaking. For he who thus introduces God into human affairs is lacking in reverence for His Greatness, nor does he maintain the Majesty and Glory of God's Worth. TRANSLATED FROM PLUTARCH'S CESSATION OF THE ORACLES. CHAPTER ix.
[55] THE ORACLE OF DODONA. NOTE T, COMMENTARY CONTINUED.

were of old in Gaul illustrious maidens [56] who transformed their entire appearance at the will of those who consulted them and who, in addition to the famous Oracles which they delivered, had a wonderful power over the waters and a salutary authority over the most incurable diseases."

"They would have treated all these fine proofs as apocryphal," said I.

"Does their antiquity render them suspect? " he reoined. "If so, you had only to adduce the Oracles which are still delivered every day."

"And in what part of the world? " said I.

"In Paris," he replied.

"In Paris!" I exclaimed.

---

[56] MAIDENS OF GAUL.--Sena being situate in the Britishe Sea, against the countrie of the Osis-Myes, is renowned with the Oracle of the God of the Galles, whose Vow-esses in number nine, are hallowed to continuall Virginitie. They call them Gallicens, and are of opinion, that through the singuler wisdom wherewith they are endued, they rayse the seas and winds with their charmes, and transforme themselves into what. Beastes theywill, and and heale such diseases as to others are incurable, knowe thinges to come and prophesie of them, but not unto any other than such as sayle thither for the nonce, and come of set purpose to demaund Counsell of them.
THE RARE AND SINGULER WORK OF POMPONIUS MELA, THAT EXCELLENT AND WORTHY COSMOGRAPHER. TRANSLATED INTO ENGLISH BY ARTHUR GOLDING, GENTLEMAN, LONDON, 1590. BOOK., III., CHAPTER vi.

"In Paris," he repeated, "'Art thou a master of Israel [57] and knowest not these things?' Do not people daily consult Aquatic Oracles in glasses of water or in basins, and Aerial Oracles in mirrors and on the hands of virgins? Do they not recover lost beads and pilfered watches? Do they not learn news from distant countries in this way, and see the absent?"

"Eh, Sir, what are you saying?" said I.

"I am recounting that which I am positive happens every day," he answered, "and it would not be difficult to find a thousand eyewitnesses of it."

"I cannot believe that Sir," I returned. "The magistrates would make an example of such culprits and people would not permit idolatry------"

"Ah! how hasty you are!" interrupted the Comte. "There is not so much evil in all this as you might suppose, and Providence will not permit the total destruction of that remnant of Philosophy which has escaped the lamentable shipwreck Truth has sustained. If there yet remains among the people any vestige of the dread power of the Divine Names[58], are you of the opinion that it should be blotted out and that they should lose the respect

---

[57] MASTER OF ISRAEL.--an official interpreter of the sacred books of the Jews. The Comte's words are quoted from the third chapter of the Gospel of St. John.

[58] DIVINE NAMES.--"It must be obsérved that these divine names were produced by scientific men energising according to a divine afflatus," THOMAS TAYLOR," THE CRATYLUS OF PLATO."

and recognition due to the great name AGLA[59],
which works all these wonders, even when invoked

[59] AGLA.--Every letter of the Hebrew alphabet has hidden or
sacred meaning, knowledge of which renders Hebrew names
self interpretative. The four letters of the word AGLA and
their significance are:--
A.--The First Cause, Positive Force.
G.--Negative Force.
L.--Objective Force.
A.--The First Cause.
Hence AGLA is seen to signify the First Cause in triple aspect
and to be a synonym of the ancient Hebrew word Al--the Sun,
(Creator of the Sun of our Solar system) . Al signifies the Sun
behind the Sun in triple aspect, the Trinity Unmanifest
symbolised thus

As in the microcosm, the physical body is informed and
animated by the invisible or spiritual man, so in the
macrocosm, the visible Sun derives its light and life from an
invisible or Spiritual Sun, whose glory and power can be
apprehended by man solely through his Solar Principle to
which the Sun behind the Sun is manifest as a radiance of
unspeakable glory realised, or participated in, as an ecstacy of
consciousness unframable in any medium of expression
known to the finite mind. In some Christian churches this
state 'is called Union with God, in the East, Yoga, and among
Initiates of all races has been striven for though rarely
attained. It is "the flight of the Alone to the Alone" says
Porphyry. "I and my Father are one," said Christ.
Agla is here used as a substitute for the Ineffable Name of the
Sun behind the Sun, which is the Lost Word of Masonry and
Sacrificial Word pronounced by the First Cause of the
Brahmins, and whose property it is to open the human
consciousness to this estate of oneness with God. Reference is
made to this Name in the Egyptian Book of the Dead "I am
the Great God existing of myself, the Creator of His Name,--I
know the Name of the Great God that is there." As in ancient
Egypt so in our own land and day there exists that spoken
Word or Name, inner key of spiritual knowledge possessed by

by the ignorant and sinful and which, spoken by a Cabalist, would perform many other miracles. Ifs you had wished to convince your gentlemen ofthe truth of the Oracles, you had only to exalt your imagination and your faith, and turning towards the East cry aloud 'AG' ------"

"Sir," I interposed, "I was careful not to advance that kind of argument to such proper folk as those with whom I was debating. They would have taken me for a fanatic for, depend upon it, they have no faith whatever in that sort of thing, and even if I had known the Cabalistic Procedure to which you refer, it would not have succeeded when pronounced by me; I have even less faith than they."

"Well, well," said the Comte, "If you lack faith we shall supply it. If you had reason to believe, however, that your gentlemen would not credit that which they can see any day in Paris, you might have cited a story of rather recent date. That Oracle, which Celius Rhodeginius[60] says he himself witnessed, delivered towards the end of the last century by that extraordinary woman who spoke and predicted the future by means of the same organ as did the Eurycles of Plutarch."

---

the hierophants of all ages, to the power of which Christ testified, saying " the works that I do in my Father's Name, they bear witness of me." COMPARE THE DIVINE POWER OF LETTERS, NOTE U, COMMENTARY CONTINUED.
[60] CELIUS RHODIGINUS AND HIS ORACLE. NOTE V, COMMENTARY CONTINUED.

"I should not have cared to cite Rhodeginius," I answered, "it would have seemed pedantic to do so, moreover they would certainly have told me that the woman was beyond question a demoniac."

"They would have said that very monachally," he replied.

"Sir," I ventured to say, "notwithstanding the

Cabalistic aversion to monks which I perceive you to entertain, I cannot help siding with them on this occasion. I believe that there would not be so much harm in absolutely denying that Oracles ever existed as there is in saying it was not the Devil who spoke through them because, in short, the Fathers and the theologians--"

"Because, in short," he interrupted, "do not the theologians agree that the learned Sambethe, the most ancient of the Sibyls was the daughter of Noah [61]?"

"Eh! what has that to do with it?" I retorted.

"Does not Plutarch say," he rejoined, "that the most ancient of the Sibyls was the first to deliver Oracles at Delphi? Therefore the Spirit which Sambethe harboured in her breast was not a devil nor was her Apollo a false god, for idolatry did not begin until long after the division of languages, and it would be far from the truth to attribute to the Father of Lies

---

[61] SAMBETHE, THE DAUGHTER OF NOAH. NOTE W, COMMENTARY CONTINUED.

the sacred books of the Sibyls[62], and all the proofs
of the true religion which the Fathers have drawn

---

[62] SACRED BOOKS OF THE SIBYLS.--Under the title of
"Oracles of the Sibyls" there exists a collection of verses in
Greek hexameter in fourteen books, which has long been
regarded as an authentic collection of the prophecies of the
pagan Sibyls. In Libri Divin-arum Rerum, Lactantius quotes
Varro as saying that these books are not all written by one
Sibyl, but are called Sibylline because by the ancients all
prophetesses were called Sibyls. And Diodorus Siculus states
that the Sibyl was actuated by the spirit of God and that the
name Sibyl signifies "being full of God."

As these books accurately prophesied the mission, teaching,
and miracles of Christ as well as his death upon the cross and
resurrection, the church fathers accepted and made use of
them without hesitation. The pleasantry of the Comte as to
the marriage of David and the Sibyl is a reference to the
words occuring in the Mass for the Dead, "Teste David cum
Sibylle." (By the witness of David and the Sibyl).

The original Sibylline Books were kept concealed in the
Capitol at Rome, and were lost when it was destroyed by fire
in 405, A.D. They were held in profound veneration and were
consulted only by decree of the Senate. Cicero bears witness
to their worth saying,"How often has our Senate enjoined the
decemvirs to consult the hooks of the Sibyls," when "
portentious events announced to the Romans terrible and
disastrous seditions. On all these occasions the diviners and
their auspices were in perfect accordance with the prophetic
verses of the Sibyl." There is a famous tradition that the first
Sibylline Book was sold to King Tarquin, one of the early
rulers of Rome, by the Sibyl who dwelt at Cumae, in Italy.

Now Justin Martyr states that it was the ancient Babylonian
Sibyl (Sambethe), who came to Cumae, and there gave
Oracles which contain the true religion, and which Plato
admired as divine. Thus Sambethe, the most ancient of the
Sibyls, is seen to have initiated the Sibylline Oracles which
guided the destinies of ancient Rome as well as the Delphic
Oracles which exercised such influence over the evolution of
ancient Greece. And if Justin Martyr's statement(GIVEN
NOTE X, COMMENTARY CONTINUED. SIBYLLINE

from them. And then, too, my Son," he laughingly continued, "it is not for you to annul the marriage of David and the Sibyl which was made by a celebrated cardinal, nor to accuse that learned personage of having placed side by side a great prophet and a wretched demoniac. Since either David strengthens the testimony of the Sibyl or the Sibyl weakens the authority of David."

"Sir," I exclaimed, "I entreat you again to become serious."

"Willingly," said he, "provided you will not accuse me of being too much so. Is it your opinion that the Devil is sometimes divided against himself and against his own interests?"

"Why not?" said I.

"Why not!" said he, "Because that which Tertullian has so felicitously and so grandly termed 'the Reason of God' does not find it fitting. Satan is never divided against himself. It therefore follows either, that the Devil has never spoken through the Oracles, or that he has never spoken through them against his own interests; and therefore if the Oracles have spoken against the interests of the

---

PROPHECY OF WORLD PEACE. NOTE II, COMMENTARY CONCLUDED.) as to the tenor of her teachings is to be believed, we must conclude that the
TRUE RELIGION EXISTED IN BOTH ROME AND GREECE PRIOR TO THE CHRISTIAN ERA AND DURING WHAT IS NOW TERMED THE PAGAN PERIOD.

Devil, it was not the Devil who was speaking through the Oracles."

"But," said I, 'has not God been able to compel the Devil to bear witness to the truth and to speak against himself?"

"But," he answered, "What if God has not compelled him to do so?"

"Ah, in that case," I replied, "you are more in the right than the monks."

"Let us look into this matter then," he continued, "and that I may proceed invincibly and in good faith, I do not care to introduce the evidence concerning Oracles cited by the Fathers of the Church, although I am aware of the veneration you entertain for those great men. Their religion and the interest they took in the matter might have prejudiced them, and seeing Truth to be rather poor and naked in their own time, their love of her might have caused them to borrow from[63] Falsehood's self some robe and ornament for Truth's adornment. They were men and consequently capable of bearing false witness, according to the maxim of the Poet of the Synagogue. I shall therefore take a man who cannot be suspected of such a motive, a Pagan, and a Pagan of a very different kind to Lucretius, or Lucian, or the Epicureans. A Pagan thoroughly imbued with the belief that there are gods and

---

[63] MAXIM OF THE POET OF THE SYNAGOGUE. "I said in my haste, all men are liars." PSALMS OF DAVID, CXV1, 11.

devils without number, immeasurably superstitious, a mighty magician, or supposedly so, and consequently a great partisan of devils namely Porphyry. Here are word for word some Oracles which he reports.

ORACLE. 64

---

[64] THE PRINCIPLE OF ALL THINGS.--BEYOND THE SUN IN THE DIRECTION OF THE DOG STAR LIES THAT INCORRUPTIBLE FLAME OR SUN, PRINCIPLE OF ALL THINGS, WILLING OBEDIENCE FROM OUR OWN SUN WHICH IS BUT A MANIFESTATION OF ITS RELEGATED FORCE. THE EXISTENCE OF THE SUN BEHIND THE SUN HAS BEEN KNOWN IN ALL AGES, as well as the fact that its influence is most potent upon earth during that period every 2000 years when it is in conjunction with the Sun of our solar system. Then gathering to itself the power of its own Source and transmitting it through our Sun to this planet, it is said to send the Sons of God into the consciousness of the earth sphere that a anew world of thought and emotion may be born in the minds of men for the stimulation of humanity's spiritual evolution. Such a manifestation marks the beginning or end of an epoch upon earth by the radiation of that divine consciousness known as the Christ Ray or Paraclete.

To the Egyptians the Sun behind the Sun was known as Osiris, (AND ALSO AS AMEN-RA, THE HIDDEN SUN.) said to be the husband of Isis (Nature) and parent of Horus (the Sun), symbolically represented as a hawk because that bird flies nearest the Sun. This ancient people knew that once every year the Parent Sun is in line with the Dog Star. Therefore the Great Pyramid was so constructed that, at this sacred moment, the light of the Dog Star fell upon the square "Stone of God" at the upper end of the Great Gallery descending upon the head of the high priest who received the Super Solar Force and sought through his own perfected Solar Body to transmit to other Initiates this added stimulation for the evolution of their Godhood. This then was the purpose of

91

Above the Celestial Fire there is an Incorruptible Flame, ever sparkling, Source of Life, Fountain of all Beings, and Principle of all Things. This Flame produces all, and nothing perishes save that which it consumes. It reveals itself by virtue of itself This Fire cannot he contained in any place; it is without form and without substance, it girdles the Heavens and from it there proceeds a tiny spark which: makes the whole fire of the Sun, Moon and Stars. This is what I know of God. Seek not to know more, for this passes thy comprehension howsoever wise thou mayest be. Nevertheless, know that the unjust and wicked man cannot hide himself from God, nor

---

the "'Stone of God,' whereon, in the Ritual, Osiris sits to bestow upon him (the illuminate) the Atf crown of celestial light." "North and South of that crown is love" proclaims an Egyptian hymn. "And thus throughout the teaching of Egypt the visible light was but the shadow of the invisible Light; and in the wisdom of that ancient country the measures of Truth were the years of the Most High."(MARSHAM ADAMS "THE BOOK OF THE MASTER." PAGE 141-2.) The adorable Fire and immense depth of Flame which the human heart must not fear to touch is that power proceeding from the Lord and Giver of Life, the Creative Principle of the Universe, the Sun behind the Sun.

Modern science partially confirms these facts as to the significance of the Great Pyramid but lacks the key to them. Dr. Percival Lowell, in a recent essay entitled "Precession and the Pyramids," says--"The Great Pyramid was in fact a great observatory, the most superb one ever erected," and "The Great Gallery's floor exactly included every possible position of the Sun's shadow at noon from the year's beginning to its end. We thus reach the remarkable result that the gallery was a gigantic gnomon or sundial telling, not like ordinary sundials the hour of the day, but on a more impressive scale, the seasons of the year."

can craft nor excuse disguise aught fröm His piercing eyes. All is full of God, God is everywhere.

"You will admit, my Son, that this Oracle is not too greatly influenced by his devil."

"At least," I answered "the Devil in this instance rather departs from his character."

"Here is another," said he, "that preaches still better."

ORACLE.

There is in God an immense depth of Flame. The heart must not, however, fear to touch this adorable Fire nor to be touched by it. It will in no wise he consumed by this gentle Flame, whose tranquil and peaceful warmth causes the union, harmony and duration of the world. Nothing exists save by this Fire, which is God himself It is uncreate, it is without mother, it is omniscient and unteachable: it is unchanging in purposes, and its Name is Inefable. This is God; as for us who are His messengers, WE ARE BUT A LITTLE PART OF GOD.

"Well! What say you to that?"

"I should say of both," I replied, "that God can force the Father of Lies to bear witness to the truth."

"Here is another," rejoined the. Comte, "which will remove that scruple."

ORACLE. [65]

Alas Tripods! Weep and make funeral oration for your Apollo. HE IS MORTAL, HE IS ABOUT TO DIE, HE EXPIRES; because the Light of the Celestial Flame extinguishes him.

"You see, my child, that whoever this may be who speaks through these Oracles, and who so admirably explains to the Pagans the Essence, Unity, Immensity and Eternity of God, he owns that he is mortal and but a spark of God. Therefore it cannot be the Devil who is speaking, since he is immortal, and God would not compel him to say that he is not. It is therefore proven that Satan is not divided against himself. Is it a way to make himself worshipped to say that there is but one God? The Oracle says that he is mortal, since when is the Devil become so humble as to deprive himself of even his natural qualities? Therefore you see, my Son, that if the principle of Him who is called par excellence the God of the Sciences exists, it cannot have been the Devil who spoke through the

---

[65] THE DELPHIC ORACLE'S PROPHECY REGARDING CHRIST.--This prophecy foretells the silence of the Oracles subsequent to the cdming of Christ, the Light of the Celestial Flame." Its fulfilment is confirmed by the following authorities. Scarcely thirty years after the supposed date of Jesus' death, Lucan in his Pharsalia states that "the greatest calamity of our century is the loss of that wonderful gift of heaven, the Delphic Oracle, which is silent." Eusebius cites Porphyry as saving that since Jesus began to be worshipped no man had received any public help or benefit from the Gods. And Plutarch wrote his treatise affirming the "Cessation of the Oracles" during the first century of the Christian Era.

Oracles." "But if it was not the Devil," said I, "either lying from gaiety of heart when he speaks of himself as mortal, or telling the truth under compulsion when he speaks of God, then to what will your Cabala ascribe all the Oracles which you maintain to have been actually delivered? Is it to an exhalation of the earth, as Aristotle, Cicero and Plutarch say?"[66]

"Ah! not to that my child," said the Comte. "Thanks to the Sacred Cabala my imagination has not led me astray to that extent."

---

[66] ARISTOTLE ON EXHALATION.--Likewise there exist in many parts of the world openings through which exhalations escape, some of these cause those who approach them to become inspired, while others make people waste away, and others again, as for instance those at Delphi and Labadea, cause them to utter oracles.
TRANSLATED FROM ARISTOTELIS DE MUNDO AD ALEXANDRUM. CHAPTER IV, §10.
CICERO ON EXHALATION.--"I believe also that there were certain exhalations of certain earths, by which gifted minds were inspired to utter oracles." CICERO, "ON DIVINATION." CHAPTER L.
PLUTARCH ON EXHALATION.--For the power of the exhalation neither has a predisposing influence over all nor does it always predispose the same people in the same way hut, as has been said, it supplies a beginning and, as it were, enkindles those spirits which are prepared and fitted to receive and suffer change under its influence. This divinatory vapour is a breath and a most divine and most holy Spirit, (literally, divine it is in very fact and supernatural). TRANSLATED FROM PLUTARCH MORALIA, "DE DEFECTU ORACULORUM" §438 C, D.

"What do you mean?" I inquired, "Do you consider that opinion so exceedingly visionary? Nevertheless its partisans are men of good sense."

"Not in this instance," he replied, "and it is impossible to attribute to an exhalation all that happened in the Oracles. For example, that man in Tacitus, who appeared in a dream to the priests of a temple ofHercules[67] in Armenia, and commanded them to make ready for him hunters equipped for the chase. Up to this point exhalation might account for it: but when those horses returned in the evening jaded, and their quivers emptied of shafts; and when the next day exactly the same number of dead beasts were found as there had been arrows in the quivers, you will perceive that exhalation could not have produced this effect, much less the Devil. For to believe that the Devil has been permitted to divert himself by chasing the hind and hare, is to have an irrational and uncabalistic idea of the misery of the enemy of God." "Then," said I, "to what cause does the Sacred Cabala ascribe all this?"

"Wait," he answered "before I reveal this mystery to you I must overcome any prejudice you might have because of this hypothetical exhalation. For, if I remember aright, you cited Aristotle, Plutarch and Cicero with emphasis. You might likewise have cited lamblichus, who very great genius though he was, laboured for a time under this delusion, but

---

[67] TEMPLE OF HERCULES IN ARMENIA. NOTE Y, COMMENTARY CONTINUED.

speedily relinquished it when he had examined the matter at close range in the Book of the Mysteries.

Peter of Aponus, Pomponatius, Levinius, Sirenius, and Lucilius Vanino were also overjoyed to find this subterfuge in some of the ancient writers. All these pseudo-geniuses who, when they treat of divine things, say rather what pleases them than what they know to be true, are unwilling to admit that there is anything superhuman in the Oracles, lest they should acknow- ledge the existence of something superior to man." They fear lest men should make of the Oracles 'a lad= der wherewith to mount to God, Whom they"dread

to acknowledge as manifesting through gradations of His spiritual creatures[68], and they prefer to

---

[68] GRADATIONS OF HIS SPIRITUAL CREATURES.--The purpose of this book is to point out to man the possibility of his own divine evolution and to make plain to him that through obedience to the highest instincts and impulses which he knows, he may evolve from darkness into light, from knowledge into understanding, and from understanding into Wisdom Found which is the consciousness of the Universal Mind.

It is true that God manifests through the gradations of His spiritual creatures, for the Creator is omnipresent in His Creation and inseparable from it. Therefore knowledge of the Creator or true religion, and knowledge of His Creation or exact science, are in their essence one. And as the scientist of to-day re- cognises as being between the vegetable and animal kingdoms, certain forms of life which demonstrably partake of the nature of, and may be claimed by both; so the scientist of the future will have power to discern that man is by nature both human and divine, possessing at once the attributes of humanity and the elements of a Godhood, the science of whose evolution is as exact and as logical as the science of

manufac ture a ladder to descend into nothingness. Instead of mounting towards heaven they delve into the earth, ;ày. and instead of seeking in Beings superior to man 'the cause if those transports which lift him above himself and restore to him a kind of divinity, they weakly ascribe to impotent exhalations this power to penetrate the future, discover hidden things, and attain to the supreme secrets of the Divine Essence."

"Such is the misery of man when possessed by the spirit of contradiction and the disposition to think differently to others. Instead of achieving his ends he becomes involved and fettered. These intellectual libertines do not wish to make man subject to substances less material than himself, and yet they make him subject to an exhalation: and disregarding the absence of any connection whatever between this chimerical vapour and the soul of man, between this emanation and future events, between this frivolous cause and these miraculous effects, the mere singularity of their theories is to them sufficient evidence of their reasonableness. They are content to deny the existence of spirits and to assume the rôle of free thinkers."

---

mathematics. Hence the religion of the future will be a knowledge of Truth which the science of the future will sublimely sustain, while the aim of both will be to instruct humanity as to its place in the Divine Plan and as to the Law of Nature, God, which wills obedience from all things. COMPARE PLATO ON MAN'S PLACE IN NATURE, NOTE Z, COMMENTARY CONTINUED.

"Then, Sir, is singularity exceeding displeasing to you?" I asked.

"Ah! my Son," said he, "'tis the bane of commonsense and the stumbling block of the greatest minds. Aristotle, great logician though he was, could not avoid the snare into which the passion for singularity leads those whom it unbalances as violently as it did him. He could not, I say, avod becoming entangled and contradicting himself. In is hook on 'The Generation of Animals'[69] and in his 'Ethics,' he says that the spirit and understanding of man come to him from without,

---

[69] THE GENERATION OF ANIMALS.--"Plainly those principles whose activity is bodily cannot exist without a body, e.g. walking cannot exist without feet. For the same reason also they cannot enter from outside. It remains, then, for the reason alone so to enter And alone to be divine, for no bodily activity has any connection with the activity of reason." ARISTOTLELIS DE GENERATIONE ANIMALIUM. BOOK II, CHAPTER iii.
ETHICS.--"But such a life will be higher than mere human nature, because a man will live thus, not in so far as he is man, but in so far as there is in him a divine Principle. And in proportion as this Principle excels his composite nature, so far does the Energy thereof excel that in accordance with any other kind of Virtue. And therefore if pure Intellect, as compared with human nature, is divine, so too will the life in accordance with it be divine compared with man's ordinary life."
"These (the Moral Virtues), moreover, as bound up with the passions, must belong to the composite nature, and the Excellences or Virtues of the composite nature are proper to man; therefore so too will be the life and Happiness which is in accordance with them. But that of the Pure Intellect is separate and distinct." ARISTOTLE'S NICOMACHEAN ETHICS. CHASE'S TRANSLATION. EXTRACTS BOOK X, CHAPTER vi.

and cannot be transmitted from father to son. And from the spirituality of the operations of man's soul he concludes it to be of a different nature to that composite material which it animates, the grossness of which only serves to becloud speculation and is far from contributing to its production. Blind Aristotle! Since you maintain[70] that the matter of which we are composed cannot be the source of our spiritual thoughts, how can youexpect a weak exhalation to be the source of sublime thought and of those soaring flights of spirit achieved by those who gave forth the Pythian Oracles? See, my child, how forcibly this genius contradicts himself, and how his craving for singularity leads him astray."

"You reason very logically, Sir," said I, enchanted to perceive that he was talking excellent sense, and hoping that his madness would not prove incurable, "God willing--"

"Plutarch,[71] so sound in other respects," he said, interrupting me, "moves me to pity in his dialogue concerning the 'Cessation of the Oracles.'

---

[70] 384 B.C. ARISTOTLE, 322 B.C., the disciple of Plato. "Aristotle and Plato are reckoned the respective heads of two schools. A wise man will see that Aristotle Platonises." (Ralph Waldo Emerson.)

[71] 45 A.D. PLUTARCH, 120 A.D.--A Greek Initiate, for many years priest of Apollo apparently at Delphi. "You know that I have served the Pythian God for many Pythiads past, yet you would not now tell me, 'you have taken part enough in the sacrifices, processions and dances, and it is high time Plutarch, now you are an old man, to lay aside your garland, and retire as superannuated from the Oracle.'"

Convincing objections are raised which he in no wise refutes. Why does he not answer what is said to him, namely, that it is the exhalation which causes these transports, all those who approach the prophetic Tripod would be seized with enthusiasm and not merely a single maiden who moreover must be virgin. But how can this vapour articulate cries through the abdomen? Besides this exhalation is a natural cause which must necessarily produce its effect regularly and at all times. Why is this maiden agitated only when consulted? And, what is more important, why has the earth ceased to breathe forth these divine vapours? Is it less earth now than then? Is it subject to other influences? Has it other seas and other rivers? Who then has stopped earth's pores or changed its nature?"

"I wonder that Pomponatius, Lucilius and the other Libertines should borrow this idea from Plutarch and cast aside his explanation. He spoke more judiciously than Cicero and Aristotle, for he was a man of great good sense and, not knowing what conclusion to draw from all these Oracles, after tedious irresolution, he decided that this exhalation, which he believed issued from the earth, was a most divine spirit. Thus he ascribed to divinity the extraordinary agitations and illuminations of the Priestesses of Apollo[72]. '*This*

---

[72] PRIESTESSES OF APOLLO.--"But the prophetess at Delphi, whether she gives oracles to mankind through an attenuated and fiery spirit, bursting from the mouth of the cavern, or whether being seated in the adytum on a brazen tripod, or on a stool with four feet, she becomes sacred to the God; which so ever of these is the case, she entirely gives herself up to a divine spirit, and is illuminated with a ray of

divinatory vapour is a breath and a most divine and most holy spirit,' said he."

"Pomponatius, Lucilius and modern atheists do not adapt themselves readily to fashions of speech which imply divinity. 'These exhalations', say they, 'were of the nature of those vapours which infect splenetics who speak languages they do not understand.' Fernelius refutes these impieties rather well, by proving that bile which is a peccant humour cannot cause that diversity of tongues which is one of the most marvellous effects under consideration and an artificial expression of thought. Nevertheless, he decided erroneously in subscribing to Psellus, and to all those who have not penetrated far enough into our Holy Philosophy for, like them, not knowing where to locate the causes of these surprising effects, he imitated the women and monks and attributed them to the Devil."

"Then to whom should one attribute them? " said I, "I have long awaited this Cabalistic secret."

---

divine fire. And when, indeed, fire ascending from the mouth of the cavern, circularly invests her in collected abundance, she becomes filled from it with a divine splendour. But when she places herself on the seat of the God, she becomes co-adapted to his stable prophetic power; and from both those preparatory operations she becomes wholly possessed by the God. And then, indeed, he is present with and illuminates her in a separate manner, and is different from the fire, the spirit the proper seat, and, in short, from all the visible apparatus of the place, whether physical or sacred." IAMBLICHUS ON THE MYSTERIES. SECTION III, CHAPTER xi. THOMAS TAYLOR'S TRANSLATION.

"Plutarch[73] has very well indicated it," he said, "and he would have been wise had he let matters rest there. Since this irregular method of expressing one's opinion by means of an unseemly organ was neither solemn enough nor sufficiently worthy of the majesty of the gods, says that Pagan, and since the sayings of the Oracles surpassed the powers of the soul of man, they have rendered great service to Philosophy, for they have established the existence of mortal beings between the gods and man to whom one can ascribe all that surpasses human weakness yet falls short of divine greatness."

---

[73] PLUTARCH ON THE ORACLES.--"We have formerly shown that he (Plutarch) owned the unity of a Godhead; whom, according to his attributes, he calls by several names, as Jupiter from his almighty power, Apollo from his wisdom, and so of the rest; but under him he places those beings whom he styles Genii or Daemons, of a middle nature, between divine and human; for he thinks it absurd that there should be no mean between the two extremes of an immortal and a mortal being; that there cannot be in nature so vast a flaw, without some intermedial kind of life, partaking of them both. As, therefore, we find the intercourse between the soul and body to be made by the animal spirits, so between divinity and humanity there is this species of daemons. Who, having first been men, and followed the stria rules of virtue, having purged off the grossness and feculency of their earthly being, are exalted into these genii; and are from thence either raised higher into an ethereal life, if they still continue virtuous, or tumbled down again into mortal bodies, and sinking into flesh after they have lost that purity which constituted their glorious being. And this sort of Genii are those who, as our author imagines, presided over oracles." A. H. CLOUGH: INTRODUCTION TO PLUTARCH'S LIVES. COMPARE SIR THOMAS BROWNE ON MAN'S PLACE IN NATURE, NOTE AA, COMMENTARY CONTINUED.

"This is the opinion held in every ancient philosophy. The Platonists and the Pythagoreans took it from the Egyptians, and the latter from Joseph the A Saviour, and from the Hebrews who dwelt in Egypt before the crossing of the Red Sea. The Hebrews used to call these beings who are between the Angels and man Sadaim, and the Greeks, transposing the letters and adding but one syllable, called them Daimonas. Among the ancient Philosophers these demons were held to be an Aerial Race, ruling over the Elements, mortal, engendering, and unknown in this century to those who rarely seek Truth in her ancient dwelling place, which is to say, in the. Cabala and in the theology of the Hebrews, who possessed the special art of holding communion with that Aerial People and of conversing with all these Inhabitants of the Air."

"Now, Sir, I think you have returned again to your Sylphs."

"Yes, my Son," he went on, "the Teraphim of the Jews was but the ceremony which had to be observed

for that communion: and that Jew Micah[74], who complains in the Book of Judges that his gods have

---

74 MICAH.--"And the man Micah had an house of gods, and made an ephod, and teraphim, and conse- crated one of his sons, who became his priest. And there was a young man out of Bethlehem-judah of the family of Judah, who was a Levite; and Micah consecrated the Levite; and the young man became his priest. And the five men that went to spy out the land went up, and came in thither, and took the graven image, and

104

been taken from him, only laments the loss of the little image through which the Sylphs used to converse with him. The gods which Rachel stole

---

the ephod, and the teraphim, and the molten image. And when they were a good way from the house of Micah, the men that were in the houses near to Micah's house were gathered together, and overtook the children of Dan. And they cried unto the children of Dan. And they turned their faces and said unto Micah, What aileth thee, that thou comest with such a company?' And he said, Ye have taken away my gods which I made, and the priest, and ye are gone away: and what have I more?'" EXTRACTS FROM BOOK OF JUDGES, CHAPTERS xvii. AND xviii.

MICHAL AND DAVID.--"Saul also sent messenger unto David's house to watch him, and to slay him in the morning: and Michal, David's wife told him. saying, If thou save not thy life to-night, to-morrov, thou shalt be slain.' So Michal let David dowr through a window: and he went, and fled, and escaped And Michal took an image, and laid it in the bed and put a pillow of goat's hair for his bolster, and covered it with a cloth." I SAMUEL, xix., 11-13.

RACHEL, JACOB AND LABAN.--"Yet wherefore has p. 108 thou stolen my gods? And Jacob answered and said to Laban, 'With whomsoever thou findest thy gods, let him not live.' For Jacob knew not that Rachel had stolen them. Now Rachel had taken the images, and put them in the camel's furniture, and sat upon them. And Laban searched all the tent, but found them not." EXTRACTS FROM BOOK OF GENESIS, CHAPTER XXXI.

TERAPHIM.--"The use of these Images was to consult with them as with Oracles, concerning things for the present unknown, or future to come. To this purpose they were made by Astrologers under certain constellations, capable of heavenly influences, whereby they were enabled to speak. The teraphims have spoken vanity, (*Zacharias x. 2*). And among other reasons why Rachel stole away her father's images, this is thought to be one, that Laban might not, by consulting with these Images, discover what way Jacob took his flight." THOMAS GODWYN.

from her father were also Teraphim. Neither Micah nor Laban are reproved for idolatry, and Jacob would have taken care not to live for fourteen years with an idolater, nor to marry his daughter. It was only a commerce with Sylphs; and tradition tells us that the Synagoge considered such commerce permissible, and that the image belonging to David's wife was but the Teraphim by virtue of which she conversed with the Elementary Peoples: for you can well imagine that the Prophet after God's own heart would not have tolerated idolatry in his household."

"These Elementary Nations, so long as God neglected the salvation of the world in punishment for the first sin, used to take pleasure in explaining to men through the Oracles what they knew of God, in teaching them how to live morally, and in giving them most wise and most profitable counsels, such as are seen in great number in Plutarch and in all historians. As soon as God took pity on mankind and was willing Himself to become their Teacher, these little Masters withdrew. Hence the silence of the Oracles."

"Then the upshot of your entire discourse, Sir," I remarked, "is that there certainly were Oracles, and that the Sylphs delivered them, and even to-day deliver them in goblets or in mirrors."

"The Sylphs or Salamanders, the Gnomes or Undines," corrected the Comte.

"If that be so," I replied, "all your Elementary Peoples are very dishonest folk."

"Why do you say that? " said he.

"Why? Could anything be more knavish," I pursued, "than all these responses with double meanings which they always give?"

"Always? " he replied. " Ah! not always. Did the Sylphid speak very obscurely who appeared to that Roman in Asia[75] and predicted to him that he would one day return to Rome with the dignity of Proconsul? And does not Tacitus say that the event occurred exactly as predicted? That inscription and a those statues famous in the history of Spain which warned unfortunate King Rodriguez[76] that his indiscretion and incontinence would be punished by men dressed and armed exactly as they were, and that those black men would take possession of Spain and rule there for many a year. Could anything have been more explicit, and was not the prophecy verified by the event in that selfsame year? For did not the Moors come to dethrone that effeminate king? You know the story, and you must admit that the Devil, who since the reign of the Messiah does not dispose of empires, could not have been the author of this Oracle: and that it was undoubtedly some great Cabalist who had it from one of the most learned Salamanders. Since the Salamanders love chastity exceedingly,

---

[75] LCOMMENTARY. THAT ROMAN IN ASIA WAS CURTIUS RUFUS. NOTE BB, COMMENTARY CONTINUED.
[76] KING RODRIGUEZ.--NOTE CC, COMMENTARY CONTINUED.

they willingly make known to us the misfortunes which must befall mankind for lack of that virtue."

"But, Sir," said I to him, "do you consider that heteroclitic organ which they made use of for the preaching of their ethics very chaste and altogether in keeping with Cabalistic modesty?"

"Ah!" said the Comte, smiling, "Your imagination is shocked, and you fail to perceive the physical reason which causes the flaming Salamander naturally to delight in the most igneous places and to be attracted by--" [77]

"I understand, I understand," I interrupted, "Do not take the trouble to explain further."

"As for the obscurity of some Oracles which you dub knavery," he went on seriously, "are not shadows the usual cloak of Truth? Is not God pleased to hide Himself in their sombre veil? And is not Holy Writ, that perpetual Oracle which He has left to His

---

[77] DUAL ASPECT OF SOLAR FORCE.--Allusion is here made to the fact that the force manifesting in generation is identical with that which, when rightly controlled, becomes the instrument of regeneration, the upbuilding of the Spiritual or Solar Body.

"In love is found the secret of divine unity: it is love that unites the higher and lower stages, and that lifts every thing to that stage where all must be one." ZOHAR.

"Oh height of love, thou openest the double Gate of the Horizon." EGYPTIAN BOOK OF THE DEAD.

"Men have called Love Eros, because he has wings the Gods have called him Pteros, because he has the virtue of giving wings." PLATO, "THE BANQUET."

children, enveloped in an adorable obscurity which confounds and bewilders the proud even as its Light guides the humble?"

"If this be your only difficulty, my Son, I advise you not to postpone entering into communion with the Elementary Peoples. You will find them very sincere folk, learned, benevolent and God-fearing. I am of opinion that you should begin with the Salamanders, for you have Mars in mid-heaven in your horoscope, which signifies that there is a great deal of fire in all your actions. And as for marriage, I rather think that you should choose a Sylphid. You would be happier with her than with any of the others, for you have Jupiter in the ascendant with Venus in sextile. Now Jupiter presides over the Air and the Peoples of the Air. You must, however, consult your own heart in this matter for, as you will one day see, a Sage governs himself by the interior stars, and the stars of the exterior heaven but serve to give him a more certain knowledge of the aspects of the stars of that interior heaven[78] which is in every creature. Thus it rests with you to tell me what your inclination is, that we may

---

[78] INTERIOR STARS.--Reference is here made to the seven principal ganglia of the sympathetic nervous system. When awakened and stimulated by the inflowing Solar Force, these centres appear to the seer as flaming rapidly revolving wheels or stars of great luminositly. In Sanskrit works the planets are held to govern these ganglia as follows: Saturn the sacral, Jupiter the prostatic, Mars the epigastric, Venus the cardiac, Mercury the pharyngeal, Moon the post nasal, Sun the pineal. COMPARE THE INMATES OF THE CAVE, OR THE STORY OF THE SEVEN SLEEPERS, AS RELATED IN THE KORAN. NOTE DD, COMMENTARY CONTINUED.

proceed to your alliance with those Elementary Peoples which are most pleasing to you."

"Sir," I replied, "in my opinion this affair demands a little consultation."

"I esteem you for that answer," said he, laying his hand on my shoulder. "Consult maturely as to this affair, and above all, with him who is called in an eminent degree the Angel of the Grand Council[79]. Go, and devote yourself to prayer, and I shall be at your house at two o'clock to-morrow afternoon."

---

[79] ANGEL OF THE GRAND COUNCIL.--when a group of souls is sent forth from the Infinite Mind to perform a desired work and to gain a definite range of experience, these souls descend into matter and lose consciousness for a time of their own true estate. A chosen member remains upon the loftiest plane of consciousness in which it is possible to fun ion while maintaining constant communication with the most highly evolved soul of the group now immersed in matter. This chosen member is the Angel of the Grand Council, whose office it is to be the channel of that Source which sent them forth in the beginning. This exalted being retains and makes known to those of his own

Order, working in the lower states
of consciousness, a knowledge
of the divine plan and purpose
for which they
incarnated. COMPARE
SLEEP. NOTE EE,
COMMENTARY
CONTINUED

We came back to Paris, and on the way I led him once more to discourse against atheists and libertines. I have never heard arguments so well supported by reason, nor such sublime and subtle ideas advanced for the existence of God, and against the blindness of those who go through life without wholly surrendering themselves to a serious and continual worship

of Him to whom we owe the gift and preservation of
our being. I was surprised at
the character of this man, and I could
not comprehend how it was
possible for him to be at
once so strong, and so
weak, so
admirable,
yet so
ridiculous

THE COMTE DE GABALIS

 AWAITED the Comte de Gabalis at my house, as we had arranged at parting. He came at the appointed hour and accosting me with a smiling air said, "Ah well, my Son, which of the Invisible Peoples does God give you most inclination for, and would you prefer an alliance with Salamanders, Gnomes, Nymphs, or Sylphids?"

"I have not yet quite made up my mind to this marriage, Sir," I replied.

"What deters you?" he inquired.

"To be frank with you, Sir," said I, "I cannot conquer my imagination, which always represents these pretended hosts of the Elements as so many imps of Satan." [80]

"Dissipate, O Lord!" cried he, "O God of Light! Dissipate the darkness in which ignorance and a perverse education have enveloped the mind of this chosen one, whom Thou hast made me know that Thou dost destine for such great things! And you, my Son, close not the door against Truth which is willing to enter in unto you. Be non-resistant. Nay, you need not be so, for it is most injurious to Truth to prepare the way for her. She knows how to break through gates of iron and how to enter where she

---

[80] SATAN CABALISTICALLY DEFINED.--St. Paul states that there is "One God and Father of all, who is above all, and through all, and in you all." (Ephesians, iv., 6;) If this be true, Satan, the so-called force of evil, can be but a manifestation of God. "The Hebrew satan is derived from the same root as séteh, 'turn away,' (*Prov. iv., 15*), it implies the notion of turning and moving away from a thing; "hence the meaning of adversary, opposer."According to our Sages the evil inclination, the adversary (satan) and the angel are undoubtedly identical, and the adversary being called 'angel,' because he is among the sons of God. "It has thus been shown to you that one and the same thing is designated by these three different terms, and that actions ascribed to these three are in reality the actions of one and the same agent." (RABBI MOSES MAIMONIDES, "GUIDE FOR THE PERPLEXED." EXTRACTS PART III., CHAPTER XX71., PAGES 298-299. 2ND EDITION OF TRANSLATION BY M. FRIEDLANDER, PH.D.) In the Book of Genesis this agent is personified as "the serpent more subtil than any beast of the field which the Lord God had made," in which allegory interpreted Satan, the serpent, is seen to be the Serpent Fire or Solar Force misgoverned by the human mind, turning away from and operating in opposition to the Law of Nature, God, which wills obedience from all things.

pleases despite all resistance of falsehood. What have you to oppose to her? Would you say that God has not, power to create in the Elements real beings such as have described?"[81]

"I have not looked into the matter," said I, "to ascertain whether the thing itself be impossible, whether a single Element can furnish blood, flesh and bones; whether temperament can exist without admixture, and action without opposing force; but assuming that God has been able thus to create, what sound proof is there that He has done so?"

"Let me convince you of it at once, without further temporising. I am going to summon the Sylphs of Cardan; and you shall hear from their own lips what they are, and what I have taught you about them."

---

[81] PLATO ON THE PEOPLE OF THE ELEMENTS.--"There are also many other animals and men upon it (the earth), some dwelling in mid-earth, others about the air, as we do about the sea, and others in islands which the air flows round, and which are near the continent: and in one word, what water and the sea are to us for our necessities, the air is to them; and what air is to us, that ether is to them. But their seasons are of such a temperament that they are free from disease, and live for a much longer time than those here, and surpass us in sight, hearing, and smelling, and everything of this kind, as much as air excels water, and ether air, in purity." SOCRATES SPEAKING. PLATO, THE PHAEDO." PAGE 195, EVERYMAN EDITION.
SYLPHS OF CARDAN. NOTE D, COMMENTARY CONTINUED.

"By no means, Sir," I exclaimed hastily. "Postpone such proof, I beg of you, until I am persuaded that these folk are not the enemies of God; for until then I would rather die than wrong my conscience by----"

"Behold the ignorance and false piety of these unhappy times," interrupted the Comte wrathfully. "Why do they not expunge the greatest of the Anchorites [82] from the Calendar of the Saints? Why

---

[82] 251 A.D. ST. ANTONY, 356 A.D., the founder of Christian monasticism, born at Coma in Egypt.
Incident to which the Comte refers.
ST. ANTONY AND THE ELEMENTARY BEING.--
"Antony was amazed, and thinking over what he had seen went on his way. Before long in a small rocky valley shut in on all sides he sees a mannikin with hooked snout, horned forehead, and extremities like goats' feet. When he saw this, Antony like a good soldier seized the shield of faith and the helmet of hope: the creature none the less began to offer him the fruit of the palm-trees to support him on his journey and as it were pledges of peace. Antony perceiving this stopped and asked who he was. The answer he received from him was this: I am a mortal being and one of those inhabitants of the desert whom the Gentiles deluded by various forms of error worship under the names of Fauns, Satyrs, and Incubi. I am sent to represent my tribe. We pray you in our behalf to entreat the favour of your Lord and ours, who, we have learnt, came once to save the world, and 'whose sound has gone forth into all the earth.' As he uttered such words as these, the aged traveller's cheeks streamed with tears, the marks of his deep feeling, which he shed in the fulness of his joy. He rejoiced over the Glory of Christ and the destruction of Satan, and marvelling all the while that he could understand the Satyr's language, and striking the ground with his staff, he said, 'Woe to thee, Alexandria, who instead of God worshippest monsters! Woe to thee, harlot city, into which have flowed together the demons of the whole world! What will you say now? Beasts speak of Christ, and you instead of God worship monsters,' He had not finished speaking when,

do they not burn his statues? It is a thousand pities people do not insult his venerable ashes and cast them to the winds, as they would those of the poor wretches who are accused of having had dealings with devils! Did he bethink himself to exorcise the Sylphs? And did he not treat them as men? What have you to say to that, scrupulous Sir, you and all your miserable doctors? And is it your opinion that the Sylph who discoursed concerning his nature to this Patriarch was an imp of Satan? Did this incomparable man confer with a hobgoblin concerning the Gospel? And will you accuse him of having profaned the adorable Mysteries by conversing concerning them with a phantom enemy of God? In that case Athanasi.us and Jerome are most unworthy of the great name accorded them by your learned men, for they have written eloquent eulogies of a man who treated devils thus humanely."

"If they had taken this Sylph for a devil they would either have concealed the adventure or have altered the sense of the sermon, or of that very pathetic apostrophe, which the Anchorite--more zealous and

as if on wings, the wild creature fled away. Let no one scruple to believe this incident; its truth is supported by what took place when Constantine was on the throne, a matter of which the whole world was witness. For a man of that kind was brought alive to Alexandria and shewn as a wonderful sight to the people. Afterwards his lifeless body, to prevent its decay through the summer heat, was preserved in salt and brought to Antioch that the Emperor might see it." ST. JEROME'S LIFE OF PAULUS THE FIRST HERMIT, CHAPTER VIII. TRANSLATED BY THE HON. W. H. FREEMANTLE, M.A.

more credulous than you--made to the cify of Alexandria.

Now if they thought him a being who had, as he affirmed, a share in the redemption as well as we ourselves, and if they considered this apparition an extraordinary favour bestowed by God upon the Saint whose life they wrote, are you rational in thinking yourself better informed than Athanasius and Jerome, and a greater Saint than the divine Antony? What would you have said to that admirable man had you been one of the ten thousand hermits to whom he recounted the conversation he had just been having with the Sylph? Wiser and more enlightened than all those terrestial Angels, you would doubtless have demonstrated to the Holy Abbot that his entire adventure was but pure illusion, and you would have dissuaded his disciple Athanasius from making known to all the world a story so little in keeping with religion, philosophy, and common sense. Is not this true?"

"It is true," said I, "that I should have thought best either to say nothing whatever about it or to tell more."[83]

---

[83] Incident to which the Abbé refers.
TEMPTATION OF ST. ANTONY.--"But the devil, who hates and envies what is good, could not endure to see such a resolution in a youth, but endeavoured to carry out against him what he had been wont to effect against others. In a word he raised in his mind a great dust of debate, wishing to debar him from his settled purpose. But when the enemy saw himself to be too weak for Antony's determination, and that

"Athanasius and Jerome," replied he, "were careful not to tell more, for that was all they knew, and even though they had known all, which is impossible if one is not of our number, they would not rashly have divulged the secrets of the Sages."

"But why not? Did not the Sylph propose to St. Antony what you are to-day proposing to me? " "What?" said the Comte laughing, "Marriage? Ah! would that have been quite fitting?"

"Probably the good man would not have accepted the offer," I ventured.

"No, certainly not," said the Comte, "for it would have been tempting God to marry at that age and to ask Him for children."

"What! " I exclaimed. "Do people marry Sylphs for the purpose of having children?"

---

he rather was conquered by the other's firmness, overthrown by his great faith and falling through his constant prayers, then at length putting his trust in the weapons (COMPARE BEHEMOTH AND LEVIATHAN. NOTE FF, COMMENTARY CONTINUED.) which are 'in the navel of his belly,' and boasting in them--for they are his first snare for the young--he attacked the young man, disturbing him by night and harassing him by day, so that even the onlookers saw the struggle which was going on between them. And the devil, uuhappy wight, one night even took upon him the shape of a woman and imitated all her acts simply to beguile Antony. But he, his mind filled with Christ and the nobility inspired by Him, and considering the spirituality of the soul, quenched the coal of the other's deceit."
ATHANASIUS' "LIFE OF ANTONY," CHAPTER V.

"Indeed! " said he, "Is it ever permissible to marry for any other purpose?"[84]

"I did not imagine," said I, "that they aspired to I' the planting of family trees. I had supposed their sole object to be the immortalisation of the Sylphids."

"Ah! you are mistaken," quoth he. "The charity of the Philosophers causes them to have as their ultimate aim the immortality of the Sylphids: but Nature makes them desire to see them fruitful. Whenever you wish you shall see these philosophic families in the Air. Happy world, if there had been no other families and if there had been no children of sin!"

"What do you mean by children of sin?" I inquired.

"They are, my Son," he explained, "all children who are born in the ordinary way, children conceived by the will of the flesh and not by the will of God, children of wrath and malediction; in a word, children. of man and woman. You are longing to interrupt me. I see exactly what you would like to say. Yes, my child, know that it was never the will of the Lord that men and women should have children in the way in which they do. The design of the Most Wise Craftsman was far nobler. He would have had the world peopled in a different manner than we see it. If wretched Adam had not grossly

---

[84] "DIVORCE should warn the age of some fundamental error in the marriage state." MARY BAKER EDDY.

disobeyed God's command not to touch Eve, and had he contented himself with all the other fruits in the garden of pleasure[85], with the beauties of the

---

[85] ALLEGORY OF EVE AND THE SERPENT.--The primordial elericity or Solar Force, semi-latent within the aura of every human being, was known to the Greeks as the Speirêma, the serpent-coil; and in the Upanishads, the sacred writings of India, it is said to lie coiled up like a slumbering serpent. In the third chapter of the Book of Genesis it is symbolised as the serpent, "more subtil than any beast of the field which the Lord God had made." Eve, when this force stirred within her, was tempted to its misapplication. Directed downward through the lower physical centres for generation, unhallowed by a consciousness of responsibility to God and the incoming soul, the Serpent Force or Fire brought knowledge of evil; directed upward toward the brain for regeneration, the formation of the deathless Solar Body, it brought knowledge of good. Hence the dual operation of the Solar Force is symbolised as the tree of the knowlege of good and evil.

The curse of the Lord upon the serpent, "upon thy belly shalt thou go, and dust shalt thou eat all the days of thy life:" makes reference to the fact that, during a certain period of human evolution, man shall remain in ignorance of the Law governing the serpent (Solar Force) which shall manifest in man's lower or earthly vehicles misgoverned by the human mind.

"And I will put enmity between thee and the woman, and between thy seed and her seed; it shall bruise thy head, and thou shalt bruise his heel." During the above mentioned cycle of evolution, in his ignorance of the Law governing the Serpent Fire, man shall continually direct it downward or bruise its head, while the Serpent Fire, thus misdirected, shall bruise man's heel, heel being a euphemism for that part of man nearest the earth, that is to say, the body, lower emotions and mortal mind.

"And the Lord God said, Behold, the man is become as one of us, to know good and evil: and now, lest he put forth his hand, and take also of the tree of life, and eat, and live for ever: "Here the tree of life symbolises the upward play of the Solar

Nymphs and Sylphids, the world would not have had the shame of seeing itself filled with men so imperfect that they seem monsters when compared with the children of the Philosophers."

"Apparently, Sir," said I, "you believe Adam's crime to have been other than that of eating the apple."

"Why, my Son," he replied, "are you one of those who are so simple-minded as to take the story of the apple literally? Ah! know that the Holy Language makes use of these innocent metaphors to prevent us from having improper ideas of an action which has caused all the misfortunes of the

---

Force for the creation of the deathless or Solar body. Hence the meaning is lest man should learn the Law governing Solar Force and, directing it upward, become immortal.

"So He drove out the man; and He placed at the east of the garden of Eden Cherubims, and a flaming sword which turned every way, to keep the way of the tree of life." Various interpretations of this passage . are possible. Cosmically speaking, the garden of Eden symbolises those realms -of higher spiritual attainment, at the gates of which, from the time of man's descent into the lower cycles of evolution, God placed Heavenly Beings charged with the duty of preventing that nature in man correspondent to their own from receiving stimulation during man's progress through the lower spheres of knowledge. The Muhammedans rightly hold that man can only be born again in Spirit through the aid of Heavenly Powers typified by the Angel Gabriel, ("GABRIEL, ONE. OF THE HOLY ANGELS, WHO IS OVER PARADISE AND THE SERPENTS AND THE CHERUBIM." BOOK OF ENOCH, CHAPTER XX., 7.) who is said by them to connect the heart of man with the soul, the lower consciousness with the higher. Then the same,force in Nature which has deterred man from premature spiritual attainment assists him in his upward evolution, the mind having been prepared through man's own effort for a further understanding of God's Mysteries.

human race. Thus when Solomon said, 'I will go up unto the palm tree and gather the fruit thereof,' [86] he had another appetite than that for eating dates. This language consecrated by the Angels, and in which they chant hymns to the living God, has no terms to express what it implies figuratively by the words apple and date. But the Sage easily deciphers these chaste figures of speech.[87] When he sees that the taste and mouth of Eve were not punished, and that she was delivered with pain, he knows that it was not the tasting which was criminal. And discovering what the first sin was, by reason of the care which the first sinners took to hide certain parts of their bodies with leaves, he concludes that God did not will men to multiply in this vile way. O Adam! thou shouldst only have begotten men like unto thyself, or have engendered none save heroes or giants."

"Eh! What expedient had he," I asked, "for either of these marvellous generations?"

"Obeying God," he replied, "and touching only the Nymphs, Gnomids, Sylphids or Salamanders: Thus there would have been none save heroes born, and the Universe would have been peopled with marvellous men filled with strength and wisdom. God has been pleased to enable us to conjecture the difference between that innocent world and the guilty one we behold to-day by now and then

---

[86] *Song of Solomon, Chapter vii:, verse 8.*
[87] *The Holy Language described by Emmanuel Swedenborg. Note gg, Commentary Continued.*

permitting us to see children born in the manner He designed."

"Then, Sir, have these children of the Elements occasionally been seen? If so, a Master of Arts from the Sorbonne, who was citing St. Augustin, St. Jerome, and Gregory of Nazianzus the other day, was mistaken in believing that no issue can spring from the love of spirits for women, or from the relationship men can have with certain demons he called Hyphialtes."

"Lactantius has reasoned better," the Comte replied, "and cautious Thomas Aquinas has learnedly determined not only that these intimacies, may be fruitful, but also that the children thus born are of a far nobler and more heroic nature. In fact, when it pleases you, you shall read of the lofty deeds of those mighty and famous men[88] whom Moses says were born in this manner. We have their records in our possession in the Book of the Wars of the Lord[89], cited in the twenty-first chapter of the Book of Numbers.

---

[88] MIGHTY AND FAMOUS MEN.--"There were giants in the earth in those, days; and also after that, when the sons of God came in unto the daughters of men, and they bare children to them, the same became mighty men which were of old, men of renown." *Genesis vi., 4.* Since the Book of Genesis is attributed to Moses, this verse is authority for the Comte's statement.
MOSES AN INITIATE. NOTE HH, COMMENTARY CONTINUED.
[89] BOOK OF THE WARS OF THE LORD. NOTE ii, COMMENTARY CONTINUED.

Meantime just think what the world would be if all its inhabitants were like Zoroaster."

"What!" said I, "Zoroaster whom people say was the inventor of necromancy?"

"The same of whom the ignorant have written that calumny," said the Comte. "He had the honour of being the son of the Salamander Oromasis and of Vesta, Noah's wife. He lived for twelve hundred years, the sagest monarch in the world, and then was carried away to the Region of the Salamanders by his father Oromasis."

"I do not doubt that Zoroaster is with the Salamander Oromasis in the Region of Fire," said I, "but I should not like to put such an affront upon Noah as you have been guilty of."

"The affront is not so great as you might think," replied the Comte; "all your patriarchs considered it a great honour to be the reputed fathers of those children whom the Sons of God were pleased to have by their wives[90], but as yet this is too much for you. Let us return to Oromasis. He was beloved by Vesta, Noah's wife. This Vesta after her death became the tutelary genius of Rome, and the Sacred Fire[91], which she desired the virgins to preserve with so much care, was in honour of the

---

[90] MARRIAGES OF THE GODS. "We are informed by Proclus in his Mss. commentary on the Parmenides of Plato, that ancient theologists mystically dominated the kindred conjunction and communion of divine causes with each other, Marriage."
[91] SACRED FIRE. NOTE JJ, COMMENTARY CONTINUED.

Salamander, her lover. Besides Zoroaster, there sprang from their love a daughter of rare beauty and wisdom, the divine Egeria, from whom Numa Pompilius received all his laws. She compelled Numa, whom she loved, to build a temple to Vesta[92], her mother, where the Sacred Fire should be maintained in honour of her father Oromasis. This is the truth concerning the fable about the

---

[92] NUMA.--When those Higher Intelligences which guide the evolution of mankind have determined upon that fixed ideal or principle which shall hold together in concord the minds of a race for a certain epoch of time, in order that a definite range of experience may be gained, they send their Messenger to mankind endowed with the radiance and life-giving powers of the Sun that its divine regenerative force may be poured into the channel determined upon, creating in the minds of men that new ideal which shall give a dynamic impulse to human evolution. Numa, Son of the Sun, was such a Messenger imparting to Roman civilisation that spiritual impulse and initiative which vitalised and guided it until the focus of the current was changed. The decline of the Roman Empire was coincident with the ebb of this current, and with the withdrawal of the Sun Force from the conjunction of planets dominated by Mars under which the Roman civilisation was generated.

When a religion is given to the world, a centre is usually established in which the pure essence of the sacred teachings is preserved intact. For as the human mind evolves in this essence it becomes tinctured so that the original teaching and instruction tend to become disintegrated by the action of human thought. Thus those whom Numa anointed with the Sacred Fire or Everliving Solar Force transmitted this power and knowledge of its mystery to their successors, who maintained their temples of worship as centres for its radiation and the regeneration of the race, until that purpose for which the religion of Numa had been instituted was fulfilled and the Force which had vitalised it was withdrawn.

Nymph Egeria which Roman poets and historians have related."

"William Postel, least ignorant of all those who have studied the Cabala in ordinary books, was aware that Vesta was Noah's wife[93], but he did not know that Egeria was Vesta's daughter, and not having read the secret books of the ancient Cabala, a copy of which the Prince de Mirande [94] bought so dearly, he confused things and believed that Egeria was merely the good genius of Noah's wife."

"In those books we learn that Egeria was conceived upon the waters when Noah was wandering upon the avenging floods which inundated the Universe. Women were at that time reduced to the small number who were saved in the Cabalistic Ark, built by that second father of mankind."

"This illustrious man, mourning over the frightful chastisement wherewith the Lord was punishing the crimes caused by Adam's love for Eve, and seeing that Adam had ruined his posterity by preferring her to the daughters of the Elements and by taking her from that Salamander or Sylph who would have gained her affection--Noah, I say, profited by the fatal example of Adam and was content that his wife Vesta should yield herself to the Salamander Oromasis, Prince of Fiery Beings; and persuaded his three sons likewise to surrender

---

[93] NOAH, VESTA AND EGERIA. NOTE KK, COMMENTARY CONTINUED.
[94] PRINCE DE MIRANDE AND THE CABALA. NOTE LL, COMMENTARY CONTINUED.

their three wives to the Princes of the three other Elements. The Universe was, in a short time, re-peopled with heroic men, so learned, so handsome, so admirable, that their posterity dazzled by their virtues has mistaken them for divinities. One of Noah's children, rebelling against his father's counsel, could not resist the attractions of his wife any more than Adam could withstand the charms of his Eve . But just as Adam's sin blackened the souls of all his descendants, so Ham's lack of complaisance for the Sylphs branded all his black posterity; whence comes the horrible complexion of the Ethiopians, say our Cabalists, and of all those hideous peoples who have been commanded to dwell in the torrid zone as punishment for the profane ardour of their father." "These are very singular fancies, Sir," said I, marvelling at the man's ravings, "and your Cabala is of wonderful service in illuminating antiquity."

"Of wonderful service," he rejoined gravely, "and without it Scripture, history, fable and Nature are obscure and unintelligible. You believe, for example, that the injury Ham did his father was what it seems literally to be; as a matter of fact, it was something quite different. Noah went forth from the Ark, and perceiving that his wife Vesta had but grown more beautiful through her love for Oromasis, fell passionately in love with her again. Ham fearing that his father was about to re-people the earth with progeny as black as his own Ethiopians, seized his 'opportunity one day when the old man was full of wine, and mercilessly maltreated him. You laugh?"

"I laugh at Ham's indiscreet zeal," said I.

"Rather," replied he, "admire the kindness of the Salamander Oromasis, whom jealousy did not prevent from taking pity upon the disgrace of his rival. He taught his son Zoroaster, otherwise known as Japhet,[95] the Name of Omnipotent God which expresses His eternal fecundity. Japhet pronounced the Redoubtable Name JABAMIAH[96] six times alternately with his brother Shem, walking backward towards the patriarch, and they completely restored the old man. This story,

---

[95] JAPHET. NOTE MM, COMMENTARY CONTINUED.

[96] JABAMIAH.--"Therefore Divine Plato in Cratylus and in Philebus commandeth to reverence the names of God more than the Images or statues of the gods: for there is a more express Image and power of God, reserved in the faculty of the mind, especially if it be inspired from above, than in the works of mens hands; Therefore sacred words have not their power in Magi-call operations, from themselves, as they are words, but from the occult Divine powers working by them in the minds of those who by faith adhere to them; by which words the secret power of God as it were through Conduite pipes, is transmitted into them, who have ears purged by faith, and by most pure conversation and invocation of the divine names are made the habitation of God, and capable of these divine influences; whosoever therefore useth rightly these words or names of God with that purity of mind, in that manner and order, as they were delivered, shall both obtain and do many wonderfull things."
THREE BOOKS OF OCCULT PHILOSOPHY, WRITTEN BY HENRY CORNELIUS AGRIPPA OF NETTESHEIM, COUNSELLER TO CHARLES THE FIFTH, EMPEROR OF GERMANY: AND JUDGE OF THE PREROGATIVE COURT. TRANSLATED OUT OF THE LATIN INTO THE ENGLISH TONGUE, BY J. F. LONDON 1651. BOOK III., CHAPTER xi. OF THE DIVINE NAMES, AND THEIR POWER AND VERTUE.

misunderstood, caused the Greeks to say that the oldest of the Gods was maltreated by one of his children; but this is the truth of the matter. Hence you[97] can see how much more humane are the ethics of the Children of Fire than our own, and even more so than those of the Peoples of the Air or the Water; for their jealousy is cruel, as the divine Paracelsus shows us in an incident he recounts, and which was witnessed by the entire town of Stauffenberg. A certain Philosopher, with whom a Nymph was engaged[98] in an intrigue of immortality, was so disloyal as to love a woman. As he sat at dinner with his new paramour and some friends, there appeared in the air the most beautiful leg in the world. The invisible sweetheart greatly desired to show herself to the friends of her faithless lover, that they might judge how wrong he was in preferring a woman to her. Afterward the indignant Nymph killed him on the spot."

---

[97] THE GREEK MYTH.--"The Goddess Night, too, in Orpheus, advises Jupiter to make use of honey as an artifice. For she says to him--
When stretch'd beneath the lofty oaks you view Saturn, with honey by the bees produc'd, Sunk in ebriety, fast bind the God. This, therefore, takes place, and Saturn being bound," is maltreated in the same manner as Noah; "the theologist obscurely signifying by this, that divine natures become through pleasure bound, and drawn down into the realms of generation." PORPHYRY, TREATISE ON THE HOMERIC CAVE OF THE NYMPHS. § 7.

[98] NYMPH OF STAUFFENBERG. NOTE NN, COMMENTARY CONTINUED.

"Ah Sir," I exclaimed, "this is quite enough to disgust me with these tender sweethearts."

"I confess," he rejoined, "that their tenderness is apt to be somewhat violent. But if exasperated women have been known to murder their perjured lovers, we must not wonder that these beautiful and faithful mistresses fly into a passion when they are betrayed, and all the more so since they only require men to abstain from women whose imperfeaions they cannot tolerate, and give us leave to love as many of their number as we please. They prefer the interest and immortality of their companions to their personal satisfaction, and they are very glad to have the Sages give to their Republic as many immortal children as possible."

"But after all, Sir," I asked. "how does it happen that there are so few examples of all that you tell me?"

"There are a great number, my child," he answered, "but they are neither heeded nor credited, in fact, they are not properly interpreted for lack of knowledge of our principles. People attribute to demons all that they should ascribe to the Elementary Peoples. A little Gnome was beloved by the celebrated Magdalen of the Cross [99], Abbess of a Monastery at Cordova in Spain. Their alliance began when she was twelve years of age; and they continued their relationship for the space of thirty years. An ignorant confessor persuaded Magdalen

---

[99] MAGDALEN OF THE CROSS. NOTE OO, COMMENTARY CONTINUED.

that her lover was a hobgoblin, and compelled her to ask absolution of Pope Paul III. It could not possibly have been a demon, however, for all Europe knew, and Cassiodorus Renius[100] was kind enough to transmit to posterity, the daily miracles wrought through the intercession of this holy maiden, and which obviously would never have come to pass if her relationship with the Gnome had been as diabolical as the venerable Dictator imagined. This same Doctor, if I mistake not, would impertinently have said that the Sylph who immortalised himself with the youthful Gertrude[101], nun of the Monastery of Nazareth in the diocese of Cologne, was some devil or other." "And so he was, no doubt," I said.

"Ah, my Son," pursued the Comte mirthfully, "If that were the case the Devil is not the least unfortunate if he has power to carry on an intrigue with a girl of thirteen, and to write her such billets doux as were found in her casket. Rest assured, my child, that. the Devil, in the region of death, has sadder employment and that more in keeping with the hatred which the God of Purity bears him; but thus do people wilfully close their eyes to the truth. We find, for instance, in Titus Livy, that Romulus[102] was the son of Mars. The sceptics say that this is a fable, the theologians that he was the son of an incubus devil, the wags that

---

[100] CASSIODORUS RENIUS. NOTE PP, COMMENTARY CONTINUED.
[101] GERTRUDE, NUN OF THE MONASTERY OF NAZARETH. NOTE QQ, COMMENTARY CONTINUED.
[102] ROMULUS. NOTE RR, COMMENTARY CONTINUED.

Mademoiselle Sylvia had lost her gloves and sought to cover her confusion by saying that a god had stolen them from her."

"Now we who are acquainted with Nature, and whom God has called out of darkness into His wonderful Light, know that this so-called Mars was a Salamander in whose sight the young Sylvia found favour, and who made her the mother of the great Romulus, that hero who, after having founded his superb city, was carried away by his father in a fiery chariot as Zoroaster was by Oromasis[103]. Another Salamander was the father of Servius Tullius [104]. Titus Livy, deceived by c the resemblance, says that he was the God of Fire. And the ignorant have passed the same judgment upon him as upon the father of Romulus. The renowned Hercule [105] and the invincible Alexander[106] were

---

[103] This statement identifies Oromasis with Osiris, and with the God of the Hebrew, Christian, and Muhammedan religions.

[104] SERVIUS TULLIUS. NOTE SS, COMMENTARY CONTINUED.

[105] HERCULES. NOTE TT, COMMENTARY CONTINUED.

[106] 356 B.C. ALEXANDER THE GREAT, 323 B.C., was the reputed son of Philip, King of Macedonia. In reality he was the son of an Egyptian high priest and Initiate, and of Philip's wife Olympias. From the age of fifteen he was for three years the pupil of Aristotle who moulded his genius for the work for which it had incarnated, namely, that initial fusing of civilisations culminating in the Roman Empire under Julius Cæsar, whereby Greek and Roman letters leavened the then known world and made a medium for the transmission of the Christ and Muhammed messages. The divine authority under which the Adept Alexander the Great accomplished what was virtually the conquest of the then known world in less than fifteen years, is explicitly acknowledged in the Koran Sura i8.

sons of the greatest of the Sylphs [107]. Not knowing this, the historians said that Jupiter was their father. They spoke the truth for, as you have learned, these Sylphs, Nymphs and Salamanders set themselves up for divinities. The historians, believing them to be so, called all those who were born of them 'Children of the Gods.'"

"Such was the divine Plato[108], the most divine Apollonius of Tyana, Hercules, Achilles, Sarpedon, the pious Æneas, and the celebrated Melchizedek. For do you know who the father of Melchizedek was?"

"No, indeed," said I, "St. Paul himself did not know."

"Rather say that he did not tell," returned the Comte, "and that he was not permitted to reveal the Cabalistic Mysteries. He well knew that Melchizedek's father was a Sylph, and that the King of Salem was conceived in the Ark by the wife

---

"They will ask thee of Dhoulkarnain (Alexander the Great), SAY: I will recite to you an account of him. We stablished his power upon the earth; and made for him a way to everything. And a route he followed.' The Angel Gabriel speaking.

[107] GREATEST OF THE SYLPHS.--The word Sylph] I4at times used'in these Discourses with the meaning, of Master or Spiritual Teacher. MASTER DEFINED. NOTE UU, COMMENTARY CONTINUED.

[108] PLATO, A SON OF THESUN.--Elearchus the Sophist, Amaxilides in the second book of his Philosophy, and Plato's nephew Speusippus, his sister's son, who succeeded him in the conduct of his academy, affirm that Plato's mother Periione was beloved by Apollo, the Sun God, who made her the mother of Plato, who was therefore a Son of the Sun.

of Shem. That Pontiff's method of sacrificing was the same as that which his cousin Egeria taught King Numa, as well as the worship of a Supreme Deity without image or statue[109], for which reason the Romans, becoming idolaters at a later period, burned the Holy Books of Numa which Egeria had dictated. The first God of the Romans was the true God, their sacrifice a true sacrifice. They offered up bread and wine to the Supreme Ruler of the Universe: but all that became perverted in course of time. In acknowledgment of this first worship, however, God gave the Empire of the World to this city which had owned His supremacy. The same sacrifice which Melchizedek------"

"Sir," I interposed, "Pray let us drop Melchizedek, [110] the Sylph that begat him, his cousin Egeria, and the sacrifice of bread and wine. These proofs seem to be rather remote. I should be greatly obliged if you would tell me some more recent news. For when someone asked a certain Doctor what had become of the companions of that species of Satyr which appeared to St. Antony and

---

[109] *Roman worship. Note vv, Commentary Continued.*

[110] MELCHIZEDEK AND SHEM.--Philo speaks of Melchizedek as "the logos, the priest whose inheritance is the true God." (*De Allegoriis Legum, iii., 26.*) And other Hebrew authorities state that the Rabbis identify Melchizedek with Shem, and say that Noah having been crippled by the lion (*Symbolic of the lower nature and passions.*) while in the Ark, Shem officiated as priest at the sacrifice of thanksgiving offered after the subsidence of the flood. They also state that Noah in blessing his two sons declared that the Shekinah (Paraclete) was to to dwell only in the tents of Shem. Melchizedek and Shem are known as Sovereign Directors of this Divine or Super Solar Force.

which you call a Sylph, I heard him say that all these folk are dead nowadays. So it may be that the Elementary Peoples have perished[111] since you own they are mortal and we hear no tidings of them."

"I pray God," exclaimed the Comte with emotion, "I pray God, who is ignorant of nothing, to be pleased to ignore that ignoramus who decides so presumptously that of which he is ignorant. May God confound him and all his tribe! Where has he learned that the Elements are abandoned and that all those wonderful Peoples are annihilated? If he would take the trouble to read history a little, and not ascribe to the Devil, as the old wives do, everything which goes beyond the bounds of the chimerical theory which has been con-structed about Nature, he would find in all ages and in all places proofs of what I have told you." "What would your Doctor say to this authentic[112] account of a

---

[111] RECENT TIDINGS OF THE ELEMENTARY PEOPLES? NOTE WW, COMMENTARY CONTINUED.
[112] THE MAN WHO THINKS, WILLS TO KNOW.--The Abbe recounts these stories as a means of pointing out the folly of accepting and affirming without reflectior the opinion of others.

Man sinks into oblivion and indifference of though and allows himself to be governed by the minds am opinions of others.
It has therefore been possible to keep him in ignorance of his true estate and to retard his spiritual progres for centuries.
The man who does not think cannot know, and he becomes the slave and property of other minds.
The man who thinks, wills to know, and tends to become the expression of the God within.

recent occurrence in Spain? A beautiful Sylphid was beloved by a Spaniard, lived with him for three years, presented him with three fine children and" then died. Shall one say that she was a devil? A clever answer that! According to what Natural Philosophy can the Devil organise for himself a woman's body, conceive, bear children and suckle them? What proof is there in Scripture of the extravagant power which your theologians are forced in this instance to accord the Devil? And with what probable reason can their feeble Natural Philosophy supply them? The Jesuit Delrio in good faith naïvely recounts several of these adventures, and without taking the trouble to give physical explanations, extricates himself by saying that those Sylphids were demons. How tirue it is that your greatest doctors very often know no more than silly women!"

"How true it is that God loves to withdraw into His cloud-enveloped throne, and deepening the darkness which encompasses His Most Awful Majesty, He dwells in an inaccessible Light, and reveals His Truths only to the humble in heart. Learn to be humble, my Son, if you would penetrate that sacred night which environs Truth. Learn from the Sages to concede the devils no power in Nature since the fatal stone has shut them up in the depths of the abyss. Learn of the Philosophers to seek always for natural causes in all extraordinary events; and when natural causes are lacking have recourse to God and to His holy Angels, and never to evil spirits who can no longer do aught but suffer, else you would often be guilty of unintentional blasphemy and would ascribe to the Devil the honour of the most wonderful works of Nature."

"If you should be told, for example, that the divine Apollonius of Tyana[113] was immaculately conceived, and that one of the noblest Salamanders descended to immortalise himself with his mother, you would.call that Salamander a demon and you would give the Devil, the glory of fathering one of

---

[113] BIRTH OF APOLLONIUS OF TYANA, 97 A.D.-- "Apollonius was born in Tyana, a town founded by Greeks in Cappodocia. He was called Apollonius from his father. Whilst his mother was with child of him, Proteus the Egyptian god appeared to her, who, as Homer writes, has the power of assuming such a variety of shapes. The woman without being much alarmed, asked him what she should bring forth? to which he replied, 'Thou shalt bring forth me.' The natives of the place affirm, that at the instant of her delivery, a thunderbolt which seemed ready to fall on the ground, rose aloft, and suddenly disappeared. By this the Gods prefigured, I think, the splendor of the child, his superiority over earthly beings, his intercourse with them, and what he was to do when arrived to manhood. All the people of the country say that Apollonius was the son of Jupiter." EXTRACTS FROM CHAPTERS IV., V. AND VI. OF PHILOSTRATUS' "LIFE OF APOLLONIUS OF TYANA." TRANSLATED FROM THE GREEK BY THE REV. EDWARD BERWICK.
ST. JEROME ON APOLLONIUS OF TYANA.--"Apollonius too was a traveller--the one I mean who is called the sorcerer by' ordinary people and the philosopher by such as follow Pythagoras. Everywhere he found something to learn, and as he was always going to new places, he became constantly wiser and better."
EXTRACTS FROM ST. JEROME'S LETTER TO PAULINUS ON THE STUDY OF SCRIPTURE. §1.

the greatest men who ever sprang from our Philosophic marriages."

"But, Sir," I remarked, "this same Apollonius is reputed amongst us to be a great sorcerer, and they have nothing better to say of him."

"Behold," exclaimed the Comte, "one of the most wonderful effects of ignorance and bad education! Because one hears one's nurse tell stories about sorcerers, every extraordinary occurrence can have only the Devil for author. The greatest doctors may strive in vain, they are not believed unless they echo the nurses. Apollonius was not born of man; he understood the language of birds; he was seen on the same day in different parts of the world. He vanished in the presence of the Emperor Domitian who wished to do him harm; he raised a girl from the dead by means of Onomancy. He announced at Ephesus, in an assembly gathered from all parts of Asia, that at that very hour they were killing the tyrant at Rome. A judgment of this man is the point at issue. The nurses say that he was a sorcerer. St. Jerome and St. Justin Martyr say that he was merely a Philosopher. [114] Jerome, Justin

---

[114] JUSTIN MARTYR ON APOLLONIUS OF TYANA.--HOW is it that the talismans of Apollonius have power over certain parts of creation? For, as we see, they arrest the fury of the waves and the violence of the winds and the attacks of wild beasts. And while the miracles wrought by our Lord are preserved by tradition alone, those of Apollonius are most numerous and manifested to us in the very moment of their occurence: why, then, should they not lead astray all beholders? QUESTION xxiv.

and our Cabalists are to be adjudged visionaries, and silly women are to carry the day. Ah! Let the ignorant perish in their ignorance, but do you, my child, save yourself from shipwreck."

"When you read that the celebrated Merlin was immaculately conceived by a nun, daughter of a king of Great Britain, and that he foretold the future more clearly than Tyresias [115], do not say with the masses that he was the son of an incubus devil, because there never have been any; nor that he prophesied through the assistance of devils, since according to the Holy Cabala devil is the most ignorant of all beings. Rather say with the Sages that the English Princess was consoled in her retirement by a Sylph who took pity on her, that he diverted her with his attentions, that he knew how to please her, and that Merlin[116], their son, was

---

Apollonius was a man well skilled in the powers of Nature and the mutual attra&ions and repulsions inherent in them, and by virtue of this skill produced the effects he did. EXTRACT FROM ANSWER xxiv. TRANSLATED FROM THE GREEK, JUSTIN MARTYRIS OPERA, 1593, PAGE 316.

[115] TYRESIAS. NOTE XX, COMMENTARY CONTINUED.

[116] MERLIN was born during the fifth century of the present era at the town now called Caermarthen, Wales, and was a professed Christian. When King Vortigern asked Merlin's mother, daughter of King Demetius, to tell him the name of her son's father, she answered " that she never had the society of any one mortal or human, only a spirit assuming the shape of a beautiful young man, had many times appeared unto her, seeming to court her with no common affection, but when any of her fellow-virgins came in, he would suddenly disappear and vanish, by whose many and urgent importunities, being at last overcome, I yielded, saith

brought up by the Sylph in all knowledge, and learned from him to perform the many wonders which English history relates of him."

"No longer cast aspersion upon the Comtes de Cleves by saying that the Devil is their father, and have a better opinion of the Sylph who, so the story goes, came to Cleves in a miraculous boat drawn by a swan harnessed with a silver chain. After having several children by the heiress of Cleves, this Sylph re-embarked on his aerial boat one day at high noon, in full view of everyone. What has he done to your doctors that constrains them to pronounce him a devil?"

"Have you so little regard for the honour of the House of Lusignan as to give your Comtes de Poitiers a diabolical genealogy? What will you say of their celebrated mother?"

"I verily believe, Sir," I declared, "that you are about to tell me the fairy tale of Melusina."

---

she, to his pleasure--and I was delivered of this soil (now in your presence) whom I caused to be called
Merlin." THE LIFE OF MERLIN, SURNAMED AMBROSIUS; HIS PROPHECIES AND PREDICTIONS INTERPRETED, AND THEIR TRUTH MADE GOOD BY OUR ENGLISH ANNALS. LONDON, 1813. PAGES 52-53.
MERLINS PROPHECY OF THE CONQUEST OF THE AIR AND OF AERIAL AND SUBMARINE WARFARE. NOTE YY, COMMENTARY CONTINUED.
MERLINS PROPHECY OF WORLD PEACE. NOTE vii, COMMENTARY CONCLUDED.

"Ah!" he replied, "If you deny the story of Melusina[117] I am inclined to think you prejudiced. But in order to deny it you must burn the books of the great Paracelsus who affirms in five or six different places that nothing is more certain than the fact that this same Melusina was a Nymph. And you must give the lie to your historians who say that since her death or, to speak more accurately, since she disappeared from the sight of her husband, whenever her descendants are threatened with misfortune, or a King of France is to die in some extraordinary way, she never fails to appear in mourning upon the great tower of the Château of Lusignan which she had built. If you persist in maintaining that she was an evil spirit, you will pick a quarrel with all those who are descended from this Nymph, or who are related to her house."

"Do you think, Sir," said I, "that these noblemen prefer to trace their origin to the Sylphs?"

"They would undoubtedly prefer to do so," he rejoined, "if they knew that which I am now teaching

---

[117] MELUSINA A NYMPH.--"Let us speak a little of Melusina. The subject should not be treated with shallowness or levity. She was not what theologians suppose, but a Nymph." LIBER DE NYMPHIS, SYLPHIS, PYGMAEIS ET SALAMANDRIS, TRACTATUS IV. TRANSLATED FROM THE LATIN EDITION OF THE WORKS OF PARACELSUS. PUBLISHED AT GENEVA IN 1658. VOL. II., PAGE 396.

you, and they would consider these extraordinary births [118] a great honour. If they had any Cabalistic Light they would know that such births are more conformable with the method whereby God, in the beginning, intended mankind to multiply. Children[119] born in this way are happier, more

---

[118] EXTRAORDINARY BIRTHS, COMPARE THE BIRTH OF JESUS AS RELATED IN THE KORAN. NOTE ZZ, COMMENTARY CONTINUED.

[119] CHILDREN OF THE PHILOSOPHERS.--The Philosophers hold that to engender children is the most sacred and filial duty of man. Both man and woman are taught by them that the aim and aspiration of union is to enter into a conscious relationship with the incoming ego or soul. Their disciples seek so to prepare and govern themselves that they may be worthy to bring a soul manifesting in the loftiest and purest levels of consciousness into incarnation on earth, thereby giving life to a more highly evolved being than it is possible for unthinking minds, impure hearts and unprepared bodies to attract. The Philosopher, being in conscious relationship with the incoming ego, affords it great assistance as it passes through the denser states of matter, and encourages and stimulates it to incarnate or enter the physical body prior to birth: for then for a space of time it cringes from assuming its dense physical vesture since, as it were, it dies to the world from which it came. Through knowledge of Nature's Law and obedience to it the Philosopher has power? to attract frôm the Heavenly World those perfected beings who come as messengers to the race.

Purity of body, mind and soul, and the worship of God through the being beloved, ever bring into life on earth a soul beautified by its own Divine Source. And if two people having physical characteristics which are ugly worship God through the being beloved with purity of mind and heart, the law of hereditary physical resemblance will be modified, and their offspring will radiate that which is of the soul.

The child which is product of unpurified, ungoverned and unhallowed passion and desire becomes the vehicle of an ego

valiant, wiser, more renowned and more blest of God. Is it not more glorious for these illustrious men to be descended from beings so perfect, wise and powerful than from some foul hobgoblin or infamous Asmodeus?"

"Sir," said I, "our theologians are far from saying that the Devil is the father of all those men who are born without one's knowing who is responsible for them. They recognise the fact that the Devil is a spirit and therefore cannot engender."

"Gregory of Nice," replied the Comte, "does not say that, for he holds that demons multiply among A themselves as men do."

"We are not of his opinion," I answered, "but it happens, our doctors say, that------"

"Ah!" the Comte interrupted, "do not tell me what they say or you will be talking very obscene and indecent foolishness as they do. What abominable evasion they have been guilty of! The way in which they have all, with one accord, embraced this revolting idea is amazing. And what pleasure they have taken in posting hobgoblins in ambush to take

---

of like character but more dominant in will, with inclinations equalling the sum of the

Ppassions and desires of the unthinking parents. Such are, in truth, the children of wrath and malediction for whose salvation the Philosophers, through reverent preparation of body, soul and spirit for parenthood, seek to bring into incarnation those Beings who are chosen vessels of the Divine Love and Wisdom.

advantage of the unoccupied lower nature of the recluse, and so hasten into the world those miraculous men whose illustrious memory they blacken by so base an origin. Do they call this philosophising? Is it worthy of God to say that He has such complaisance for the Devil as to countenance these abominations, granting them the grace of fecundity which He has denied to great Saints, and rewarding such obscenity by creating for these embryos of iniquity, souls more heroic than for those formed in the chastity of legitimate marriage?"

"If I dared to break in upon your declamation, Sir," said I, "I would own, in order to pacify you, that it were .greatly to be desired that our doctors had hit upon some solution less offensive to such pure ears as yours. Indeed, they have been obliged altogether to deny the facts upon which the question is founded."

"A rare expedient! " he rejoined. "How is it possible to deny manifest truths? Put yourself in the place of an ermine-furred theologian and suppose the blessed Danhuzerus comes to you as the Oracle of his religion------"

At this point a lackey came to say that a certain young nobleman had come to visit me. "I do not care to have him see me" remarked the Comte. "I ask your pardon, Sir," said I, "but as you can readily judge from this nobleman's name, I cannot say that I am not at home to anyone; therefore may I trouble you to go into this closet?"

"It is not worth while," said he, "I am about to make myself invisible."

"Ah! Sir," I exclaimed. "A truce to deviltry, I beg of you, I am not prepared to jest about it."
"What ignorance," said the Comte, smiling and shrugging his shoulders, "not to know that to become invisible one has only to place before oneself the opposite of the light! " He went into my closet and the young nobleman entered at almost the same moment. I now ask his pardon for not speaking to him of my adventure

Ancient Persian Monument

By permission of the Directorate, R. R. Gallerie Di Firenze.

Ancient Persian Monument.

ANCIENT PERSIAN MONUMENT.--Throughout antiquity it was usual symbolically to represent the lower nature and passions of man, or accurately speaking the Solar Force manifesting in them ungoverned, as a lion, [120] the king of beasts, whose conquest must precede all spiritual development. Thus the first labour of the Greek saviour Hercules is said to have been the slaying of a huge lion, his lower physical nature. And the initial exploit of the Hebrew hero Samson is described as follows: "And, behold, a young lion roared against him. And the Spirit of the Lord came mightily upon him, and he rent him as he would have rent a kid,, and he had nothing in his hand." This subordination of the lower nature to the higher in man or government of the generative force that it may ascend and be employed for regeneration, the upbuilding of the Solar or Spiritual Body, is here represented. The lion symbolises the lower nature of man, and the serpent the Solar Force directed upward which is overcoming it. "I said in mine heart concerning the estate of the sons of men, that God might manifest them, and that they might see (literally, that they might clear God, and see) that they themselves are beasts. Who knoweth the spirit of man that goeth upward, and the spirit of the beast that goeth downward to the earth?" ECCLESIASTES iii., 18, 2I.

---

[120] *A lion. An emblem of the Solar Light both to believers and idolaters. Parkhurst, Hebrew Lexicon.*

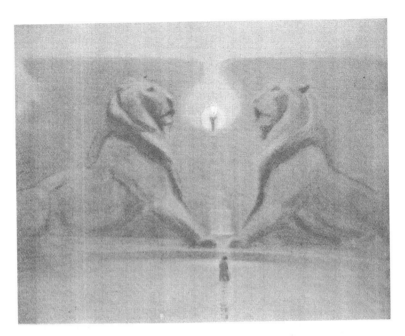

WHEN the illustrious personage had taken his departure, on my return from accompanying him to the door, I found the Comte de Gabalis in my study.

"It is a great pity," said he, "that the nobleman who has just left you is one day to become one of the seventy-two Princes of the Sanhedrin of the New Law[121], else he would be a great subject for our Holy Cabala. His mind is profound,

---

[121] SANHEDRIN OF THE NEW LAW.--On February 9th, 1807, one hundred and thirty-seven years after the publication of the first edition of these Discourses, the "Grand Sanhedrin " convened at Paris. This French Sanhedrin was

pure, broad, lofty and fearless. Here is the geomantic[122] figure which I cast for him while you were talking together. I have never seen happier aspens nor those denoting a finer soul. Just look at

---

the Jewish high court convoked by the Emperor Napoleon I. for the purpose of giving legal sanction to those principles of government which he desired to establish as the basis of the future status of the Jews and of his New Law for them.

[122] GEOMANCY.--"A forecast of the future by means of dots made in the sand. It is mentioned by many English writers-- by Chaucer and Dryden--and is at present largely practised in China, in the Soudan and in Egypt, where its practitioners may daily be seen making signs in the dust at the corners of the streets. Instead of making marks on the earth itself, it has been the habit in Europe--one may say for centuries--for the marks to be made by pen or pencil on a sheet of paper."

"'Geomancy,' according to M. de Cattan, (*La Geomance do Seigneur Christofe de Cattan, Gentilhomme Genevois. Paris, 1567*.) 'is a science and an art which consists of points and lines representing the four elements and the stars and planets of the sky.' The instruments of this art are a pen, ink and paper, or a small stick, and earth, dust or well-cleaned sand. This method was used by the Chaldeans, Persians, Hebrews, and Egyptians before ink and paper were invented. The science therefore retains the name of geomancy."

"The great professors of the art assert for geomancy the widest possible extension to all subjects."

"This was the distraction that Sir Edward Lytton often sought in the intervals of business and study."

Mother and Daughter are terms denoting the so-called houses in a geomantic figure. Further particulars as to the practice of this art, together with Sir Edward Lytton's own geomantic tables and instruction, as well as an international forecast of importance made by him and since verified by the event, are to be found in the book from which the quotations given above are made. "RAMBLING RECOLLECTIONS," BY SIR HENRY DRUMMOND WOLFF. VOL. I., PAGE 298 AND FOLLOWING.

this 'Mother'--what magnanimity it gives him; and this 'Daughter' will procure him the purple. Bad luck to her and to destiny since they deprive Philosophy of a subject who might perhaps surpass you. But where were we when he came in?"

"You were speaking, Sir," said I, "of a Saint whom I have never seen in the Roman Calendar. I think you called him Danhuzerus."

"Ah! I remember," he replied, "I was bidding you put yourself in the place of one of your doctors and suppose that the Blessed Danhuzerus had just laid bare to you his conscience and said, 'Sir, the fame of your learning has brought me from beyond the mountains. I have a slight scruple which is troubling me. A Nymph holds her court in a mountain in Italy: and a thousand Nymphs almost as beautiful as their Queen attend upon her. The handsomest and most learned and most worthy men resort thither from all the habitable globe. They love these Nymphs and are beloved by them; they lead the most delightful life in the world; the Nymphs whom they love bear them very fine children; they worship the living God, injure no. one and hope for immortality. I was one day walking upon this mountain and found favour in the eyes of the Queen of the Nymphs, who appeared to me and showed me her charming court. The Sages perceiving that she loved me, reverenced me almost as their Prince. They exhorted me to yield to the Nymph's sighs and beauty. She told me of her martyrdom, and left unsaid nothing which might touch my heart, and in short convinced me that she would die if I did not love her, and that if I loved her she would be indebted to me for her immortality. The arguments of those learned men prevailed over my principles, even as the charms of the Nymph won my heart. I love her and she has borne me children of great promise, but in the midst of my felicity I am sometimes troubled by the recollection that the Church of Rome might not approve of all this. I have come to consult you, Sir, about this Nymph, those Sages, these children and the state of my conscience.' Well, Mr. Doctor, what answer would you make to my Lord Danhuzerus?"

"I should say to him," I answered, "With all due respect to you, Lord Danhuzerus, you are letting your imagination run away with you, or else your vision is an enchantment, your children and your mistress are hobgoblins, your Sages are fools, and I must say that your conscience is thoroughly cauterized."

"By such an answer, my Son, you might achieve a doctor's hood, but you would not merit admission to our Order," rejoined the Comte with a deep sigh. " Such is the barbarous tendency of all your doctors nowa-days. A poor Sylph would never dare show himself lest he be straightway mistaken for a hobgoblin; a Nymph cannot labour to become immortal without passing for an impure phantom; and a Salamander[123] would not dare appear for fear

---

[123] ST. BENEDICT AND THE SALAMANDER.--The truth of this statement is verified by the following extract from "The Life of St. Benedict, by St. Gregory the Great."(*Chapter viii.*) "The castle called Casaino is situated upon the side of a high

of being taken for the Devil himself, while the pure flames of which he is composed would be thought the hell fire which ever attends upon the Prince of Darkness. To dissipate these Most injurious suspicions they vainly make the sign of the cross on appearing, bow the knee at Divine Names, and even pronounce them with reverence. All these precautions are futile. They cannot succeed in changing their reputation for being enemies of the God whom they worship more devoutly than do those who flee from them."

---

mountain, which containeth as it were, in the lap thereof, the same castle, and riseth into the air three miles high so that the top seemeth to touch the very heavens: on this stood an old temple where Apollo was worshipped by the foolish country people, according to the custom of the ancient heathens. Round about it, likewise, grew groves, in which even until that time the mad multitude of infidels offered idolatrous sacrifices. The man of God coming to that place broke down the idol, overthrew the altar, burn't the groves, and, of the temple of Apollo, made a chapel to St. Martin, and where the profane altar had stood, he built a chapel of St. John; and, by continual preaching, converted many of the people thereabout. But the old enemy not bearing this silently, did pre- sent himself, not covertly or in a dream but openly and visibly in the sight of the Father, and with great cries complained of the violence he had suffered, in as much that the brethren heard him though they could see nothing. For, as the venerable Father told his disciples, the wicked fiend represented himself to his sight all on fire, and, with flaming mouth and flashing eyes, seemed to rage against him. And, then, they all heard what he said, for first, he called him by his name, and, when the man of God would make him no answer, he fell to reviling him. And whereas before, he cried: 'Benedict, Benedict,' and he saw that he could get no answer, then he cried Maledict, not Benedict, what hast thou to do with me, and why dost thou persecute me?'"

"But seriously, Sir," said I, "do you really believe these Sylphs to be such extraordinarily devout folk?"

"Most devout," he answered, "and most zealous for Divinity. The superlatively excellent discourses upon the Divine Essence which they deliver to us, and their wonderful prayers edify us greatly."

"Have they prayers as well? " said I. "I should very much like to hear one of their making."

"It is easy to gratify you," he rejoined, "and that I may not quote anything of questionable authority, and that you may be unable to suspect me of having fabricated it, listen to the prayer which the Salamander who gave answers in the Temple of Delphi was pleased to teach the Pagans, and which is recorded by Porphyry. It contains a sublime theology from which you will perceive that if mankind did not worship the true God, it was through no fault of these Sage Beings.

PRAYER OF THE SALAMANDERS.

Immortal, Eternal, Inejble and Sacred Father of all things, Thou who art borne upon the ceaselessly-rolling chariot of the ever-turning worlds. Thou Ruler of the Etherial Countries where the Throne of Thy power is raised, from the summit whereof Thy formidable eyes discover all things, and Thine excellent and holy ears hear all things. Hearken nto Thy children whom Thou hast loved from the birth of time; for Thy golden, mighty, and eternal Majesty shines above the world and above the firmament of the Stars. Thou art exalted above them, O radiant Fire! There Thou kindlest Thyself and maintainest Thyself by Thine own Splendour, and there go forth from Thine Eternal Essence inexhaustible streams of Light which nourish Thine Infinite Spirit. Thine Infinite Spirit produces all things and causes the inexhaustible treasure of matter, which can never fail in that generation which forever environs it, because .of the forms without number wherewith it is pregnant and wherewith Thou in the beginning didst fill it. From this Thy Spirit, likewise, are born those Holy Kings who stand about Thy Throne, and[124] who compose Thy court, O Universal Father! O Thou Unique God! O Father of mortal and immortal Saints![125]

---

[124] HOLY KINGS.--These Hierarchal Beings called Kings are in reality states of consciousness or energy within which are governing intelligences having jurisdiction over the seven planets.

"But the Mind, The God, being masculine-feminine, originating Life and Light, begat by Word another Mind Creator, Who being God of the Fire and the Spirit, created some Seven Administrators, encompassing in circles the sensible world; and their administration is called Fate." HERMES TRISMEGISTUS. POEMANDRES I, §9.

"Grace be unto you, and peace, from Him which is, and which was, and which is to come; and from the seven Spirits which are before His throne." THE APOCALYPSE OR REVELATION OF ST. JOHN. CHAPTER I., VERSE 4.

[125] PRAYER.--There is a mansion above through which shines down the great central Light of the Paraclete or Holy Spirit, and through this descending column the prayers of those who seek the Light ascend to the higher spheres. The gateway of this mansion, known to Cabalists as the Sixth House or Hierarchy, is guarded by two Wonderful Beings. (*Cherubim. Note aaa, Commentary Continued.*) These Beings symbolise

Thou hast in particular created Powers which are marvellously like unto Thine Eternal Thought, and unto Thine Adorable Essence. Thou hast set them higher than the Angels who announce to the world Thy Will. Lastly Thou hast created in the Elements a third rank of Sovereigns. Our continual exercise is to praise Thee and to worship Thy Will. We burn with desire to possess Thee, O Father, O Mother, who art tenderest of Mothers, O wonderful exemplar of the sentiments and tenderness of Mothers, O Son,

---

the union between the human and divine, for prayer is but the bringing together of these opposites. The divine mingles with the human so that it also may become divine: and man's thoughts ascending into the the Light are taken up by these Intelligences who judge them and summon the Hosts of their Realm to grant, according to Law, the requests made.

When you pray, think! Shut out all lower thoughts. Approach God as you would the entrance to the Holy Place. Ask if it be well to demand to be given wisdom according to Law. Be strong in purpose and firm in demand, for as you seek and demand power of a spiritual nature you will balance that power in self on the lower planes.. It is to penetrate beyond these lower planes or spheres of illusion that Jesus said, (*Luke xi., 2. Compare Proclus on Prayer. Note bbb, Commentary Continued.*) "When you pray, SAY" these things. You have by a direct and positive effort to reach the higher spheres of consciousness, therefore let your thought be clear . and concise, for a sincere, positive and well-defined prayer harmonises man with God. On the other hand, an idle or unthinking prayer without definite expression becomes an affliction to the mind and destroys its receptivity to the Light. A fervent prayer to the Deity crystallises the mind so that other forms of thought cannot enter, and prepares it to receive a response from the God within.

Prayer or concentration on the Highest Source man is capable of imagining is a path to Wisdom Found.

the flower of all Sons, O Form of all Forms, Thou Soul, Spirit, Harmony and Number of all things!

"What say you to this prayer of the Salamanders? Is it not exceedingly learned, lofty and devout?"

"And exceedingly obscure as well," I answered. "I once heard it paraphrased by a preacher who proved thereby that the Devil, in addition to his other vices, is above all else a great hypocrite."

"Alas!" exclaimed the Comte, "Poor Elementary Peoples! What resource is left you? You tell marvellous things concerning the Nature of God, the Father, Son, and Holy Ghost, the Assisting Intelligences, Angels and Heavens. "You make wonderful prayers and teach them to man; yet after all you are nothing but hypocritical hobgoblins!"

"Sir," I hastily observed, "it makes me uncomfortable to have you thus apostrophise these Peoples." "Nay, my Son," he replied, "do not fear lest I summon them, but rather lest your faintheartedness should in the future prevent you from having any realisation beyond that of amazement that you see fewer examples of their alliance with men than you could wish for. Alas! Where is the woman whose imagination has not been beclouded by your doaors, and who does not look with horror upon this relationship, and who would not tremble at the appearance of a Sylph?. Where is the man with least pretension to being good who does not flee the sight of them? Do we find, save very rarely, a man of worth who would care to be on familiar terms with them? Only profligates, misers, ambitious men or knaves court this honour to which, however, PRAISE GOD, they shall never attain; 'for the fear of the Lord is the beginning of Wisdom.'"

"Then what is to become of all these flying Nations," I inquired, "now that honest folk are so prejudiced against them?"

"Ah!" said he, "The arm of God is in no wise shortened, and the Devil does not derive all the advantage he anticipated from the ignorance and error which he has spread to their detriment; for in addition to the fact that the Philosophers, of whom there are a great number, do their utmost to remedy it by absolutely renouncing women, God has given all these Peoples permission to make use of every innocent artifice of which they can bethink themselves in order to converse with men without their knowledge."

"What do I hear, Sir?" I exclaimed.

"You hear nothing but the truth," he replied. "But I have a much greater secret to communicate to you. Know, my Son, that many a man believes himself to be the son of a man, who is really the son of a Sylph. Did I not tell you the other day that the Sylphs and other Lords of the Elements are overjoyed that we are willing to instruct them in the Cabala? Were it not for us their great enemy the Devil would alarm them exceedingly, and they would have difficulty in immortalising themselves without the knowledge of the maidens."

"I cannot sufficiently wonder at the profound ignorance in which we live," I remarked. "It is currently believed that the Powers of the Air sometimes help lovers to attain their desires. Apparently the contrary is true; the Powers of the Air require the assistance of men in their love affairs."

"Quite so, my Son," the Comte went on, "the Sage lends assistance to these poor people who, were it not for him, would be too wretched and too weak to resist the Devil. But when a Sylph has learned from us

to pronounce Cabalistically the potent Name NEHMAHMIHAH[126], and to combine it in mantric

---

[126] NEHMAHMIHAH.--The three-syllabled word which is communicated to Master Masons as a substitute for the Master's word, "until wiser ages shall discover the true one," resembles Nehmahmihah: and one need not travel far to find further indication of the identity of the esoteric teachings of Masonry with. the Philosophy of the Comte. The following confirmation of this fact is drawn from a manuscript on the subjea of Freemasonry now in the Bodleian Library, and entitled "Certayne Questyons, with Answeres to the same, concerning the Mystery of Maçonrye; written by the hande of kynge Henrye, the sixthe of the name, and faithfullye copyed by me Johan Leylande, Antiquarius, by the commaunde of his Highnesse." Wherein King Henry VI, himself A Mason, says of the Craft:
"They concelethe the arte of kepynge secrettes, that soe the worlde mayeth nothinge concele from them. Thay concelethe the arte of wunderwerckynge, and of foresayinge thynges to comme, that so thay same artes may not be usedde of the wyckedde to an evyell ende. Thay also concelethe the ante of chaunges, the wey of wynnynge the facultye of ABRAC (God), the skylle of becommynge gude and parfyghte wythouten the

158

form with the delicious name Eliael, all powers of darkness take flight and the Sylph peacefully enjoys the society of his loved one."

"When these gentlemen are immortalised, they labour earnestly and live most piously that they may not lose their recently-acquired right to the possession of the Supreme Good. They therefore desire the person to whom they are allied to live with exemplary innocence, as is apparent in that celebrated adventure of a young Lord of Bavaria[127]. He was inconsolable at the death of his wife, whom he loved passionately. A certain Sylphid was advised by one of our Sages to assume the likeness of the wife. She had confidence in the Sage and presented herself to the sorrowing young man, saying that God had raised her from the dead to console him in his extreme aflfliction. They lived together many years and had several beautiful children. The young nobleman, however, was not a good enough man to retain the gentle Sylphid; he used to blaspheme and use had language. She often warned him, but seeing that her remonstrances

---

holpynges of fere and hope (religion); and the universelle longage of maçonnes."
Additional proof is found in the following statement: "Freemasonry proclaims, as it has proclaimed from its origin, the existence of a creative principle, under the name of the great Architect of the universe."
"PROCEEDINGS OF THE SUPREME COUNCIL OF SOVEREIGN GRAND INSPECTORS-GENERAL OF THE THIRTY-THIRD AND LAST DEGREE, ETC., HELD AT THE CITY OF NEW YORK, AUGUST 15, 1876."
[127] LORD OF BAVARIA. NOTE CCC, COMMENTARY CONTINUED.

were unavailing she disappeared one day, and left him nothing but her petticoats and the regret of having been unwilling to follow her pious counsel. Thus you see, my Son, that Sylphs sometimes have reason to disappear. You see too that neither the Devil nor the fantastic caprices of your theologians can prevent the People of the Elements from working with success for their immortality when they are helped by one of our Sages."

"But honestly, Sir," I asked, "are you persuaded that the Devil is so great an enemy of these seducers of young girls?"

"A mortal enemy," said the Comte, "especially of the Nymphs, Sylphs and Salamanders. As for the Gnomes, he does not hate them nearly so much because, as I believe you have already learned, the Gnomes, frightened by the howlings of the Devils which they hear in the centre of the earth, prefer to remain mortal rather than run the risk of being thus tormented should they acquire immortality. Thence it comes to pass that these Gnomes and the demons, their neighbours, have a good deal to do with one another. The latter persuade the Gnomes, who are naturally most friendly to man, that it is doing him a very great service and delivering him from great danger, to compel him to renounce his immortality. In exchange, they promise the man whom they can persuade to this renunciation that they will provide him with all the money he asks for, will avert the dangers which might threaten his life during a given period, or will grant any other condition pleasing to him who makes this wretched covenant. Thus the Devil, wicked fellow that he is, through the mediation of a Gnome, causes the soul[128] of such a man to become mortal and deprives it of the right to eternal life."

"Then, Sir," cried I, "in your opinion those covenants, of which demonographers cite so many examples, are not made with the Devil at all?"

"No, assuredly not," replied the Comte, "Has not the Prince of the World[129] been driven out? Is he not confined? Is he not bound? Is he not the *terra damnata et maledicta* which is left at the bottom of the retort of the Supreme and Archetype Distiller? Can he ascend into the Region of Light and spread

---

[128] SOUL.--The word Soul is used with the meaning of spiritual vesture throughout these Discourses, and in their terminology may be said to be the Air and Water bodies taken together, and in contradistinction to the Earth body and Fire body or spirit which they unite. "For the Spirit is an invisible thing nor doth it ever appear without another garment, which garment is the Soul." EIRENAEUS PHILALETHES, 44RIPLEY REVIV'D," LONDON, 1678. PAGE 8.

[129] PRINCE OF THE WORLD.--And God said to Raphael: "Go Raphael, and bind Azalzel; chain him Hand and Foot, and cast him into Darkness; open the Desart that is in the Wilderness of Dudael, and go, and plunge him in there; cover him with sharp and rugged Stones; involve Darkness over him, which he shall inhabit to Eternity: Obstruct his Sight, that he may not see the Light, and that he may be brought out in the Day of Judgment, to be consum'd by Fire." THE HISTORY OF THE ANGELS AND THEIR GALLANTRY WITH THE DAUGHTERS OF MEN. WRITTEN BY ENOCH THE PATRIARCH. PUBLISH'D IN GREEK, BY DR. GRABE, MADE ENGLISH, LONDON, 1715.

there his concentrated darkness? He can do nothing against man. He can only inspire the Gnomes, his neighbours, to come and make these propositions to those among mankind whom he most fears may be saved, to the end that their souls may die with their bodies."

"Then," said I, "according to you these souls do die?"

"They die, my child," he answered.

"And are not those who enter into such covenants damned?"

"They cannot be damned," said he, "for their souls die with their bodies."

"Then they are let off easily, and' they are very lightly punished for so heinous a crime as that of renouncing the saving grace of their Baptism, and the Death of Our Lord."

"Do you call it being lightly punished," said the Comte, "to return into the black abyss of nonexistence? Know that it is a greater punishment than that of being damned, and that there is still a remnant of mercy in the justice which God exercises towards the sinners in Hell: it is a great grace not to let them be consumed by the fire which burns them. Nonexistence[130] is a greater evil than

130 NON-EXISTENCE. -- The inner meaning of these teachings is that man, by yielding to the temptations of his lower or Gnome nature, gradually weakens the link which the

Hell. This is what the Sages preach to the Gnomes when they assemble them to make them understand the wrong they do themselves in preferring death to immortality and nonexistence to the hope of a blessed eternity, which they would have the right to possess if they would only ally themselves to men without exacting from them such criminal renunciation. Some yield to our persuasions and we marry them to our daughters."

"Then, Sir, do you evangelise the Subterranean Peoples?" I inquired.

"Why not?" he replied. "We are instructors to them as well as to the Peoples of the Fire, Air and Water; and Philosophic charity is extended without distinction to all these children of God. As they are more subtile and more enlightened than the generality of mankind, they are more tractable and amenable to discipline, and listen to the divine truths with a reverence which charms us."

---

immortal or Solar Principle is able to maintain between itself and man's soul. Continued degeneration irrevocably severs this link, and the Spirit or Solar Principle withdraws into the Divine Essence whence it came. Once this withdrawal of the Spirit is accomplished the soul and physical body of man follow the trend of all mortal evolution and die or disintegrate, reverting to the great treasury of matter and becoming for a time an unconscious and therefore, from the standpoint of consciousness, a non-existent part of the Divine Plan.

"It must be charming indeed," I exclaimed mirthfully, "to see a Cabalist in the pulpit holding forth to these gentlemen!"

"You shall have that pleasure, my Son, whenever you wish," said the Comte, "and if you so desire I will assemble them this very evening and will preach to them at midnight."

"At midnight," I protested, "I have been told that that is the hour of the Sabbat."[131]

The Comte began to laugh. "You remind me," he said, "of all the imbecilities related by the demonographers in that chapter on their imaginary Sabbat. You are not going to tell me that you also believe in it, that would indeed be a joke!"

"Oh!" I retorted, "as for those tales of. the Sabbat, I assure you I do not believe one of them."

"That is right, my Son," said he, "for I repeat that the Devil has not power thus to amuse himself at the expense of mankind, nor to enter into covenants with men, still less to make himself worshipped as the Iniquisitors believe. What has given rise to the popular rumour is that the Sages, as I have just told you, assemble the Inhabitants of the Elements to preach their Mysteries and Ethics to them. And as it usually happens that some Gnome turns from his gross error, comprehends the horrors of non-existence and consents to become immortalised, they bestow upon him one of our daughters; he is

---

[131] SABBAT. NOTE DDD, COMMENTARY CONTINUED.

married and the nuptials are celebrated with all the rejoicing called for by the recent conquest. There are dances and those shouts of joy which Aristotle says were heard in certain isles [132] where, nevertheless, no living being was visible. The mighty Orpheus was the first to convoke these Subterranean Peoples. At his first lecture SABAZIUS, the most ancient of the Gnomes, was immortalised; and from that SABAZIUS [133] was

---

[132] ENCHANTED ISLES.--In one of the seven islands called the Islands of Aeolus, Lipara by name, there is, so they say, a tomb, concerning which many wonder- ful things are told; but in this more especially all are agreed, that it is not safe to approach the place by night. For the sound of drums and cymbals is clearly heard proceding thence, together with laughter and clamour and the clapping of hands. TRANSLATED FROM ARISTOTELIS DE MIRABILIBUS AUSCULTATIONIBUS, §838b.

[133] TO SABAZIUS.

The fumigation from aromatics.

Hear me, illustrious father, daemon fam'd,

Great Saturn's offspring, and Sabazius nam'd;

Inserting Bacchus, bearer of the vine,

And sounding God, within thy thigh divine,

That when mature, the Dionysian God

Might burst the bands of his conceal'd abode,

And come to sacred Tmolus, his delight,

Where Ippa' dwells, all beautiful and bright.

Blest Phrygian God, the most august of all,

Come aid thy mystics, when on thee they call.

FROM THE MYSTICAL HYMNS OF ORPHEUS. TRANSLATED FROM THE GREEK, AND DEMONSTRATED TO BE THE INVOCATIONS WHICH WERE USED IN THE ELEUSINIAN MYSTERIES, BY THOMAS TAYLOR.

"But the older Greeks considered the Eleusinian mysteries as much above all other religious services as the Gods are superior to heroes." PAUSANIAS, BOOK X., PHOCIS.

derived the name of this Assembly wherein the Sages were wont to address a speech to him as long as he lived, as is apparent in the Hymns of the divine Orpheus."

"The ignorant have confounded things, and have made them the occasion of a thousand impertinent tales, and of defaming an Assembly which we convene solely to the glory of the Supreme Being."

"I should never have imagined the Sabbat to be a devotional assembly," said I.

"And yet it is a most holy and Cabalistic one;" he rejoined, "a fact of which it would not be easy to persuade the world. But such is the deplorable blindness of this unjust age; people are carried away by popular rumour and do not in the least wish to bd undeceived. Sages speak in vain, fools are more readily believed than they. In vain does a Philosopher bring to light the falsity of the chimeras people have fabricated, and present manifest proofs to the contrary. No matter what his experience, nor how sound his argument and reasoning, let but a man with a doctor's hood come along and write them down as false,--experience and demonstration count for naught and it is henceforward beyond the power of Truth to re-establish her empire. People would rather believe in a doctor's hood than in their own eyes. There has been in your native France a memorable proof of this popular mania. The famous. Cabalist

Zedechias, [134] in the reign of your Pépin, took it into his head to convince the world that the Elements are inhabited by these Peoples whose nature I have just described to you. The expedient of which he bethought himself was to advise the Sylphs to show themselves in the Air to everybody; they did so sumptuously. These beings were seen in the Air in human form, sometimes in battle array marching in good order, halting under arms, or encamped beneath magnificent tents. Sometimes on wonderfully constructed aerial ships, whose flying squadrons roved at the will of the Zephyrs. What happened? Do you suppose that ignorant age would so much as reason as to the nature of these I' marvellous spectacles? The people straightway believed that sorcerers had taken possession of the Air[135] for the purpose of raising tempests and bringing hail upon their crops. The learned theologians and jurists were soon of the same opinion as the masses. The Emperors believed it as well; and this ridiculous, ;a; chimera went so far that the wise Charlemagne, and after him Louis

---

[134] *Zedechias. Note eee, Commentary Continued.*

[135] STORM WIZARDS.--In these regions nearly all men, noble and of low degree, town folk and country folk, old and young, think that hail and thunder can be produced at the will of man. For on hearing thunder and seeing lightning, they say, "It is a raised breeze." When asked what they mean by "raised," they aver, some shamefacedly, others with confidence, as is the manner of the unexperienced, that the storm has been raised by the incantations of certain men who are called storm wizards, and hence the expression. Whether this common belief agrees with the facts is a matter to be proved by the authority of Holy Scripture. TRANSLATED FROM AGOBARD, LIBER DE GRANDINE ET TONITRUIS, CHAPTER i.

the Débonnaire, imposed grievous penalties upon all these supposed Tyrants of the Air. You may see an account of this in the first chapter of the Capitularies of these two Emperors."[136]

"The Sylphs seeing the populace, the pedants and even the crowned heads thus alarmed against them, determined to dissipate the bad opinion people had of their innocent fleet by carrying off men from every locality and showing them their beautiful women, their Republic and their manner of government, and then setting them down again on earth in divers parts of the world. They carried out their plan. The people who saw these men as they were descending came running from every direction, convinced beforehand that they were sorcerers who had separated from their companions in order to come and scatter poisons on the fruit and in the springs. Carried away by the frenzy with which such fancies inspired them, they hurried these innocents off to the torture. The great number of them who were put to death by fire and water throughout the kingdom is incredible."

"One day, among other instances, it chanced at Lyons that three men and a woman were seen descending from these aerial ships. The entire city gathered about them, crying out that they were magicians[137] and were sent by Grimaldus, Duke of

---

[136] CAPITULARIES, "KAROLI MAGNI ET LUDOVICI PII CHRISTIONES CAPITULA." NOTE FFF, COMMENTARY CONTINUED.
[137] MAGICIANS SENT BY GRIMALDUS, DUKE OF BENEVENTUM. NOTE GGG, COMMENTARY CONTINUED.

Beneventum, Charlemagne's enemy, to destroy the French harvests. In vain the four innocents sought to vindicate themselves by saying that they were their own country-folk, and had been carried away a short time since by miraculous men who had shown them unheard-of marvels, and had desired them to give an account of what they had seen. The frenzied populace paid no heed to their defence, and were on the point of casting them into the fire when the worthy Agobard, Bishop[138] of Lyons, who having been a monk in that city had acquired considerable authority there, came running at the noise, and having heard the accusations of the people and the defence of the accused, gravely pronounced that both one and the other were false. That it was not true that these men had fallen from the sky, and that what they said they had seen there was impossible."

"The people believed what their good father Agobard said rather than their own eyes, were pacified, set at liberty the four Ambassadors of the Sylphs[139], and received with wonder the book which

---

[138] AGOBARD, BISHOP OF LYONS. NOTE HHH, COMMENTARY CONTINUED.

[139] THE FOUR AMBASSADORS OF THE SYLPHS.--We have, however, seen and heard many men plunged in such great stupidity, sunk in such depths of folly, as to believe and say that there is a certain region, which they call Magonia, whence ships sail in the clouds, in order to carry back to that region those fruits of the earth which are destroyed by hail and tempests; the sailors paying rewards to the storm wizards and themselves receiving corn and other produce. Out of the number of those whose blind folly was deep enough to allow them to believe these things possible, I saw several exhibiting, in a certain concourse of people, four persons in

Agobard wrote to confirm the judgment which he had pronounced. Thus the testimony of these four witnesses was rendered vain."

"Nevertheless, as they escaped with their lives they were free to recount what they had seen, which was not altogether fruitless for, as you will recall, the age of Charlemagne was prolific of heroic men. This would indicate that the woman who had been in the home of the Sylphs found credence among the ladies of that period and that, by the grace of God, many Sylphs were immortalised. Many Sylphids also became immortal through the account of their beauty which these three men gave; which compelled the people of those times to apply themselves somewhat to Philosophy; and thence are derived all the stories of the fairies which you find in the love legends of the age of Charlemagne and of those which followed.

All these so-called fairies were only Sylphids and Nymphs. Did you ever read those histories of heroes and fairies?"

"No Sir," said I.

"I am sorry to hear it," he replied, "for they would have given you some idea of the state to which the

---

bonds--three men and a woman who they said had fallen from these same ships; after keeping them for some days in captivity, they had brought them before the assembled multitude, as we have said, -in our presence to be stoned. But truth prevailed. TRANSLATED FROM AGOBARD, LIBER DE GRANDINE ET TONITRUIS, CHAPTER ii.

Sages are one day determined to reduce the world. Those heroic men, those love affairs with Nymphs, those voyages to terrestial paradise, those palaces and enchanted woods and all the charming adventures that happen in them, give but a faint idea of the life led by the Sages and of what the world will be when they shall have brought about the Reign of Wisdom[140]. Then we shall see only

---

[140] MARRIAGE IN THE REIGN OF WISDOM.--There is an ancient Hermetic saying, "As above, so below," as in the universe so in man, as in the universal principle and finer bodies of man, so in the gross physical body. We cannot divorce the Creator from His Creation. In like manner we cannot divorce the Divine Principle in man from man when considering him, and must regard the physical body as the vesture and manifestation of the God within.

It is therefore significant that Aristotle and anatomists prior to his day and in our own have recognised the fact that the human body is androgynous, and accurately speaking neither male nor female, but bisexual. In the male body the female organs of sex exist in a state of latent development; and in the female organism the male organs of sex are present in rudimentary form. Thus we find upon the physical plane an evidence that a dual force, male and female, positive and negative, is manifesting in every human being. And we must inevitably conclude that the attraéion between the sexes, since it is of a magnetic character, is the result of the effort universal in Nature to balance these positive and negative forces.

The existence of a dual force operative in man and its balance in the perfect man, Adarn, is plainly stated in the first chapter of Genesis, verse 27. " So God created man in His own image, in the image of God created He him; male and female created He them," and more explicitly in chapter v., verses z and 2, "In the day that God created man, in the likeness of God made He him; male and female created He them;

PO and blessed them and called their name Adam, in the day when they were created."

heroes born; the least of our children will have the strength of Zoroaster, Apollonius or Melchizedek; and most of them will be as accomplished as the children Adam would have had by Eve had he not sinned with her."

"Did you not tell me, Sir," I interposed, "that God did not wish Adam and Eve to have children, that

---

This verse reveals the Fatherhood and Motherhood of God, making known to us that the Divine or Solar Force is both positive and negative in its manifestation, yet at its Source maintained in a unity of sublime harmony and balance.

If the ultimate goal of the individual soul's evolution on this planet is the formation of a deathless Solar Body which can only evolve when a perfect balance of the positive and negative currents of Solar Force has been achieved, then marriage or the effort of the soul to balance self with its opposite-, thereby attaining a transitory equilibrium, must be in its essence spiritual. Swedenborg affirms this truth regarding the polarisation of the sexes when he says, "Love that is truly conjugal in its first essence is love to the Lord." And Plato expands this divine reality in the Phaedrus.

But whenever one who is fresh from those mysteries, who saw much of that heavenly vision, beholds in any god-like face or form a successful copy of original beauty,--he is inspired with a reverential awe, and did he not fear the repute of exceeding madness, he would offer sacrifice to his beloved as to the image of a god."

Thus the Sages of our Order teach their disciples to worship God through the being beloved as a means of purifying the mind and of creating chaste thought in the world. For the person who, thinking of his beloved one, prays to God through that being, recognising in him or in her that divinity which is of God, breaks no law; for one cannot approach God through the being that one loves with impure thought.

"Praise the name of thy Lord THE MOST HIGH, Who hath created and balanced ALL THINGS." THE KORAN, SURA lxxxvii.

Adam was to think only of Sylphids, and Eve only of some Sylph or Salamander?"

"It is true," said the Comte, "that they ought not to have had children in the way in which they did."

"Then Sir," I continued, "your Cabala empowers man and woman to create children otherwise than by the usual method?"

"Assuredly," he replied.

"Ah Sir," I entreated, "teach this method to me, I beg of you."

"You will not find it out to-day, and it please you," said he smilingly, "I wish to avenge the People of the Elements for your having been so hard to undeceive regarding their supposed deviltry. I do not doubt that you are now recovered from your panic terrors. Therefore I leave you that you may have leisure to meditate and to deliberate in the presence of God as to which species of Elementary Beings will be most appropriate to His glory and to your own, as a participant in your immortality."

"Meanwhile I go to meditate in preparation for the discourse you have made me long to deliver to the Gnomes to-night."

"Are you intending to explain a chapter of Averroes. to them?" said I.

"I believe that it might be well to introduce something of the sort," said the Comte, "for I intend to preach to them on the excellence of man, that I may influence them to seek his alliance. Like Aristotle, Averroes held two theories which it would be well for me to explain, one as to the nature of the understanding, and the other as to the Chief Good. He says that there is only one created understanding which is the image of the uncreated, and that this unique understanding suffices for all men; that requires explanation. And as for the Chief Good, Averroes says that it consists in the conversation of Angels, which is not Cabalistic enough. For man, even in this life[141] can, and is created to, enjoy God, as you will one day understand and experience when you shall have reached the estate of the Sages."

Thus ends the Discourse of the Comte de Gabalis. He returned the next day and brought the speech that he had delivered to the Subterranean Peoples. It was marvellous! I would publish it with the series of Discourses which a certain Vicomtesse and

---

[141] FOR MAN, EVEN IN THIS LIFE CAN, AND IS CREATED TO, ENJOY GOD.--"He is known when realized by an acute intellect, purified by meditation and self-control. By a knowledge of Him assuredly man attains to bliss even in the flesh. By a proper and thorough cultivation and development of the powers of his soul he becomes vested with a SINGULAR ENERGY, (Solar Force.) and by a true realization of the nature of the Supreme Being by means of contemplation, he attains to beatitude on the dissolution of the physical body. If God is known and understood in this life, the supreme object of existence is attained; if missed in this life, the loss is indescribable." KAINOPNISHAT. TRANSLATED INTO ENGLISH BY CHHAJJU SINGH. PAGES 13-14.

I have had with this Illustrious Man, were I certain that all my readers would have the proper spirit, and not take it amiss that I amuse myself at the expense of fools. If I see that people are willing to let my book accomplish

the good that it is capable of doing, and are
not unjustly suspeéting me of seeking to give
credit to the Occult Sciences under
pretence of ridiculing them, I
shall continue to delight in
Monsieur le Comte,
and shall soon be
able to publish
another
volume[142]

---

[142] ANOTHER VOLUME.--Noel Argonne, in the second edition of his Mélanges Vigneul-Marville, published in 1725, about fifty years after the supposed death of the Abbé de Villars, includes a criticism of the Comte de Gabalis. He says, "The world has never known whether the author merely wished to jest or whether he spoke in good faith. The second volume which he promised would have settled the question." This statement made by a representative man of letters thoroughly in touch with the literary happenings of his day, may be taken as proof that those who were best qualified to judge did not regard the various sequels published with

the later editions of the Comte de Gabalis as the
work of its author, but knew them for the
obvious forgeries which a careful study
of their internal evidence and style
reveals them to be. The Comte
de Gabalis may be said to
stand alone as the only
one of the Abbé de
Villar's writings
on occultism
thus far
given
out

COMMENTARY
CONTINUED.

A.

MAP OF THE HOROSCOPE.

 HE charted observation which an astrologer makes of the state of the heavens at the hour of a child's birth and from which he seeks to determine the events of the child's life. By Initiates, the planetary aspects at the moment of birth are considered of utmost importance. In ancient times Astrology was regarded as one of the most sacred of the sciences and was taught only to those Initiates admitted to the Greater Mysteries, for it was considered essential that the astrologer should have such spiritual discernment as would enable him to check any astrological calculations by visualising the effect of the planetary influences playing at any moment upon the native or person for whom the horoscope was cast. As the ebb and flow of the tides are due to the influence of the moon, so the currents in man's superphysical bodies are subject to planetary influence and their fludtuations are visible to the seer.

B.

HARMONY OF THE WORLD.

Throughout the universe there vibrates a resonant tone known to Occultists as the Bindery Note. When man, by discipline of the mind, is able to shut off all sense perception, he becomes conscious of an ever-vibrating rhythmic throb or pulsation which manifests as a distinct and audible sound. As the earth and planets . have each their own note or sound vibration, this pulse of the universe creates a respondent chord from the spheres. When the different planets approach the earth their respective notes are apparent to the consciousness of the Adept as distinct tones predominant in the Harmony of the World.

C.

NUMBERS OF PYTHAGORAS.

A Greek Initiate of the sixth century B.C., known as the Son of Apollo the Sun God, or Son of the Sun, and the first to take the name of Philosopher, lover of Wisdom. Pythagoras publicly recognised the power of woman to achieve Initiation by associating his wife Theano with him in the teaching of a brotherhood which he founded at Crotona, and by entrusting the conduct of this work to her at his death. To facilitate the mastery of mind, every disciple entering this school took a vow of five years' silence. During this period a system of numbers and symbols, preserved intact in the Order to this day, was imparted, concentration on which opened the mind of the disciple to different states of consciousness. Pythagoras held that numbers are the principle of the universe and a key to the cosmic or Solar Consciousness in man.

D.

1501 A.D. JEROME CARDAN, 1576 A.D.

The son of Facius Cardan, a learned jurist and mathematician of Milan, Italy. During his lifetime he was celebrated as an occultist, mathematician and physician. To-day he is remembered chiefly for his treatise on Algebra, published at Nuremberg in 1545, which is the first example of the application of algebraical reasoning to geometrical problems.

SYLPHS OF CARDAN.

Here I will add a story which is more wonderful than all the rest, and which I have heard my father, Facius Cardan (who confessed that he had had a familiar spirit for nearly thirty years) recount not once but many times. Finally I searched for his record of this event, and I found that which I had so often heard, committed to writing and to memory as follows. August 13, 1491. When I had completed the customary rites, at about the twentieth hour of the day, seven men duly appeared to me clothed in silken garments, resembling Greek togas, and wearing, as it were, shining shoes. The undergarments beneath their glistening and ruddy breastplates seemed to be wrought of crimson and were of extraordinary glory and beauty. Nevertheless all were not dressed in this fashion, but only two who seemed to be of nobler rank than the others. The taller of them who was of ruddy complexion, was attended by two companions, and the second, who was fairer and of shorter stature, by three. Thus in all there were seven. He left no record as to whether their heads were covered. They were about forty years of age, but they did not appear to be above thirty. When asked who they were, they said that they were men composed, as it were, of air, and subject to birth and death. It was true that their lives were much longer than ours, and might even reach to three hundred years duration. Questioned on the immortality of our soul, they affirmed that nothing survives which is peculiar to the individual. They said that they themselves were more closely related to the gods than mankind, but were yet separated from them by an almost immeasurable distance. They are either more blessed or more wretched than we are, just as we ourselves are more so than the brutes. They said that no hidden things were unknown to them, neither books nor treasures, and that the basest of them were the guardian spirits of the noblest of men, just as men of low degree are the trainers of good dogs and horses. They have such exceedingly subtle bodies that they can do us neither good nor harm, save through apparitions and terrors or by conveying knowledge. The shorter of the two leaders had three hundred disciples in a public academy, and the other, two hundred. Indeed both were in the habit of lecturing publicly. When my father asked them why they did not reveal treasures to men if they knew where they were, they answered that it was forbidden by a peculiar law under the heaviest penalties for anyone to communicate this knowledge to men. They remained with my father for over three hours. But when he questioned them as to the cause of the universe they were not agreed. The tallest of them denied that God had made the world from eternity. On the contrary, the other added

Air that God created it from moment to moment, so that should He desist for an instant the world would perish. To prove this he brought forward certain statements from the Disquisitions of Averroes, although that particular book had not then been found. He referred, and by name, to certain books, some of which had been found and others which up to that time had remained undiscovered. They were all works of Averroes. Indeed he openly declared himself to be an Averroeist. Be this fad or fable, so its stands. TRANSLATED FROM JEROME CARDAN, "DE SUBTILITATE," BOOK XIX.

E.

1126 A.D. AVERROES, 1198 A.D.

An Arabian philosopher born at Cordova in Spain, and at one time Cadi of Seville. He revered Aristotle, and translated his works into Arabic with commentaries which express his conception of the relation between philosophy and religion. Averroes holds the highest bliss of the soul to be union in this life with that actual intelledt or consciousness which is one and continuous in all individuals, who differ solely in the degree of their illumination through its manifestation. Mediævalism misinterpreted Averroes, pronounced him an arch heretic, and his name became the synonym for scoffer and sceptic.

F.

DISCOURSE II.

AINT PAUL AN INITIATE. Authority for this statement is found in St. Paul's own I CORINTHIANS, ll., 6, 7. We speak wisdom among the initiated, not the wisdom of this age (but of the life-giving Force), nor of the archons of this age who pass away (but of the archons of the life-giving Force who do not pass away), but we speak the Wisdom of God in a secret made known to the initiated, the wisdom kept secret, which God ordained before the ages for (the upbuilding of) our spiritual body.

Σοφίαν δὲ λαλοῦμεν ἐν τοῖς τελείοις. *We speak wisdom among the initiated,*

Bishop Lightfoot states that "τέλεοις is properly that of which the parts are fully developed. Hence it signifies full-grown,' and accordingly τέλεοις is used by St. Paul as opposed to νήπιος.[143] Pythagoras also is said to have distinguished his disciples as τέλειοι and νήπιοι. But besides this meaning of full development,' the term here most probably bears the collateral sense of 'initiated' according to its classical usage, illustrating ἐν μυστηρίῳ below.

---

[143] *Infant, little child.*

These words have been the subject of much dispute. On the one hand they have been adduced to justify the distinction of an exoteric and an esoteric dodrine, as though there were certain secrets withheld from the generality. The idea of a higher and a lower teaching seems early to have gained ground even among orthodox writers, and Clement of Alexandria (*Eusebius H.E. v. 11*) especially says that Christ communicated the inner γνῶσις to a few chosen disciples. This distinction became the starting-point of Gnosticism. It is clear from the whole context, especially iii. I, 2, that St. Paul was speaking of an actual distinction in the teaching addressed to the less and the more advanced believer." J. B. LIGHTFOOT, D.D., D.C.L., L.L.D., LORD BISHOP OF DURHAM. EXTRACTS FROM "NOTES ON EPISTLES OF ST. PAUL," FIRST EPISTLE TO THE CORINTHIANS, PAGES 173-4.

σοφίαν δὲ οὐ τοῦ αἰῶνος τούτου. *Not the wisdom of this age,*

But the wisdom of the life-giving Breath or Force is here implied. "αἰών is so connected with ἄημι, *to breathe, blow,* as to denote properly *that which causes life, vital force;*" (or life-giving Force).[144] GREEK-ENGLISH LEXICON OF THE NEW TESTAMENT, EDITED BY JOSEPH HENRY THAYER, D.D. PAGE 18. This passage is a subtle play upon words conveying one meaning to the Initiate who has knowledge of the life-giving Force and its manifestation for the uphuilding of man's spiritual body, and quite another to the ordinary

---

[144] Solar Force.

hearer for whom the primary significance of the word αἰών has become obliterated through its customary usage with the meaning of age.

οὐδὲ τῶν ἀρχόντων τοῦ αἰῶνος τούτου τῶν καταργουμένων. *Nor of the archons of this age who pass away,*

But of the Archons of the life-giving Force who do not pass away is here implied. The Century Dictionary defines archon as "a chief magistrate of some states in ancient Greece, and particularly Athens," and as "In various Gnostic systems, one of several spiritual powers superior to angels, believed to be the rulers of the several heavens." The word archon is here used by St. Paul with double significance. While actually speaking of the Greek magistrates of the period who are uninitiated and therefore ignorant of the mysteries of the life-giving Force, he has in mind those heavenly Archons,or Rulers of this Divine Power.

ἀλλὰ λαλοῦμεν θεοῦ σοφίαν ἐν μυστηρίῳ. *But we speak the Wisdom of God in a secret made known to the initiated,* "μυστήριον has its ordinary sense of 'a secret made known to the initiated.'" ARTHUR PENRHYN STANLEY, D.D., DEAN OF WESTMINSTER. "THE EPISTLES OF ST. PAUL TO THE 'CORINTHIANS," PAGE 48, NOTE 7.

τὴν ἀποκεκρυμμένην. *The wisdom kept secret,* this is the passive of the verb to conceal, to hide or keep secret. ἣν προώρισεν, ὁ θεὸς πρὸ τῶν αἰώνων. *Which God ordained before the ages.*

The word αἰών is again used with dual meaning. In its primal sense, as used in the Mysteries, "which God ordained before the life-giving Forces or Breaths," it makes reference to the Cabalistic doari;e of the existence of the Archetypal Plan before its manifestation in Breaths or Emanations.

εἰς δόξαν ἡμῶν. *For (the upbuilding of) our spiritual body.*

In considering the utterances of St. Paul it is necessary to bear in mind that he was a Jew and a Cabalist, and that he used Greek words rather as translations of the Hebrew words with which he was familiar than in the sense in which they are usually employed by Greek writers. Thus Eis εἰς δόξαν. "δόξα. As a translation of the Hebrew, in a use foreign to Greek writing, splendor, brightness; used of the heavenly brightness, by which God was conceived of as surrounded," and here applied to the heavenly brightness by which the God in man is clothed, or the spiritual body. "By which heavenly beings were surrounded when they appeared on earth, with which the face of Moses was once made luminous, and also Christ in his transfiguration, in the Targum and Talmud, Shekinah or Shechinah, *the glory of the Lord.*"

EXTRACTS FROM GREEK-ENGLISH LEXICON OF THE NEW TESTAMENT, PAGE 156.

G.

429 B.C. PLATO, 347 B.C.

HIS PLACE AS A PHILOSOPHER.

"Yes, there is a mother-dotrine, a synthesis of religions and philosophies. It develops and deepens as the ages roll along, but its foundation and centre remain the same. We have still to show the providential reasons for its different forms, according to race and time. We must re-establish the chain of the great initiates, who were the real initiators of humanity. Then, the might of each of them will be multiplied by that of all the rest, and the unity of truth will appear in the very diversity of its expression. Like everything in nature, Greece has had her dawn, the full blaze of her sun, and her decline. Such is the law of days, of men, and nations, of earths and heavens. Orpheus is the initiate of the dawn, Pythagoras the initiate of the full daylight, and Plato that of the setting sun of Greece, a setting of glowing purple which becomes the rose of a new dawn, the dawn of humanity. Plato follows Pythagoras, just as the torch-bearer followed the great hierophant in the mysteries of Eleusis." EXTRACTS, PAGES 61, 62.

PLATO MEETS HIS MASTER.

"At the age of twenty-seven he had written several tragedies and was about to offer one for competition. It was about this time that Plato met Socrates, who was discussing with some youths in the gardens of the Academy. He was speaking about the Just and the Unjust, the Beautiful, the Good, and the True. The poet drew near to the philosopher, listened to him, and returned on the morrow and for several days afterwards. At the end of a few weeks, his mind had undergone a complete revolution. . . . Another Plato had been born in him, as he listened to the words of the one who called himself 'the one who brings souls to birth.' The important thing, he (Socrates) said, was to believe in the Just and the True, and to apply them to life. Plato had received from Socrates the great impulse, the active male principle of his life, his faith in justice and truth. He was indebted for the science and substance of his ideas to his initiation into the Mysteries, and his genius consists in the new form, at once poetic and dialectic, he was enabled to give to them." EXTRACTS PAGES 69, 72, 83, EDOUARD SCHURE, "HERMES AND PLATO." TRANSLATED BY F. ROTHWELL, B.A.

H.

BENVENUTO CELLINI SEES A SALAMANDER.

The People of the Elements have power over matter which enables them to transform their appearance at will. They frequently make themselves visible under the form of animals as did Melusina. Hence interest attaches to the following testimony as to the existence of a living creature whose habitat was fire taken from the Autobiography of Benvenuto Cellini.

"When I was about five years old my father happened to be in a basement chamber of our house, where they had been washing, and where a good fire of oak-logs was still burning; he had a viol in his hand, and was playing and singing alone beside the fire. The weather was very cold. Happening to look into the fire, he spied in the middle of those most burning flames a little creature like a lizard, which was sporting in the core of the intensest coals. Becoming instantly aware of what the thing was, he had my sister and me called, and pointing it out to us children, gave me a great box on the ears, which caused me to howl and weep with all my might. Then he pacified me good-humouredly, and spoke as follows: 'My dear little boy, I am not striking you for any wrong that you have done, but only to make you remember that that lizard which you see in the fire is a salamander, a creature which has never been seen before by anyone of whom we have credible information.' So saying he kissed me and gave me some pieces of money."

JOHN ADDINGTON SYMONDS, "THE LIFE OF BENVENUTO CELLINI," BOOK FIRST, CHAPTER IV.

I.

BOOK OF ENOCH.

I"Enoch the great grandfather of Noah, who had that surname (Edris) from his great knowledge, for he was favoured with no less than thirty books of divine revelations, and was the first who wrote with a pen, and studied the sciences of astronomy and arithmetic." This quotation is an approved Muhammedan commentary upon the following references to Enoch in the Koran. "And remember Edris in the same book; for he was a just person and a prophet, and we exalted him to a high place." SURA 19, MARY.

"The History which follows is taken from Dr. Grabe's Spicilegium Patrum, and supposed by him to be the Genuine Work of Enoch the Patriarch, whose Name it bears. Many of the first Fathers of the Church were of this Opinion, who often produce Citations out of it, and allow it to be of the best Authority. Tertullian, speaking of the Habit of. Women, uses this Expression The same Angels who introduc'd Gold and Silver, and the mixture of Colours, which advance the Lustre of Female Beauty, are now condemn'd by God, as Enoch informs us. Clemens Alexandrinus discoursing upon the disobedient Angels, agrees to the Testimony of Enoch, and says, That the Rebellious Spirits were the Inventors of Astronomy and Divination, as Enoch delivers the Account. And St. Jude (who cites a Prophecy out of the Writings of Enoch in the fourteenth and fifteenth Verses of his Epistle) may be supposed to have recourse to this

194

Fragment before us, when he records in the Sixth Verse, That the Angels who kept not their first Estate, but left their own Habitation, are reserv'd in Everlasting Chains under Darkness, unto the Judgment of the Great Day."

THE HISTORY OF THE WATCHMEN,

(Or the Angels).

WRITTEN BY ENOCH THE PATRIARCH.

And it came to pass, when the Sons of Men were increas'd, that very Beautiful Daughters were born to them: With these the Watchmen were in Love, and burnt with Desire toward them, which drew them into many Sins and Follies. They communed with themselves: "Let us, say they, choose us Wives out of the Daughters of Men upon the Earth." Semiazas, their Prince, made Answer: "I fear, says he, you will not execute your Resolution; and so I shall derive upon myself alone the Guilt of this Impiety." They all reply'd, and said; "We will bind ourselves with an Oath to perform our Purpose, and invoke dreadful Imprecations upon our Heads, if we depart from our Enterprize before it be accomplished." So they oblig'd themselves with an Oath; and implored an Arrest of Vengeance upon one another.

They were two Hundred, who in the Days of Jared came down upon the Top of Mount Hermon. The Mountain receiv'd that Name from the Oath by which they bound themselves, and the Imprecations they wilfully submitted themselves under. The Names of their Princes were these: 1. Semiazas, the Chief of them. 2. Atarcuph. 3. Araciel. 4. Chobabiel. 5. Horammame. 6. Ramiel.7. Sampsich. 8. Zaciel. 9. Balciel. 10. Azalzel. 11. Pharmarus. 12. Amariel. 13. Anagemas. 14. Thausael. 15. Samiel. 16. Sarinas. 17. Eumiel. 18. Tyriel. 19. Jumiel. 20. Sariel. These, and all the rest of them, took to themselves Wives, in the Year of the World One Thousand one Hundred and Seventy, and were infiam'd with Lust toward them till the Floud. The Offspring of these Women were of three sorts: The first race were Giants, or Tall Men: They begat the Naphelims, and from them came the Eliudæans; and their Number increased, according to the Proportion of their Bodies. They instructed their Wives and Children in Sorcery and Inchantments. Azalzel, the Tenth in the Order of the Princes, was the first In ventor of Swords and Breastplates, and all Military Appointments: He taught his Posterity the Art of extracting Metals out of the Earth, and the Curiosity of working in Gold and Silver, to make Ornaments and Female Decorations: He diredted and shew'd them to polish, and give a Lustre to choice Stones, and to Colours: The Sons of Men soon furnish'd themselves and their Daughters with these Vanities; and breaking through the Commands of God, they drove the Pious and Just into Miscarriages; insomuch that a monstrous Appearance of Impiety stalk'd over the Face of the whole Earth. Semiazas, their Prince, discover'd the Art of Hatred, to reserve Envy in the Mind, and to infuse Misfortunes upon others by the Roots of Herbs. Pharmarus, the Eleventh Prince, found out

Witchcraft, Charms, and Inchantments. The Ninth revealed the Course of the Stars. The Fourth the Science of Astrology. The Eighth the Inspection of the Air. The Third of the Earth. The Seventh of the Sun. The Twentieth explain'd the Signs of the Moon. All of them display'd these Secrets of Knowledge to their Wives and Sons. The Giants soon after began to feed upon Human Flesh, which made the number of Men to decrease, and sensibly to decay.

Those who were left being harass'd with so many Instances of Wickedness, raised their Voice to Heaven, and implor'd, That their Memory might be preserv'd in the Sight of God.

The Four Great Archangels, Michael, Uriel, Raphael, and Gabriel, being affected with their Cries, look'd down upon Earth from the Holiness of Heaven; and beholding a general Effusion of Blood, and a Spirit of Universal Impiety, had this Communication among themselves: "The Spirits and Souls of Men implore our Aid, in Agonies of Sorrow; Introduce (they cry) our Prayers to the Highest." Then the Four Archangels calling upon God, deliver'd themselves thus: "Thou art God of Gods and Lord of Lords, King of Kings, and God of Men: The Throne of thy Glory endures to all Ages, and thy Name is Holy and Blessed for evermore; for Thou art the Creator of all things; Thy Power is over all things; all things are open and manifest before Thee, nor can anything be conceal'd from Thee. Thou seest the Actions of Azalzel; the Misfortunes he has occasioned; the Wickedness and abominable Practices he has taught upon the Earth; how he has corrupted it with Fraud and Villainy. He has divulg'd the great Arcana of Heaven; and the Sons of Men are led, by his Example, to inspeél the Celestial Mysteries: Semiazas Thou hast ordained to be the Prince of those who are about I him; but they have all turned themselves to the Daughters of the Men of the Earth, and polluting themselves with Women have discovered to them all the Methods of Impiety, and instructed them to perpetrate all degrees of Abomination: And now, behold, the Daughters of Men have born a Gigantic Offspring to them; a foul Blemish of Corruption has infected the whole Earth, and the World is full of Injustice. Lo, the Spirits of the Souls of Men who have been dead, attend thee: Their Groans have arriv'd as far as the Gates of Heaven, and they cannot depart, by reason of the exceeding Impiety that is committed upon the Earth: Yet Thou knewest these things before they were effected: Dost Thou see them, and say nothing? What must be done upon this Occasion?"

The Highest made answer, and the Holy Great One reply'd; and sent Uriel to the Son of Lamech, saying: "Go to Noe, and acquaint him in My Name, Hide thyself: And inform him, that the End approaches, for the whole Earth shall perish. And tell him, a Deluge shall overspread the whole Earth, and all Things shall be destroy'd upon the Face of it. Instruct the Just Son of Lamech what he shall do, and he shall preserve his Soul unto Life; and he shall be safe in his Generation: From him shall a new Race be deriv'd and established, and shall continue to all Ages." THE HISTORY OF THE ANGELS, AND THEIR GALLANTRY WITH THE DAUGHTERS OF MEN. WRITTEN BY ENOCH THE PATRIARCH. PUBLISH'D IN GREEK BY DR. GRABE. MADE ENGLISH, LONDON, MDCCXV. ENOCH'S PROPHECY OF WORLD PEACE, COMMENTARY CONCLUDED.

J.

THE EGG AND SERPENT SYMBOL.

"The serpent, separate or in combination with the j circle, egg, or globe, has been a predominant symbol among many primitive nations. It prevailed in Egypt, Greece, and Assyria, and entered widely into the superstitions of the Celts, the Hindoos, and the Chinese. It even penetrated into America; and was conspicuous in the mythology of the ancient Mexicans, among whom its significance does not seem to have differed materially from that which it possessed in the old world. The fad that the ancient Celts, and perhaps other nations of the old continent, erected sacred structures in the form of the serpent, is one of high interest. Of this description was the great temple of Abury, in England,--in many respects the most imposing ancient monument of the British islands."[145]

A celebrated example of the egg and serpent symbol is found in Adams County, Ohio, United States of

---

[145] *Smithsonian Contributions to Knowledge. Vol. I, page 97.*

America. It is an enduring witness to the fad that knowledge of the God-Mystery existed in North America at an early period. "It is situated on a high spur of land, which rises a hundred and fifty feet above Brush Creek. 'Conforming to the curve of the hill, and occupying its very summit, is the serpent, its head resting near the point, and its body winding back for seven hundred feet, in graceful undulations, terminating in a triple coil at the tail. The entire length, if extended, would be not less than one thousand feet. The work is clearly and boldly defined, the embankment being upwards of five feet in height, by thirty feet base at the centre of the body, but diminishing somewhat toward the head and tail. The neck of the serpent is stretched out, and slightly curved, and its mouth is opened wide, as if in the ad of swallowing or ejeting an oval figure, which rests partially within the distended jaws. This oval is formed by an embankment of earth, without any perceptible opening, four feet in height, and is perfectly regular in outline, its transverse and conjugate diameters being one hundred and sixty, and eighty feet respectively.' When, why, or by whom these remarkable works were erected, as yet we know not. The present Indians, though they look upon them with reverence, can throw no light upon their origin."

SIR JOHN LUBBOCK, "PRE-HISTORIC TIMES." EDITION 1890. PAGE 276-277.

K.

THOSE RESERVED FOR GREATER THINGS.

Reference is here made to those great souls, priests "for ever after the order of Melchizedek" or the Unspoken Name. They are Christs of former periods of evolution bound to earth by their desire to lift mankind to their own level of consciousness. These are the Masters of the Masters. Melchizedek was himself the Master to whom Moses said, "Shall I follow thee that thou teach me, for guidance, of that which thou too hast been taught?" KORAN SURA 18.

St. Paul says of him, "For this Melchizedek, king of Salem, priest of the most high God,--without father, without mother, without descent, having neither beginning of days, nor end of life; but made like unto the Son of God; abideth a priest continually." And of Christ he declares, After the similitude of Melchizedek there ariseth another priest, who is made, not after the law of a carnal commandment, but after the power of an endless life." HEBREWS viii. 1, 3; 15, 16.

MOSES MEETS HIS MASTER MELCHIZEDEK.

HEN found they one of our servants to whom we had vouch-safed our mercy, and whom we had instructed with our knowledge.

And Moses said to him, 'Shall I follow thee that thou teach me, for guidance, of that which thou too hast been taught?'

He said, 'Verily, thou canst not have patience with me;

How canst thou be patient in matters whose meaning thou comprehendest not?'

He said, 'Thou shalt find me patient if God please, nor will I disobey thy bidding.'

He said, 'Then, if thou follow me, ask me not of aught until I have given thee an account thereof.'

So they both went on, till they embarked in a ship, and he--*the unknown*--staved it in. 'What!' said Moses, 'hast thou staved it in that thou mayest drown its crew? a strange thing now hast thou done!'

He said, 'Did I not tell thee that thou couldst not have patience with me?'

He said, 'Chide me not that I forgat, nor lay on me a hard command.'

Then went they on till they met a youth, and he slew him. Said Moses, 'Hast thou slain him who is free from guilt of blood? Now hast thou wrought a grievous thing!' He said, Did I not tell thee that thou couldst not have patience with me?'

Moses said, 'If after this I ask thee aught, then let me be thy comrade no longer; but now hast thou my excuse.'

They went on till they came to the people of a city. Of this people they asked food, but they refused them for guests. And they found in it a wall that was about to fall, and he set it upright. Said Moses, 'If thou hadst wished, for this thou mightest have obtained pay.'

He said, This is the parting point between me and thee. But I will first tell thee the meaning of that which thou couldst not await with patience.

'As to the vessel, it belonged to poor men who toiled upon the sea, and I was minded to damage it, for in their rear was a king who seized every ship by force. As to the youth his parents were believers, and we feared lest he should trouble them by error and infidelity. And we desired that their Lord might give them in his place a child, better than he in virtue, and nearer to filial piety. And as to the wall, it belonged to two orphan youths in the city, and beneath it was their treasure: and their father was a righteous man: and thy Lord desired that they should reach the age of strength, and take forth their treasure through the mercy of thy Lord. And not of mine own will have I done this. This is the interpretation of that which thou couldst not bear with patience.'" THE KORAN, SURA IS, THE CAVE, EVERYMAN'S LIBRARY EDITION, PAGES 186-188.

L.

PANIC TERRORS. ORIGIN OF THE TERM.

"For having privily taken the measure of Osiris's body, he (Typho) caused a chest to be made exactly of the same size with it, as beautiful as might be, and set off with all the ornaments of art. This chest he brought into his banqueting room; where, after it had been much admired by all who were present, Typho as it were in jest, promised to give it to anyone of them, whose body upon trial it might be found to fit. Upon this the whole company, one after another, got into it, but as it did not fit any of them, last of all Osiris lays himself down in it, upon which the conspirators immediately ran together, clapped the cover upon it, and then fastened it down on the outside with nails, pouring likewise melted lead over it. After this, they carried it away to the river-side, and conveyed it to the sea by the Tanaïtic mouth of the Nile; which for this reason is still held in the utmost abomination by the Egyptians, and never named by them but with proper marks of detestation. These things, say they, were thus executed upon the 17th day of the month Athyr, when the Sun was in Scorpio, in the 28th year of Osiris's reign; though there are others, who tell us that he was no more than 28 years old at this time.

The first who knew the accident which had befallen their king, were the Pans and Satyrs who inhabited the country about Chemmis; and they immediately

acquainting the people with the news gave the first occasion to the name of *Panic Terrors*, which has ever since been made use of to signifie any sudden afright or amazement of a multitude."'
PLUTARCH, "Isis AND OSIRIS," §13, 14. TRANSLATED BY SAMUEL SQUIRE, A.M.

M.

THE GREAT PAN IS DEAD.

Cleombrotus continued saying: "And what is more, it was not alone Empedocles who said that there were evil spirits, hut also Plato, Xenocrates, and Chrysippus. Democritus, too, when he desired and prayed that he might meet fortunate spirits, showed clearly that he believed there were others perverse and evil, having-bad intentions and violent affetions. And as to whether or not they are mortal, I have heard a story related by a personage who is neither a fool nor a liar,--namely Epithersis, father of Æmilianus the orator, whom some of you may have heard declaim. This Epithersis was from the same city as myself, and had been my grammar teacher. He related that he embarked for a voyage to Italy upon a ship loaded with sundry merchandise and a great number of passengers, and he said that toward evening the wind failed them near the Echinades Islands, and their ship drifted so much that it came near the Isles of Paxos, and that the majority of the passengers were awake and many were still drinking after supper, when suddenly a voice was heard proceeding from one of the Paxi Islands, which called Thamus. so loudly that they were all amazed. This Thamus was an Egyptian pilot whom few of those on board knew by name. The two first times that he was called he made no answer, but at the third he replied, and then he who was calling, raising his voice cried out that when he reached the shoals, he should announce that the Great Pan was dead. Epithersis told us that all who heard the cries of that voice were greatly astonished, and forthwith entered into a dispute as to whether it would be better to do what it commanded, or to let things alone and not trouble. Finally, Thamus decided that if there were a good wind when they were passing the place specified, he should sail outside it without saying a word; but if, perchance, there were a calm, and no wind whatever, he should cry aloud what he had heard. When they reached the shoals and flats it chanced there was not a breath of wind, and the sea was exceedingly smooth, wherefore Thamus, looking over the prow towards the land, repeated in a loud voice what he had heard, that the Great Pan was dead. He had scarcely finished speaking when a mighty groaning was heard, not made by a single person but by a great number, who lamented and were altogether amazed. And inasmuch as many were present, the news of this event was immediately spread throughout the city of Rome in such fashion that the Emperor Tiberius Cæsar sent for Thamus and reposed such great faith in his story that he began to inquire as to who this Pan could be: and the men of letters, of whom there were a goodly number at court, were of the opinion that it must be that Pan who was the son of Penelope and Mercury. Moreover Phillipos had among the company present witnesses who had heard the story from the old man Æmilianus." TRANSLATED FROM PLUTARCH'S "CESSATION OF THE ORACLES," CHAPTER 17.

N.

JANSENISTS.

1585 A.D. CORNELIUS JANSEN, 1638 A.D.

Bishop of Ypres, Holland. His principal work "Augustinus," based upon a profound study of St. Augustine's doctrines of grace, free will and predestination, gave rise to the doctrine called Jansenism, which tends to limit the free will of man and maintains that the grace of salvation is only accorded to chosen souls for whom alone Christ died.

O.

1530 A.D. JEAN BODIN, 1596 A.D.

The celebrated French publicist, "regarded as the father of Political Science in France, and if one except Machiavelli, in Europe as well," whose book, "The Republic," "made him the Montesquieu of the sixteenth century." This learned man believed implicitly in the existence of superphysical spirits, and wrote a book concerning them entitled "D; monomanie des Sorciers." This book was inspired by his having been called upon to assist at the trial of Jean Hervillier, a native of Verbery, near Compiegne, who was burned alive the last of April, 1582.

P.

MOSES AND ELIAS FASTED FORTY DAYS.

Moses.--"And he was there with the Lord forty days and forty nights; he did neither eat bread, nor drink water. And he wrote upon the tables the words of the covenant, the ten commandments." EXODUS xxxiv, 28.

Elias.--"And the angel of the Lord came again the second time, and touched him, and said, Arise and eat; because the journey is too great for thee. And he arose, and did eat and drink, and went in the strength of that meat forty days and forty nights unto Horeb the mount of God." I KINGS xix, 7, 8.

Q.

BACCHUS AND OSIRIS THE SAME.

"Now that *Osiris* is really the same with Bacchus, nobody can be supposed to know better than you, *O Clea*, not only as you are chief of his priestesses at *Delphi*, but moreover as you are initiated, in right of both your parents, into the service and religion of *Osiris*--As others, however, may not be so well satisfied in this point; to omit the evidence which may be brought in proof of it from those more secret rites which are not to be divulged, do not those very cere- monies, which the priests perform in public, when they carry the *Apis* on a raft to his funeral, correspond entirely with what we see done in the festivals of *Bacchus?* They hang round them the skins of hinds, they carry javelins in their hands crowned with ivy, make the same sort of howlings, and use the same kind of gesticulations as the votaries of *Bacchus* are wont to do, whilst they are celebrating the orgies of their God. Hence likewise is it, that so many of the Greeks, in their statues of *Bacchus*, have given him *the visage of an ox;* that the women of *Elis* in their prayers to him, call upon the *God with the oxe's feet* to come unto them; and that the people of *Argos* not only give him the appellation of *Ox-begotten*, but likewise invoke him, and endeavour to raise him from his watry dwelling by the sound of the trumpet, throwing at the same time a lamb into the deep, as a kind of fee to the porter, who keeps the door of the infernal regions for letting him pass: these trumpets are concealed by them under boughs of ivy, as *Socrates* relates in his treatise concerning the *Delphic Hosii*--So again, the histories upon which the most solemn feasts of *Bacchus*, the *Titania* and *Nuktelia*, are founded, do they not exactly correspond with what we are told of the cutting in pieces of *Osiris*, of his rising again, and of his new life? Nor does what relates to his burial any way contradict this notion; for whilst the Egyptians, as has been already observed, show many places as the sepulchres of their *Osiris*, the *Delphians* pretend that the relics of *Bacchus* are deposited with them, and that they lye near the oracle.: and in consequence of this opinion, the *Hosii*, or priests appointed for that purpose, perform a secret sacrifice in the temple of *Apollo*, whilst at the same time the *Thyades*, or priestesses of *Bacchus*, with their hymns endeavour to raise their God, whom they at that time distinguish by the name of the *Winnower*. Now that the Greeks themselves do not look upon *Bacchus* as the Lord or President of wine only, but of all kind of humidity in general, may be sufficiently proved from the testimony of *Pindar*, where he says "may bountiful *Bacchus*, the bright glory of the year, make all my trees fruitful;" thus likewise the votaries of *Osiris* are expressly forbidden to destroy any fruit-tree, or to mar any springs of water.

But to resume a while our former argument concerning the identity of *Bacchus* and *Osiris;* as a farther proof of this point, we may mention the *Ivy*, which as it is esteemed by the Greeks sacred to *Bacchus*, so is it likewise stiled by the Egyptians, in their language, *Chenosiris*, that is, as some interpret it, *the plant of Osiris*. In like manner

Aristo, who wrote a treatise of the Athenian Colonies, tells us, he somewhere met with an epistle of *Alexarchus*, wherein *Bacchus* was expressly said to have been the son of Isis, and to heve been named by the Egyptians not *Osiris*, but *Asiris*, with an A; a word, in the language of that country, signifying *strong and mighty:* and this is farther confirmed by the testimony . of *Hermaeus*, who, in his first book concerning the Egyptians, gives us a similar explication of the name *Osiris* himself. . . . there is no need of any other evidence than that I have formerly made use of, drawn from the similarity, which may be observed, between the festivals and. sacred rites of these two Gods, a proof much more strong and convincing than any authorities whatever can be."

PLUTARCH'S TREATISE OF ISIS AND OSIRIS, §35, §37. TRANSLATED BY SAMUEL SQUIRE, A.M., 1744.

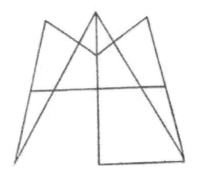

R.

571, A.D. MUHAMMED. 632, A.D.

PROPHET OF GOD AND BRINGER OF LIGHT TO ISLAM.

"The word this man spoke has been the life-guidance now of a hundred-and-eighty millions of men these twelve-hundred years. The hundred-and-eighty millions were made by God as well as we. A greater number of God's creatures believe in Mahomet's word at this hour, than in any other word whatever." [146]

In the Koran, 'the light giving Book,' transmitted to Muhammed by the Angel Gabriel from the Lord "that He may stablish those who have believed, and

---

[146] THOMAS CARLYLE. THE HERO AS PROPHET. MAHOMET: ISLAM.

as guidance and glad tidings to the Muslims," it is written:

"It beseemeth not a man, that God should give him the Scriptures and the Wisdom, and the gift of prophecy, and that then he should say to his followers, 'Be ye worshippers of me, as well as of God;' but rather, 'Be ye perfect in things pertaining to God, since ye know the Scriptures, and have studied deep.' God doth not command you to take the angels or the prophets as lords.

Say: WE BELIEVE IN GOD, AND IN WHAT HATH BEEN SENT DOWN TO US, and what hath been sent down to Abraham, and Ismael, and Isaac, and Jacob, and the tribes, AND IN WHAT WAS GIVEN TO MOSES, AND JESUS, AND THE PROPHETS, FROM THEIR LORD. WE MAKE NO DIFFERENCE BETWEEN THEM. And to Him are we resigned (Muslims)." [147]

---

[147] THE KORAN SURA III, THE FAMILY OF IMRAN. EVERYMAN'S LIBRARY EDITION, PAGES 393-4.

S.

KING SAUL.

Now Samuel was dead, and all Israel had lamented him, and buried him in Ramah, even in his own city. Then said Saul unto his servants, "Seek me a woman that hath a familiar spirit, that I may go to her, and inquire of her." And his servants said to him, "Behold, there is a woman that hath a familiar spirit at En-dor." And Saul disguised himself, and put on other raiment, and he went. Then said the woman, "Whom shall I bring up unto thee?" And he said, "Bring me up Samuel." And Samuel said to Saul, "Why hast thou disquieted me, to bring me up?" And Saul answered, "I am sore distressed; for the Philistines make war against me, and God is departed from me, and answereth me no more, neither by prophets, nor by dreams: therefore I have called thee, that thou mayest make known unto me what I shall do." Then said Samuel, "Wherefore then dost thou ask of me, seeing the Lord is departed from thee, and is become thine enemy? Moreover the Lord will also deliver Israel with thee into the hand of the Philistines: and to-morrow shalt thou and thy sons be with me: the Lord also shall deliver the host of Israel into the hand of the Philistines."

EXTRACTS FROM I SAMUEL, xxviii.

T.

THE ORACLE OF DODONA.

"They went therefore in their consternation to consult the Oracle at Dodona; for those who dwell on this mainland, as the Aetolians and their neighbours the Acarnanians and Epirots, believe in the oracular responses they get from doves and the oak there.[148] "The Peleae ('doves') at Dodona, also prophesied by divine inspiration." PAUSANIAS, BOOK X, CHAPTER xii.

---

[148] *Book vii, Chapter xxi.*

U.

DIVINE POWER OF LETTERS.

The sacred significance of the letters of the Hebrew alphabet is paralleled by that attached to those of the Sanskrit alphabet as used in the Sacred Writings of India. "The god said--'Out of the will-power of the Supreme Being there originated a force whose exponents are the fifteen letters of the alphabet and from whom the universe has subsequently emanated. By worshipping that force, O goddess, I have come to know of all the knowables and I shall presently discuss the congery of Mantras that have arisen out of the five principal ones composed of the above said letters. These Mantras, O goddess, are the life and soul of all other Mantras. They form the back bone as it were, of the Vedas, Rik, Sam, Yajur, and the Arthava. The Mantras known as the Sadyajatas, etc., are but the different combinations of the abovesaid forms revealed in the phonetic energy of the abovesaid five letters (Mantras). Through them the gods such as Brahma, Vishnu, and Rudra, etc., have come into being. They are identical with the gods called Isha, Saptashikha, etc. The vowels A.E.I.O.U. are but the five phases of the supreme god head (Brahma). . . . . Oh Brahman, as fire potentially lying in the bosom of firewood remains invisible unless kindled in the proper way, so the divine energy (Shiva-Shakti) lies latent in the body of a man quite in the dark about its very existence even." "THE WEALTH OF INDIA," VOL. viii, PART I. AGNI PURANAM, PAGE 498.

V.

1450 A.D. CELIUS RHODIGINUS, 1525 A.D. LOUIS RICCHIERI RHODIGINUS.

An Italian philologist who made a valuable and ably annotated collection of the opinions of the ancient Greek and Latin scholars on occult and other subjects.

ORACLE OF CELIUS RHODIGINUS.

Lest any one think that this story ought to be laughed at as fabulous, I desire it to be put on record, now at this time, and indeed while I am dealing with the matter, that there was in my native country a woman of humble origin named Jacoba from whose abdomen, I myself, yes and numberless others, not only at Rovigo but throughout well nigh the whole of Italy, heard the voice of an unclean spirit, excessively thin, to be sure, but nevertheless when it so desired articulate and perfectly intelligible. It would frequently happen that men of high position being eager to know the future, would send for the ventriloquist, and after having had her stripped of all clothing in order that no secret fraud might be concealed, they would watch and listen to her with great eagerness.

Little Cincinnatus was the name of the demon, an appellation in which he took great pleasure and to which he would immediately reply when called upon.

If you inquired about matters of the past or present, however hidden they might be, he often gave marvellous answers; but if you asked about the future he was always a hopeless deceiver, sometimes he used to reveal his ignorance by a doubtful whispering or more unmistakably by an unintelligible buzzing.

LUDOVICI COELII RHODIGINI, LECTIONUM ANTIQUARUM LIBRI TRIGINTA. BOOK viii, CHAPTER 10.

W.

SAMBETHE, DAUGHTER OF NOAH.

The theologian's opinion that the most ancient of the Sibyls was the daughter of Noah is based upon the following internal evidence of the Sibylline Books. "'O the great Joy that I had when I escap'd the great Destruction, when my Husband with me, and his Brothers, and Father, and Mother, and their Daughters-in-law, suffer'd much by being long toss'd by the Flood!'" (BOOK I.) [149] and "'for when the World was drowned, and only one Man of worth was left in his wooden House, swimming on the Waters with the wild and tame Beasts, that the World might replenish again by them; I was his Daughter-in-Law, and of his Blood.'" (BOOK III.) [150] SIR JOHN FLOYER, KNIGHT, "THE SIBYLLINE ORACLES." LONDON, 1713.

---

[149] *Pages 13, 14.*
[150] *Page 83.*

X.

JUSTIN MARTYR'S STATEMENT.

"Neither will it be difficult for you to learn the true religion in some measure from that antient Sybil, who, by a very powerful inspiration, instructs you in her oracular responses, and which come nearest to the dodtrine of the prophets.

Of this Sybil it is reported that she was driven out of Babylon: that she was the daughter of Berosus who wrote the history of the Chaldeans: that by some means or other, she came and settled at Cumæ in Campania, six miles from the hot baths at Baiæ, where she delivered her oracles. And when we were at Cumæ, we saw the place, wherein was a prodigious Basilic all cut out of one stone, a stupendous and amazing work. Here this Sybil gave forth her oracles, as the people, from an unquestioned tradition of their forefathers, informed us. In the midst of this Basilic were three cisterns hewn out of the Basilic itself, in which, being filled with water, the Sybil used to bathe: then, slipping on her loose garb, retired into the inmost recess of the Basilic, which also was cut out of the same stone; where sitting on an exalted throne, she delivered her oracles.

Many have made mention of this Sybil, as of an undoubted Oracle, particularly Plato in his Phaedrus: for it seems to me that Plato, meeting with her oracles, ascribed an inspiration to the author. He saw her predictions accomplished, and, struck with admiration, in his book to Menon, speaks in praise of the prophetess in this punctilious manner: 'If we rightly account those persons divine who are endowed with the gift of prophecy, are not those also inspired and agitated by a divine impulse, and possessed of the God, who declare many things about the most weighty affairs very justly, at the same time not understanding any of those things whereof they then speak.'

It is very clear and evident that Plato in this had an eye to the Sybil's verses: for she had not, like the poets, a power to revise and correct her own works, and thereby adjust them to poetical measures: but she, in the very time of her inspiration, finished her prophecy; and the moment that that inflatus ceased, that moment she forgot all she had said; for which reason the measures of her verses are not all of them entire.

Finally, O Grecians, unless you esteem the deceitful representation of the imaginary gods of these men, as more precious than your own salvation, hearken, as I said before, to what that antient Sybil saith (whose books are preserved throughout the world) of those who are called gods, for she instructs you, by a powerful inspiration, in her oracles that there are no gods, and moreover clearly foretold the coming of our Saviour Jesus Christ, and all those things which he should perform: for the knowledge of these things will be a necessary preparatory induction to the holy scriptures."

ST. JUSTIN, THE PHILOSOPHER AND MARTYR: HIS EXHORTATIONS TO THE GENTILES. TRANSLATED FROM THE GREEK BY THE REV. MR. THOMAS MOSES, ONE OF THE MINISTERS OF ST. PAUL'S CHAPEL IN ABERDEEN. ABERDEEN, 1757. EXTRACTS PAGES 58, 59, 61.

JUSTIN MARTYR MEETS A MASTER.

Justin Martyr lived at Neapolis during the reign of Marcus Aurelius, and suffered death for the faith of his Fathers the Philosophers, about 165 A.D. From youth he sought ardently for knowledge of the Truth, and in his own writings gives an account of his receiving the "Salutation of the Sages." He states that his investigation into the various philosophies of the day resulted in conviction that he would find the true path to God through Platonism. He therefore gave himself up to the rigorous mental discipline and meditation which that school enjoined upon its neophytes. During this period "Wishing to be filled with quietness and to shun the paths of men, I used to walk by myself in a field near the sea. One day an old man of gentle and venerable appearance followed me at a little distance. I stopped and turning round fixed my eyes keenly upon him."

"Dost thou know me?" he asked.

I replied that I did not.

"Why then dost thou look so intently at me?"

"Because," I said, "I had not expected to see any man here."

"I am anxious," he replied, "about some absent members of my family, and I am come to look out whether they would come in sight from any quarter."

A remarkable discussion ensued in which the messenger of the Sages made plain to Justin the futility of an intellectualism unvivified by spirit, such as was manifest in the Stoic, Peripatetic, Pythagorean, and even Platonic philosophies at that period. At last Justin said, as so many other baffled thinkers have done before and since, "Whom then, shall a man take as his Master, or whence shall he derive any instruction if the truth is not with these philosophers?"

"There once lived men called prophets," answered his instruolor, "who were anterior to any of those who are considered philosophers and who were blessed, just, and beloved by God. They were filled with the Divine Spirit and foretold future events which are now atually taking place. And they alone knew and taught the Truth neither regarding nor fearing any man, nor being carried away by personal love of glory but declaring only those things which they saw and heard when filled with the Divine Spirit. Their writings are extant, and whoever reads them will derive much instrution about the first principles and the end of things, together with all that a philosopher ought to know when he believes them. They have not indeed used demonstration in their treatises for they were verily as faithful witnesses of the Truth above all demonstration. . . They glorified God, the Father and Creator of all things and proclaimed His Son, the Christ whom He has sent. *Pray therefore above all things that the gates of light may be opened to thee,* for these things cannot be perceived or understood by all, but only by him to whom God and His Christ have given understanding."

"When he had thus spoken he went away; and I saw him no more. But straightway *a flame was kindled in my Soul,* and a love of the Prophets and of the friends of Christ took possession of me; and revolving his words in my mind I found this Philosophy alone to be sound and profitable." FROM "THE DIALOGUES OF ST. JUSTIN MARTYR WITH TRYPHO THE JEW." § 104, § I09. TRANSLATION BASED UPON EDWARD BACKHOUSE, "EARLY CHURCH HISTORY," PAGES 29-31.

In the early Christian Church the word Christ was used as a synonym for the Solar Principle in man. "But if Christ is in you, though your body must die because of sin, yet your Spirit has life because of righteousness." ROMANS viii, 10.

Y.

TEMPLE OF HERCULES IN ARMENIA.

"In their march they captured the city of Ninos, the most ancient capital of Assyria, and a fortress, historically famous, as the spot where in the last battle between Darius and Alexander the power of Persia fell. Gotarzes meantime was offering vows to the local divinities on a mountain called Sambulos, with special worship of Hercules, who at a stated time bids the priests in a dream equip horses for the chase and place them near his temple. When the horses have been laden with quivers full of arrows, they scour the forest and at length return at night with empty quivers, panting violently. Again the god in a vision of the night reveals to them the track along which he roamed through the woods, and every where slaughtered beasts are found." "ANNALS OF TACITUS," BOOK xii, §13. CHURCH AND BRODRIBB'S TRANSLATION.

Z.

PLATO ON MAN'S PLACE IN NATURE.

"But with respect to the most principal and excellent species of the soul, we should conceive as follows: that divinity assigned this to each of us as a dæmon; and that it resides in the very summit of the body, elevating us from earth to an alliance with the heavens; as *we are not terrestial plants, but blossoms of heaven.* And this indeed is most truly asserted. For from whence the first generation of the soul arose, from thence a divine nature being suspended from our head and root, directs and governs the whole of our corporeal frame. In him therefore who vehemently labours to satisfy the cravings of desire and ambition, all the conceptions of his soul must be necessarily mortal; and himself as much as possible must become entirely mortal, since he leaves nothing unaccomplished which tends to increase his perishable part. But it is necessary that he who is sedulously employed in the acquisition of knowledge, who is anxious to acquire the wisdom of truth, and who employs his most vigorous exertions in this one pursuit;--it is perfectly necessary that such a one, if he touches on the truth, should be endued with wisdom about immortal and divine concerns; and that he should participate of immortality, as far as human nature permits, without leaving any part of it behind. And besides, as such a one always cultivates that which is divine, and has a dæmon most excellently adorned residing in his essence, he must be happy in the most eminent degree. But the culture of all the parts is indeed entirely one, and consists in assigning proper nutriment and motion to each. But the motions which are allied to the divine part of our nature, are the cogitative energies and circulations of the universe. These therefore each of us ought to pursue; restoring in such a manner those revolutions in our head (which have been corrupted by our wandering about generation), through diligently considering the harmonies and circulations of the universe, that the intellective power may become assimilated to the objet of intelligence, according to its ancient nature. For when thus assimilated, we shall obtain the end of the best life proposed by the gods to men, both at present and in all the future circulations of time." "THE TIMAEUS OF PLATO." TRANSLATED BY THOMAS TAYLOR. PAGES 550-551, EDITION 1793.

AA.

SIR THOMAS BROWNE ON MAN'S PLACE IN NATURE.

"We are onely that amphibious piece between a corporal and spiritual Essence, that middle form that links those two together, and makes good the Method of God and Nature, that jumps not from extreams, but unites the incompatible distances by some middle and participating natures. That we are the breath and similitude of God, it is indisputable, and upon record of Holy Scripture; but to call ourselves a Microcosm, or little World, I thought it only a pleasant trope of Rhetorick, till my neer judgement and second thoughts told me there was a real truth therein. For first we are a rude mass, and in the rank of creatures which onely are, and have a dull kind of being, not yet priviledged with life, or preferred to sense or reason; next we live the life of Plants, the life of Animals, the life of Men, and at last the life of Spirits, running on in one mysterious nature those five kinds of existences, which comprehend the creatures, not onely of the World, but of the Universe. Thus is Man that great and true Amphibium, whose nature is disposed to live, not onely like other creatures in divers elements, but in divided and distinguished worlds: for though there be but one to sense, there are two to reason, the one visible, the other invisible." SIR THOMAS BROWNE, "RELIGIO MEDICI." EVERYMAN'S LIBRARY EDITION, PAGES 38, 39.

BB.

CURTIUS RUFUS.

"Of the birth of Curtius Rufus, whom some affirm to have been the son of a gladiator, I would not publish a falsehood, while I shrink from telling the truth. On reaching manhood he attached himself to a quæstor to whom Africa had been allotted, and was walking alone at midday in some unfrequented arcade in the town of Adrumetum, when he saw a female figure of more than human stature, and heard a voice, 'Thou, Rufus, art the man who will one day come into this province as proconsul.' Raised high in hope by such a presage, he returned to Rome, where, through the lavish expenditure of his friends and his own vigorous ability, he obtained the quæstorship, and, subsequently, in competition with well-born candidates, the prætorship, by the vote of the emperor Tiberius, who threw a veil over the discredit of his origin, saying, 'Curtius Rufus seems to me to be his own ancestor.' Afterwards, throughout a long old age of surly sycophancy to those above him, of arrogance to those beneath him, and of moroseness among his equals, he gained the high office of the consulship, triumphal distinéions, and, at last, the province of Africa. There he died, and so fulfilled the presage of his destiny." "ANNALS OF TACITUS," BOOK XI §2I. CHURCH AND BRODRIBB'S TRANSLATION.

CC.

KING RODRIGUEZ WARNING, 711 A.D.

"Now it came to pass that the King Don Rodrigo called to mind how he had been required to put a lock upon the doors of the house which was in Toledo. And after they were unlocked, the king pushed the door with his hand, and he went in, and the chief persons who were there with him, and they found a hall made in a square, and in it there was a bed richly fur nished, and there was laid in that bed the statue of a man, exceeding great, and armed at all points, and he had the one arm stretched out, and a writing in his hand. And the king went to him, and took it from his hand, and opened it and read it, and it said thus, Audacious one, thou who shalt read this writing, mark well what thou art, and how great evil through thee shall come to pass, for even as Spain was peopled and conquered by me, so by thee shall it be depopulated and lost. And I say unto thee, that I was Hercules the strong, he who conquered the greater part of the world, and all Spain; and having seen this they went to behold another apartment. He opened the door, and when it was opened they found Hebrew letters which said, This house is one of the wonders of Hercules; and when they had read these letters they saw . . . a coffer of silver, and it was fastened with a lock of mother-of-pearl. *And the king* said, Within this coffer lies that which I seek to know, and which Hercules has so strongly forbidden to be known. And when the lock was broken, a:nd the coffer open, they found nothing

233

within, except a white cloth folded between two pieces of copper; and he took it and opened it, and found Moors pourtrayed therein with turbans, and banners in their hands, and with their swords round their necks, and their bows behind them at the saddlebow, and over these figures were letters which said, When this cloth shall be opened, and these figures seen, men apparelled like them shall conquer Spain and shall be Lords thereof." EXTRACTS FROM SOUTHEY'S TRANSLATION OF "CHRONICA DEL REY DON RODRIGO." PART I, CHAPTERS 28-30.

DD.

THE INMATES OF THE CAVE, OR THE STORY OF THE SEVEN SLEEPERS.

"Hast thou reflected that the Inmates of THE CAVE and of Al Rakim were one of our wondrous signs?

When the youths betook them to the cave they said, "O our Lord! grant us mercy from before thee, and order for us our affair aright."

Then struck we upon their ears *with deafness* in the cave for many a year:

Then we awaked them that we might know which of the two parties could best reckon the space of their abiding.

We will relate to thee their tale with truth. They were youths who had believed in their Lord, and in guidance had we increased them;

And we had made them stout of heart, when they stood up and said, "Our Lord is Lord of the Heavens and of the Earth: we will call on no other God than Him; for in that case we had said a thing outrageous.

These our people have taken other gods beside Him, though they bring no clear proof for them; but, who more iniquitous than he who forgeth a lie of God?

So when ye shall have separated you from them and from that which they worship beside God, then betake you to the cave: Your Lord will unfold His mercy to you, and will order your affairs for you for the best."

And thou mightest have seen the sun when it arose, pass on the right of their cave, and when it set, leave them on the left, while they were in its spacious chamber. This is one of the signs of God. Guided indeed is he whom God guideth; but for him whom He misleadeth, thou shalt by no means find a patron, director.

And thou wouldst have deemed them awake, though they were sleeping: and we turned them to the right and to the left. And in the entry lay their dog with paws outstretched. Hadst thou come suddenly upon them, thou wouldst surely have turned thy back on them in flight, and have been filled with fear at them.

So we awaked them that they might question bne another. Said one of them, "How long have ye tarried here?" They said, "We have tarried a day or part of a day." They said, "Your Lord knoweth best how long ye have tarried: Send now one of you with this your coin into the city, and let him mark who therein bath purest food, and from him let him bring you a supply: and let him be courteous, and not discover you to anyone.

For they, if they find you out, will stone you or turn you back to their faith, and in that case it will fare ill with you for ever."

And thus made we their adventure known to their *fellow citizens*, that they might learn that the promise of God is true, and that as to "the Hour" there is no doubt of its coming. When they disputed among themselves concerning what had befallen them, some said, "Build a building over them; their Lord knoweth best about them." Those who prevailed in the matter said, "A place of worship will we surely raise over them."

Some say, "They were three; their dog the fourth," others say, "Five; their dog the sixth," guessing at the secret: others say, "Seven; and their dog the eighth." SAY: My Lord best knoweth the number: none, save a few, shall know them.

Therefore be clear in thy discussions about them, . . . And when thou hast forgotten, call thy Lord to mind; and say, "Haply my Lord will guide me, that I may come near to *the truth* of this *story* with correctness."

THE KORAN, SURA 18, THE CAVE. EVERYMAN'S LIBRARY EDITION, PAGES 181-182.

INTERPRETATION.

In sacred writings the aas of the principal characters are often symbolic, revealing to the Initiated an inner meaning. The Story of the Seven Sleepers is related for the purpose of conveying a profound spiritual truth to those prepared to receive and make it their own. The Inmates of the

Cave symbolically represent the seven ganglia of the sympathethic nervous system.

"Hast thou reflected that the Inmates of THE CAVE and of Al Rakim were one of our wondrous signs?"

Every letter of the word Rakim has a sacred or hidden meaning, the sum of which is equivalent to the true meaning of the word:--

R. External manifestation.
A. The Divine Principle.
K. Concavity or turning. [151]
I. Extension.
M. Amplitude or evolution. Thus translated and interpreted Rakim is seen to be the external manifestation of the Divine Principle in man, the focussing centres for its extension through evolution, or the ganglia of the sympathetic nervous system through which the [152]Divine Force passes in its external manifestation.

"When the youths betook them to the cave they said, 'O our Lord! grant us mercy from before thee, and order for us our affair aright.' Then struck we [153] upon their ears *with deafness* in the cave for many a year:"

---

[151] *The energised ganglia may be described as concave rotating disks.*
[152] *Solar Force Defined*
[153] *Angel Gabriel speaking.*

During the passage of the Sun through the upper signs of the Zodiac, the centres correspondent to them in man were in a state of activity, but with the descent of the Sun into Libra, the sign of the balances, and the correspondent descent of the Divine Principle into matter and balance of the divine and material natures in man, their activity was stilled in preparation for the new cycle of evolution. The evolution of the animal man reached its zenith in the Golden Age and has been followed by a gradual decline or somnolence of the masses prior to regeneration in the coming spiritual cycle. Thus the statement is made by St. Paul, "The first man Adam became a living animal (*Gen. ii, 7*); the last Adam is a life-giving spirit."[154] And in the Koran, Sura xcv, The Fig, it is written "Of goodliest fabric we created man, then brought him down to be the lowest of the low;--save who believe and do the things that are right, for theirs shall be a reward that faileth not." "NEW TESTAMENT IN MODERN SPEECH." R. F. WEYMOUTH, D.LIT.

"Then we awaked them that we might know which of the two parties could best reckon the space of their abiding."

The two parties are the higher and lower nature of man. [155]

---

[154] 1 CORINTHIANS, XV, 45.

[155] *"The soul and the mind. The 'sacred war,' the greater, is the putting down of the mind (resignation to the unknown) in order that the soul may be master over it. Islam may be translated, resigned to the soul."*

"We will relate to thee their tale with truth. They were youths who had believed in their Lord, and in guidance had we increased them; And we had made them stout of heart, when they stood up and said,

"Our Lord is Lord of the Heavens and of the Earth: we will call on no other God than Him; for in that case we had said a thing outrageous. These our people have taken other gods beside Him, though they bring no clear proof for them; but, who more iniquitous than he who forgeth a lie of God?"

The enlightened members of the Muhammedan faith define Allah (God) as Nature the Indefinable. The awakening of the ganglia through the play of Solar Force bears witness to man of Allah, Nature, giving him a knowledge of the Divine Mystery which creeds and theologians oft-times misinterpret.

"So when ye shall have separated you from them and from that which they worship beside God, then betake you to the cave: Your Lord[156] will unfold his mercy to you, and will order your affairs for you for the best."

The Cave may be said to mean the recesses of man's own nature or being. The Cave symbolises the dormant lower nature which shuts out the light of the Sun and its manifestation in man prior to Initiation. In many lands and ages caves have been the places chosen for the performance of the Rites of Initiation.

---

[156] *The Divine Self.*

"And thou mightest have seen the sun when it arose, pass on the right of their cave, and when it set, leave them on the left, while they were in its spacious chamber. This is one of the signs of God."

Reference is here made to the path of the Sun through the signs of the Zodiac and to the passage of the Solar Force through the centres corresponding to them in man.

"Guided indeed is he whom God guideth; but for him whom He misleadeth, thou shalt by no means find a patron, director."

The statement is made that Allah (God) both guides and misleads man. Therefore Allah is here acknowledged as the Source of both good and evil. Allah, as the patron and director of man, may be said to be Nature's Force made manifest in man as the illuminator of the mind and giver forth of knowledge. Allah as the misleader of man is Nature's Force manifesting in man misgoverned by the human mind. "Thus (Allah) God misleadeth whom He will, and whom He will doth He guide aright."[157] KORAN, SURA, lxxiv, "THE ENWRAPPED." EVERYMAN'S LIBRARY EDITION, PAGE 23.

"And thou wouldst have deemed them awake, though they were sleeping:"

Man believes these ganglia to be awake and alive while they are stirred by the slow moving nerve force,

---

[157] *Compare Satan Cabalistically Defined*

not realising that when compared with the augmentation of life wherewith the inflowing Solar Force endues them, their present atrophied state is sleep or death in life.

"and we turned them to the right and to the left."

May be interpreted as meaning and we turned them for good and for evil.'

"And in the entry lay their dog with paws outstretched."

A commentary upon the Koran states of the dog that "One of its traditional names is Katmir, a word whose letters, it should be observed, are with one exception identical with Rakim." The added letter T has the meaning of sequel or continuation. Therefore Katmir, the dog, is seen to be the sequel or continuation of the external manifestation of the Divine Principle in man,--the body, lower nature, emotions and mind which, as it were, sleeping, lie across the threshold of man's Divine Nature and its evolution. In ancient Greece the lower nature and its three aspects were in like manner symbolised by a dog, Cerberus, a monster with three heads having the tail of a serpent, and said to guard the entrance to Hades.

"Hadst thou come suddenly upon them, thou wouldst surely have turned thy back on them in flight, and have been filled with fear at them."

This is an allusion to the fad that premature awakening of these centres in man is sometimes fraught with much physical and mental suffering.

"So we awaked them that they might question one another."

The agents of Allah, God manifesting in Nature, awaken these ganglia in man and establish their natural relationships through the medium of the divine or Solar Force.

"Said one of them, 'How long have ye tarried here?' They said, 'We have tarried a day or part of a day.' They said, 'Your Lord knoweth best how long ye have tarried: Send now one of you with this your coin into the city, and let him mark who therein hath purest food, and from him let him bring you a supply:

This passage has several meanings, the most obvious being that when man consciously enters upon the awakening of his centres through the right use of Solar Force he should send this coin or Force throughout his city or system,--and should seek through taking only pure materials into the body, pure emotions into the heart, and pure thoughts into the mind, to prepare and strengthen them to sustain their part in his divine evolution.

"'and let him be courteous, and not discover you to anyone.'"

Man should seek in self the knowledge of his own evolution. Divinity must be experienced and cannot be engrafted.

"'For they, if they find you out, will stone you or turn you back to their faith, and in that case it will fare ill with you forever.'"

Man through Initiation becomes a law unto himself, by virtue of communion with the Lord within;--and this experience of truth is superior to creeds or faiths which often persecute or seek to proseletyse the Lord-enlightened man.

"And thus made we their adventure known to *their fellow citizens*, that they might learn that the promise of God is true, and that as to 'the Hour' there is no doubt of its coming."

The fellow citizens are the centres of the cerebro-spinal system whose awakening reveals to man those higher states of consciousness in which he is able to apprehend the Divine or Cosmic Plan and consciously to participate in it.

"When they disputed among themselves concerning what had befallen them, some said, 'Build a building over them; their Lord knoweth best about them.' Those who prevailed in the matter said, 'A place of worship will we surely raise over them.'"

The truest form of worship of Allah, God manifesting in Nature, is obedience to Its Divine

Purpose by seeking to further Its manifestation in self. "The temple of God is holy, which temple ye are." ST. PAUL.

"Some say, 'They were three; their dog the fourth:'

Some say that the Fire, Air, Water and Earth bodies of man are signified by the Sleepers and their dog.

"others say, 'Five; their dog the sixth,' guessing at the secret: others say, 'Seven; their dog the eighth.' SAY: My Lord best knoweth the number: none, save a few, shall know them. Therefore be clear in thy discussions about them. . . And when thou has forgotten, call thy Lord to mind; and say, 'Haply my Lord [158] will guide me, that I may come near to *the truth* of this *story* with correctness.'"

May this story bear witness that the Koran is a book of great mystery concealing that truth which only the pure in heart shall fathom and make their own; for Islam and Christianity received their illumination from the same source--Allah, Nature, God.

---

[158] *Divine Self.*

EE.

SLEEP.

"In sleep the soul is vigorous, and free from the senses, and the obstruction of the cares of the body, which lies prostrate and deathlike.... When we are not asleep, our faculties are employed on the necessary affairs of life, and so are hindered from communication with the Deity by the bondage of the body.... When the soul of man is disengaged from corporeal impediments and set at freedom,--in sleep,--it beholds those wonders which, when entangled beneath the veil of the flesh, it is unable to see," says Cicero in his treatise "On Divination." [159] And this truth regarding the emergence of the Soul from the body during sleep, as well as the Soul's consequent closer union with the Divine Principle, is also set forth in the Koran Sura xxxix, The Troops. " God taketh souls unto Himself at death; and during their sleep those who do not die: and He retaineth those on which He hath passed a decree of death, but sendeth the others back till a time that is fixed. Herein are signs for the refledting."

Freed from the bondage of the body and the trammels of space and time in sleep, the soul desiring light is able to seek those great souls and sources ever flooding humanity with the out-pourings of divine love and wisdom. Thus are the words of Christ fulfilled, "Ask, and it shall be given you; seek, and ye shall find; knock, and it shall be

---

[159] *Chapters xxx, xlix, lvii.*

opened unto you: For every one that asketh receiveth; and he that seeketh findeth; and to him that knocketh it shall be opened." [160] Whatever the limitations of an individual's temporal experience, they cannot fetter the immortal spirit and soul, which in sleep attain those realms of consciousness whose memories, because of the imperfetions of the instrument, may filter but dimly into the waking mind, yet inevitably tindure it and the entire life of the man.

"In a dream, in a vision of the night, when deep sleep falleth upon men, in slumberings upon the bed;

Then He (God) openeth the ears of men, and sealeth their instrudtion." JOB xxxiii, 15, 16.

---

[160] *St. Matthew vii, 7, 8.*

Thotmes III, showing on the brow the uraeus or Sacred Serpent,

emblem of the Double Bridle of Leviathan.
British Museum. Photograph, Mansell & Co., London.

FF.

BEHEMOTH AND LEVIATHAN.

In Athanasius' " Life of St. Antony," at the words, "the weapons which are 'in the navel of his belly,'" reference is made to the parallel passage in Job xl, 16, where the Lord says of Behemoth, "his force is in the navel of his belly," and it is stated that "the descriptions of behemoth and leviathan are allegorically referred to Satan." Therefore we hope to give some clue to the identity of Behemoth and Leviathan, what they are, and how they manifest.

EHEMOTH. JOB xl, 6.--Then answered the Lord unto Job out of the whirlwind, and said,

14. Then will I also confess unto thee that thine own right hand can save thee.

This verse states that man may become his own saviour, affording a key to the allegory which follows.

15. Behold now behemoth, which I made with thee;

"Bĕhēmōth is no doubt an intensive plural form, and means 'a colossal beast.'" [161] Behemoth symbolises the beast in man, the vital energy or Solar Force

---

[161] *Enyclopœdia Biblica. Edited by the Rev. T. K. Cheyne, M.A., D.D., Vol. I, page 519.*

manifesting ungo,verned in the lower or animal nature of man. [162] he eateth grass as an ox.

Grass here signifies the flesh or carnal nature. "All flesh is grass." ISAIAH xl, 6. The ox is an unsexed animal, hence "he eateth grass as an ox" is equivalent to saying that Behe moth (the vital energy) can, or was intended to, consume the carnal nature of man by manifesting unsexed; for regeneration as opposed to ungoverned sex expression or generation.

16. Lo now, his strength is in his loins,

Loins in Hebrew as in Greek is used as a euphemism for the organs of generation. During the present cycle of evolution the strength or power of the Solar Force is manifesting in sex expression.

and his force is in the navel of his belly.

"The shining, vital energy which is the manifestation of life . . . is sleeping like a serpent, having three and a half coils." [163] The first stirring or uncoiling of this force prior to its passage through and energising of the ganglia of the sympathetic system manifests in the abdomen in the region of the navel. In chapter xxxii, 18, 19; 8, of the Book of Job, the Initiate Elihu describes this stirring of the vital energy or Solar Force when speaking under divine inspiration, "the spirit of my belly constraineth me, Behold, my belly is as wine which hath no vent; it is ready to burst like new

---

[162] *Behemoth is the Lion*
[163] *Lalita Sahasranama with Bhashararaya's Commentary. Translated into English by R. A. Sastri page 75.*

250

bottles. I will speak, that I may be refreshed, but there is a spirit in man: and the inspiration of the Almighty giveth them understanding."

18. His bones are pipes of copper; his bones are like tubes of iron. [164]

The bones of Behemoth are the net work of nerves which are the channels of the Solar Force. Prior to Initiation these nerves are in the atrophied or, relatively speaking, hardened state here typified as copper and iron. In Sanskrit writings these channels are similarly termed pipes or tubes (nadis). The Uttara Gita states that these nadis "are like pipes, are hollow and in this space there exists a certain substance, like oil, in which the Chaitanya (Divine Energy) reflects." [165] In the fourth chapter of Zechariah the word "pipes" is used in this sense. "And I said, I have looked, and behold a candlestick (the spine) all of gold, with a bowl upon the top of it," ("The golden bowl is the brain," [166] or accurately speaking the *medulla oblongata* which is a reservoir of vital force,) and his seven lamps thereon, (the seven principal ganglia), and seven pipes to the seven lamps."

"And I answered again, and said unto him, What be these two olive branches which through the two golden pipes empty the golden oil" (namely the nerve fluid in which the radiance of the Solar Force is reflected or manifested). ZECHARIAH iv, 2, 12.

---

[164] *Jewish School and Family Bible, Vol. iv, Job xl, 18.*
[165] *Page 27, D. K. Laheri's Translation.*
[166] *Royal Masonic Cyclopcedia, page 675.*

19. He is chief of the ways of God: he that made him can make his sword to approach unto him.

Behemoth is the chief manifestation to man of Nature, God. The God in man can govern Behemoth. The sword is the symbol of authority, government and the Great Law of Nature, God.

20. Surely the mountains bring him forth food,

In sacred writings the word 'mountain' is often used to signify those higher levels of consciousness wherein the Seeker attains to communion with God, and the Divine Self is able to instruct the man through the instrument of the mind. Thus Moses went up into the mount to receive the Law: and Isaiah foretells that spiritual enlightenment which is the destiny of the race in these words, "And in this mountain (the higher consciousness) shall the Lord of hosts make unto all people a feast,--And he will destroy in this mountain the face of the covering cast over all people, and the wail (of forgetfulness) that is spread over all nations. And it shall be said in that day, Lo, this is our God; we have waited for him, and he will save us: For in this mountain shall the hand of the Lord rest." [167] The Divine Principle manifesting in the higher consciousness of man shall bring him into harmony with the Law of Nature, God.

20. where all the beasts of the field play.

---

[167] EXTRACTS ISAIAH, XXV, 6, 7, 9, 10.

Presumably a reference to those streams of consciousness or Divine Force playing through the signs of the Zodiac known as the ram, bull, and goat--of which the spirit of man when functioning in the mountain or higher states of consciousness is aware, and from which he can gain knowledge of of the government of Behemoth.

23. he trusteth that he can draw up Jordan (salvation) into his mouth.

Behemoth, the Solar Force manifesting in lower nature of man trusteth that it can, through upward direction approach and quicken the Solar Principle in man and through the evolution of man's divine nature achieve his salvation.

24. He taketh it with his eyes:

The eyes of Behemoth are the seven principal ganglia of the sympathetic nervous system. " Those seven; they are the eyes of the Lord," Zechariah, iv, 10. Man works out his own salvation through the awakening of these centres.

24. his nose pierceth through snares.

Already the Solar Force seeks to manifest in upward direction for the regeneration of man and the race, though ensnared by the baser inclinations and ignorance.

EVIATHAN. JOB xl, 1.--Canst thou draw out leviathan with an hook?

The word Leviathan in Hebrew is made up of two roots, Levi and Than. "ThN, Than, which is the root of Serpent or Dragon. [168] Than will be the symbol of transgression, but a symbol also of influence and of power." [169] Since the root meaning of Than is serpent, Leviathan means literally the Than or serpent of Levi. Of this word Levi "The root, we may suppose, describes the coils of the serpent, perhaps the metallic gleam of its scales."[170] For Levi was the serpent tribe, bred for generations to the knowledge and control of the World Serpent, Solar Force. Leviathan or the Serpent of Levi signifies the Solar Force governed and direted upward through the spine by the priests of the tribe of Levi for regeneration, the upbuilding of the deathless Solar Body. [171] Accurately speaking, Leviathan is the Solar Force manifesting in the cerebrospinal nervous system after its passage through the ganglia of the sympathetic system.

5. or his tongue with a cord which thou lettest down?

---

[168] KABBALA DENUDATA. THE KABBALAH UNVEILED BY SIMEON BEN JOCHAI. TRANSLATED BY S. L. MACGREGOR MATHERS. PAGE 237.
[169] THE SAME. EXTRACTS
[170] SKIPWITH IN JEWISH QUARTERLY REVIEW, VOL. xi, PAGE 264.
[171] The Solar Body is the Spiritual Body.

substantiates this statement. For it is only after the upward passage of the Solar Force through the spine that the tongue of Leviathan can be drawn out. When the Solar Force is directed upward it passes through an opening in the top of the head called by the Brahmins the "door of Brahma," and by the first Christians the "door of Jesus," and is visible to the seer as a tongue of brilliant flame.

The following verses make reference to the various temptations which beset Job, overcoming of which mark different degrees in his Initiation.

3. Will he make many supplications unto thee? will he speak soft words unto thee?

Will you even now be tempted to misapply this force? The current would descend if possible, for it becomes either a regenerator or a destroyer, intensifying the lower nature.

5. or wilt thou bind him for thy maidens?

Until a man is able so to govern his lower nature, mind, and body as to express his higher or Divine Self in sex relationship he has not passed that stage in the evolution of his Godhood typified in ancient myths as the slaying of the lion or dragon. [172] Samson slew the lion after his lower nature had been roused by his love for a daughter of the Philistines. And Hercules

---

[172] *"Hail dragon, lion dynamic by nature and first principle of fire!" Translated from Dr. Carl Wessely, Griechische Zauber Papyrus. 1889 Page 68, line 939.*

overcame the Nemean lion after the fifty daughters of King Thespius had been given him as wives. This verse alludes to a definite degree of Initiation, an experience wherein the passions are overcome by a manifestation of the God in man.

6. shall they part him among the merchants?

Will you sell the superhuman powers where with the God in self endows you for personal advantage or money?

7. Wilt thou fill . . . the cabin of fishes with his head? [173]

The word "Dag" or "the Fish" is frequently used in the Talmud for the Messiah or regenerative spiritual force. When man becomes his own saviour this force passes upward to the brain, where its currents unite for the perfecting of the Solar or spiritual body. The cabin of fishes would seem to designate the skull containing the brain where the currents of the Solar Force focus for regeneration. Thus "there is no head above the head of a serpent" [174] *Ecclesiasticus, 25, 15*, Will you be able to fill the reservoir of regenerative force situated in the brain? is the meaning of this verse.

8. Lay thine hand upon him, remember the battle, do no more.

---

[173] TRANSLATION OF ST. GREGORY THE GREAT. MORALS ON THE BOOK OF JOB. VOLUME iii, PT. ii, PAGE 590. PUSEY LIBRARY OF THE FATHERS.
[174] *The Serpent is the Solar Force.*

These words indicate that Leviathan is a conquered or governed force; indeed, Leviathan is Behemoth governed and augmented. The battle or test referred to is supreme and terrible. Plato says in the Phaedrus, "But whenever one who is fresh from those mysteries" beholds beauty of face and form "he first of all feels a shuddering chill, and there creep over him some of those terrors that assailed him in that dire struggle." In the elder Edda, that voice of the ancient religions of the north, this degree of Initiation is described as follows: "Comes forth the glorious offspring of Earth, Thor, to strive with the glistening Serpent. . . . Lone Serpent-slayer, and Shield of Men, he baited his hook with the head of the ox, and he whom the gods hate gaped thereat, the Girdle lying all lands beneath. Then Thor drew mightily--swift in his doing--the poison-glistening snake to the side. His hammer he lifted and struck from on high the fearful head. . . . Moaned the wild monster, the rocks all rumbled, the ancient earth shrank into itself. . . . Then sank the serpent down in the deep."

THE ELDER OR POETIC EDDA. OLIVE BRAY'S TRANSLATION, PAGES 295, I 21. THE LAY OF HYMIR. PROPHECY OF WORLD PEACE FROM THE ELDER EDDA, COMMENTARY CONCLUDED.

10. None is so fierce that dare stir him up: who then is able to stand before me?

None is so fierce that dare stir him up:--meaning Leviathan or the Solar Force governed, who then is able to stand before me, the Architet of the Universe, and before my manifestation the Super Solar Force?

11. Who hath prevented me, that I should repay him?

Repay is here used in the Hebrew with the sense of "give an equivalent for." What has prevented the substitution of the Super Solar Force for the Solar Force, of immortality for mortality?

PART II.

At this point the allegory changes in character. Hitherto Leviathan or the Initiatory Force has been described figuratively and somewhat ambiguously. Henceforward the writer intends to make a more explicit and unmistakeable revelation of his meaning.

12. I will not conceal his parts, nor his power, nor his comely proportion.

13. Who can strip off his outer garment?

The outer garment of Leviathan is the voltage of Solar Force manifesting in the sympathetic nervous system. Who can replace this by the voltage necessary to open. and perfect the centres of the cerebro-spinal system?

13. or who can come to him with his double bridle?

After passing through the centres of the sympathetic nervous system, the positive and negative currents of Solar Force meet in the forehead where, as it were, their balance registers; so that at this degree of evolution the Initiate can sense whether the balance is perfedf, or whether positive or negative current predominates. This power to sense and govern the currents is hère called the double bridle of Leviathan. And the Adept Kings of Egypt bore upon their foreheads the uraeus, or sacred serpent, emblem of this bridle, to signify that they had achieved this power. Hence "The Chaldee Paraphrase understands 'leviathan that piercing serpent' to refer to Pharaoh." (*Isaiah xxvii, 1,*) Leviathan is also thought to personify the King of Egypt in Psalm lxxiv, 14, "Thou brakest the heads of leviathan in pieces, and gayest him to be meat to the people inhabiting the wilderness," meaning that Moses transmitted as meat to the children of Israel knowledge of the Serpent Fire or Solar Force, hitherto the prerogative of Egypt's Adept Kings and their priests:

15. His scales are his pride, shut up together as with a close seal.

The word translated scales has the literal meaning in Hebrew of 'strong pieces of shields,' and is used to designate the ganglia which "are shut up together as with a close seal" prior to Initiation. The word seal is used similarly in the Apocalypse when St. John says of the seven principal ganglia of the sympathetic system, "I saw when the Lamb (the immortal mind) opened one of the seven seals." REVELATION vi, 1.

18. By his neesings a light doth shine,

The neesings of Leviathan characterise what may be described as the whisking of the Solar Force through and about the Initiate which at every pronounced increase of voltage causes greater illumination, to the seer, actually visible as light. See Frontispiece.

21. His breath kindleth coals,

The Divine Energy or Fire [175] enkindles the ganglia. Or this verse may be taken literally, for when the Solar Force has reached and energised a certain ganglion the Initiate is able to enkindle substances by directing the Solar Force upon them through the medium of the breath.

22. and sorrow is turned into joy before him.

The suffering experienced in the physical body during the period when the centres are energised is transmuted into the joy of divine realisation.

27. He esteemeth iron as straw, and brass as rotten wood.

his is an allusion to xl, 18, the "pipes of copper and tubes of iron," or the nervous systems, channels of the Divine Energy, which adapt themselves for the conveyance of this Force.

33. Upon earth there is not his like, who is made without fear.

Literally to 'those who behave themselves without fear,' who can fearlessly govern Leviathan.

---

[175] *Solar Force.*

Job xlii, 1. Then Job answered the Lord, and said,

2. I know that thou canst do everything, and that no thought of thine can be hindered. [176]

Job after his Illumination recognises and is non-resistant to the Law of Nature, God, which wills obedience from all things.

---

[176] *Literal translation.*

GG.

THE HOLY LANGUAGE DESCRIBED BY EMMANUEL SWEDENBORG.

"The most ancient manner of writing was that of representing things by persons, and by words, by which was understood something altogether different from what was expressed. In such manner, indeed, that nothing was literally true just as it was written, but under these narratives something allegorical was understood. Thus they set forth the various affections under the forms of gods and goddesses, to which the heathen nations afterwards instituted Divine worship; which may be known to every scholar, since such ancient books are still extant. This method of writing they derived from the most ancient people, who lived before the flood, and who represented to themselves things heavenly and Divine, by such as are visible on the earth and in the world, and thus filled their minds and souls with joyous and delightful perceptions. The most ancient people as they had communication with spirits and angels, had no other speech than this, which was full of representatives, and in every expression of which there was a Spiritual sense. . . . Hence it may appear how far man afterwards removed himself from heaven: when, at this day, he does not even know that there is in the Word anything else than what appears in the letter, not even that there is a spiritual sense; and whatever is mentioned beyond the sense of the letter is called mystical, and rejected on that account. Hence also it is that communication with heaven is at this day intercepted, insomuch that few believe there is any heaven, and, what is surprising, much fewer amongst the learned and erudite than amongst the simple." ARCANA COELESTIA, TRANSLATION OF COUNTESS OF CAITHNESS IN "THE MYSTERY OF THE AGES," PAGES 488-9.

SAMSON.

Of "these marvellous men filled with strength" was Samson. Concerning his mother, the wife or Manoah, of Zorah, of the family of the Danites, we read the following in the Book of Judges, xiii, verses 6, 7, and 24. "Then the woman came and told her husband, saying, A man of God came unto me, and his countenance was like the countenance of an angel of God, very terrible: but I asked him not whence he was, neither told he me his name: But he said to me, Behold, thou shalt conceive, and bear a son; and now drink no wine nor strong drink, neither eat any unclean thing: for the child shall be a Nazarite to God from the womb to the day of his death. " And the woman bare a son, and called his name Samson "--which is to say " Serving like the Sun."

HH.

MOSES AN INITIATE.

No less an authority than St. Paul, himself an Initiate, declares that "Moses was learned. in all the wisdom of the Egyptians," (*Acts vii, 22*). The Greek word Sophia (Wisdom) has the same root and cabalistically the same number (780) as the Greek word Ophis, (Serpent), and often signifies Wisdom of the Serpent, Solar Force, and is here used by St. Paul in this sense. We must, therefore, conclude that Moses was an Initiate, which conclusion is confirmed by Manetho, "high priest and scribe of the sacred adyta in Egypt and a citizen of Heliopolis" in the reign of Ptolemy, who makes the following statement, "It is said also that the priest, who ordained their polity and laws, was by birth of Heliopolis, and his name Osarsiph, from Osiris the god of Heliopolis: but that when he went over to these people his name was changed, and he was called Moyses." [177] In the Egyptian language the word Moses is spelled MSS, and means child, which word is not infrequently used in sacred writings with the meaning of Child of God or Initiate. [178] Accurately speaking, Moses is neither a surname nor a patronymic, but a title bestowed upon the leader of Israel by his followers in recognition of his God-enlightenment or Initiation. Thus we perceive Moses to have been an Initiate and a priest of Osiris, as well as the servant of Jehovah, and a channel through which the esoteric

---

[177] I. P. CORY, "ANCIENT FRAGMENTS," PAGE 181.
[178] COMPARE *Isaiah lxv., 20, Luke xviii., 17.*

teachings of Egypt flowed into the Jewish, Christian and Muhammedan religions, moulding their inner Truth in its own likeness. "That which is called the Christian Religion existed among the ancients, and never did not exist, from the beginning of the race until Christ came in the flesh, at which time the true religion which already existed began to be called Christianity." (*St. Augustine*).

THE BRAZEN SERPENT.

In sacred writings letters not only have hidden meanings but numerical values as well. And the key to many sacred allegories is concealed in the numbers represented by the words used. Thus we find a clue to the meaning of the story of the Brazen Serpent in the fact that, according to the Rabbis, the number of the word Messiah and of the Hebrew word for serpent are identical, being 358.

Book of Numbers, chapter xxi, verses 5-9.

5. "And the people spake against God, and against Moses, Wherefore have ye brought us up out of Egypt to die in the wilderness? for there is no bread,Ineither is there any water; and our soul loatheth this light bread." In this verse the children of Israel are portrayed as turning from divine direction and giving way to the desires of the carnal nature.

6. And the Lord sent fiery serpents among the people, "The Hebrew word here used for serpent is

Saraph, which properly signifies to burn," [179] and may he literally translated as Serpent Fire, Solar Force. And the Lord sent the Serpent Fire among the people, and because they had given way to their lower natures, the manifestations of this Force "bit (burned) the people, and much people of Israel died."

7. "Therefore the people came to Moses, and said, We have sinned, for we have spoken against the Lord, and against thee; pray unto the Lord, that he take away the serpents from us. And Moses prayed for the people.

8. And the Lord said unto Moses, Make thee a fiery serpent, and set it upon a pole: and it shall come to pass, that every one that is bitten, when he looketh upon it shall live." This verse states plainly that Moses was direéed to place before his followers the image of the serpent lifted up, or direted upward upon a pole, that "those who were bitten," those in whom the Serpent Fire was manifesting ungoverned to their destruction, might have knowledge of its upward diretion, govern it, be regenerated and live.

9. And Moses made a serpent of brass, and put it upon a pole, and it came to pass, that if a serpent had bitten any man, when he beheld the serpent of brass, he lived. In the Gospel of St. John, [180] iii, 14, we read "and just as Moses lifted high the serpent in the Desert, so must the Son of Man be. lifted up

---

[179] *Cruden's Concordance, Page 628, Ed. 1855.*
[180] *Testament in Modern Speech.*

266

in order that every one who trusts in him may have the Life of the Ages" (literally of the Solar Force). [181] This verse intimates that the serpent and the Son of Man or Messiah are manifestations of the same Divine Force, a fact which their identity of numerical value indicates and which Masonry confirms, "In the Templar and Philosophical degrees, the serpent is an emblem of Christ." *The Royal Masonic Cyclopædia, page 663.*

---

[181] *Compare Saint Paul an Initiate*

II.

BOOK OF THE WARS OF THE LORD.

"Wherefore it is said in the book of the Wars of the Lord, What he did in the Red Sea, and in the brooks of Arnon." NUMBERS xxi, 14.

This is the only known reference to this work extant. From its title, Hebrew scholars conclude that the Book of the Wars of the Lord contained songs celebrating the victories of the Israelites under the leadership of J HWH. Modern critics regard Numbers xxi, verses 17-18, 27, and following, as extracts from this book.

JJ.

SACRED FIRE.

As for the sacred fire, the vestal virgins took it up, together with other holy relics and fled away with it: though some will have it, that they have not the charge of any thing but that ever-living fire which Numa appointed to be worshipped. as the principle of things. It is indeed the most alive thing in Nature. PLUTARCH'S " LIFE OF CAMILLUS."

KK.

NOAH, VESTA AND EGERIA.

Among all races there exists the tradition of a great flood. And in the more evolved civilisations and religions a profound allegory has been framed upon this circumstance, the mystery of which is somewhat illuminated by the Comte's pleasantries. Since Oromasis is the Sun behind the Sun, [182] and since Vesta is the Essence of all things, to state that Vesta is the bride of Oromasis is equivalent to saying that Vesta is the feminine or negative aspect of Primordial Force or Fire. Thus Noah is seen to symbolise the spiritual evolution of man in relation to the Divine Force in its positive and negative aspects, union of which generates the Solar consciousness on earth, and in man when non-resistant to the divine will. Zoroaster and Egeria typify supreme manifestations of this Force..

---

[182] *Plato, The Cratylus.*

LL.

PRINCE DE MIRANDE AND THE CABALA.

GIOVANI FRANCESCO PICO DELLA MIRANDOLA,

1463 A.D.--1494. A.D.

In the year 1486, this celebrated Italian Philosopher, fell in with an impostor who showed him sixty Hebrew Codices and persuaded him that they had been compiled by order of Esdra, and contained the most recondite mysteries of religion and philosophy. In his "Apologia," the Prince de Mirande writes, "When I had bought these books at no moderate price, and had read them with utmost diligence and with indefatigable toil, I saw in them as God is my witness not so much Mosaic. as Christian religion."

MM.

JAPHET.

The Comte's identification of Zoroaster with Japhet is merely a manner of stating that these names represent equivalent manifestations of the same Divine Force. In Masonry the Cabalistic tradition as to this Force has been maintained. When the order of Knights Templar was founded, supposedly by Hugh, Godfrey and others, their leader was in reality a Master whose true name and identity remained unknown,--in reverent memory of whom, as the source from which they received their instruéion, they erected in the seven towered walls of their cities of refuge, one tower higher than the rest, and facing towards the East which they called the tower of Japhet.

ZOROASTER.

"'The sun is sometimes called in Persian *Zartushti* or *tasht-i-zer*, the golden orb (zer, gold; tasht, a disk). And in honour of the sun, I conceive, was named the celebrated philosopher *Zerdusht*, whom the Greeks have called *Zoroaster*, retaining the first part of his name, but altering the -se.cond, into Αστρον, equivalent in their language to the Persian *tasht*, an orb or disk.' It may be added, that the first Zoroaster was evidently mythical (probably a mere name for the sun himself)." THE JOURNAL OF THE ROYAL ASIATIC SOCIETY OF GREAT BRITAIN AND IRELAND. NEW SERIES, VOL. iii, PART I, 1867, PAGES 10, 11. CONTRIBUTIONS TOWARDS A GLOSSARY OF THE ASSYRIAN LANGUAGE BY H. F. TALBOT.

NN.

NYMPH OF STAUFFENBERG.

Now we will add a true story concerning a Nymph of Stauffenberg. She was of marked beauty and took her seat by the roadside waiting for the master whom she had chosen for herself. These things, it is true, are thought by some theologians to be mere mockeries and trickeries of the Devil--not however by true theologians. What can be more important in the Scriptures than to negleft nothing, to weigh everything honestly and faithfully, to digest with a sober and attentive judgement, to scrutinize everything every where with accuracy, and to despise nothing unknown. Whence it is clear that these persons lightly and supinely pass over these things, being ignorant of the truth, and pleading detersions of the Devil though the Devil himself is not known to them. It should be reflected that such marvels are permitted by God to the end that we may not all of us marry and live with Nymphs, but only one here and one there, so that the wonderful works of God among his creatures may be revealed and a surer knowledge of them spread abroad. Had these been the works of the Devil, doubtless they had deserved contempt. But they are not. The Devil cannot do such things, but only God. But let us return to our story. This Nymph had been a Water Nymph, and had married this citizen of Stauffenberg already mentioned. . . . Many other events of like nature have occurred, but by an evil example are passed over with contempt. From which the signal folly of men is abundantly clear.

PARACELSI LIBER DE NYMPHIS, ETC., TRACTATUS iv.
Translated from the Latin edition of the works of Paracelsus.
Published at Geneva in 1658. Vol. ii.

OO.

MAGDALEN OF THE CROSS.

"The mention of these Nunnes puts me in mind of that famous story in Wierus of Magdalena Crucia, first a Nunne, and then an Abbatesse of a Nunnery in Corduba in Spain. Those things which were miraculous in her were these; that she could tell allmost at any distance how the affairs of the world went, what consultations or transactions there were in all the nations of Christendome, from whence she got to herself the reputation of a very Holy woman and a great Prophetesse. But other things came to pass by her, or for her sake, no lesse strange and miraculous; as that at the celebrating of the Holy Eucharist, the Priest should allwayes want one of his round wafers, which was secretly conveyed to Magdalen, by the administration of Angelis, as was supposed, and shee receiving of it into her mouth ate it; in the view of the people, to their great astonishment and high reverence of the Saint. At the elevation of the Host Magdalen being near at hand, but yet a wall betwixt, that the wall was conceived to open and to exhibite Magdalen to the view of them in the chappell, and that thus she partaked of the consecrated bread. When this Abbatesse came into the chappell herself upon some special day, that she would set off the solemnity of the day by some notable and conspicuous miracle: For she would sometimes be lifted up above the ground three or foure cubits high; other sometimes bearing the Image of Christ in her armes, weeping savourly, she would make her haire to increase to that length and largenesse that it would come to her heels, and cover her all over and the Image of Christ in her armes, which anon notwithstanding would shrink up again to its usuall size." DR. HENRY MORE THE PLATONIST, FELLOW OF CHRIST COLLEGE, CAMBRIDGE. "AN ANTIDOTE AGAINST ATHEISM." EDITION 1653, PAGES 117-18.

PP.

CASSIODORUS RENIUS OR REYNA,

1520-30 A.D.--1594 A.D.

Was born at Seville in Spain. His chief work was pp a scholarly translation of the Old and New Testaments into Spanish. His defence of Magdalen of the Cross occurs in a rare treatise on the fourth chapter of St. Matthew, "de periculis piorum ministrorum verbi in tempore cavendis," published with his "Evangelium Joannis" in 1573 at Frankfurt, where he lived for some years prior to his death.

QQ.

GERTRUDE, NUN OF THE MONASTERY OF NAZARETH IN THE DIOCESE OF COLOGNE.

"Now this evil had begun with a certain Gertrude who had been shut up in the monastery at the age of fourteen. . . Moreover, I found out that the said girl had written to her lover outrageous letters, which were later discovered during the course of the investigation made by me in the same college on 25th May, A.D. 1565, in the presence of that man of eminent nobility and wisdom Constantine of Lyskerk, a most worthy magistrate, of John Altena formerly Dean of Cleves, of John Echte a most accomplished physician, and of my son Henry, doctor of philosophy and medicine, that these letters, however, were produced by her while possessed of the devil and not in her sound senses is open to no reasonable doubt." TRANSLATED FROM "JOANNIS WIERI OPERA OMNIA," AMSTERDAM, 1660, PAGE 305.

RR.

ROMULUS.

BIRTH.--But, in my opinion, the origin of so great a city, and the establishment of an empire next in power to that of the gods, was due to the Fates. The vestal Rhea, being deflowered by force, when she had brought forth twins, declares Mars to be the father. . . . TITUS LIVY, HISTORY OF ROME. BOOK I, CHAPTER IV.

TRANSLATION.--"On the nones of Qintilis or on the Quirinalia, as the king was reviewing his people, the Sun withdrew its light; and while the earth lay in darkness, Mars descended in a hurricane and tempest, and bore away his perfected son in a fiery chariot to heaven." B. G. NIEBUHR, THE HISTORY OF ROME, VOL. i, PAGE 197.

SS.

SERVIUS TULLIUS.

"The birth of Servius Tullius was as marvellous as it was humble. Ocrisia, a handmaid of the queen, and one of the captives taken at Corniculum, when bringing some cakes as an offering to the household genius, saw an apparition of the god in the fire on the hearth: Tanaquil commanded her to array herself as a bride and shut herself up in the chapel. She became pregnant by a god: many Romans called the household genius the father of Servius, others Vulcan (God Of Fire)." HISTORY OF ROME BY B. G. NIEBUHR. TRANSLATED BY J. C. HARE, M.A., AND C. THIRLWALL, M.A., VOLUME I, PAGE 311.

"At that time, a prodigy occurred in the palace, wonderful both in its appearance and in its result. They relate, that the head of a boy, called Servius Tullius, as he lay fast asleep, blazed with fire in the sight of many persons. That by the very great noise made at so miraculous a phenomenon, the royal family were awakened; and when one of the servants was bringing water to extinguish the flame, that he was kept back by the queen, and after the confusion was over, that she forbade the boy to be disturbed till he should awake of his own accord. As soon as he awoke the flame disappeared. Then Tanaquil, taking her husband into a private place, said, 'Do you observe this boy whom we bring up in so mean a style? Be assured that hereafter he will be a light to us in our adversity, and a proteIor to our palace in distress. From henceforth let us, with all our care, train up this youth, who is capable of becoming a great ornament publicly and privately.' From this time the boy began to be treated as their own son, and instructed in those arts by which men's minds are qualified to maintain high rank. The matter was easily accomplished, because it was agreeable to the gods." TITUS LIVY, HISTORY OF ROME, BOOK I, CHAPTER 39.

TT.

HERCULES.

Throughout the world's history, the life stories of the supreme Spiritual teachers, or Saviours of mankind, have been so identical in incident that a thoughtful comparison of them leads inevitably to the conclusion that to be *"a priest forever after the order of Melchizedek " is to fill a definite office and to perform a predetermined work in the transmission of spiritual force for the liberation of human souls.* For example, the parallelism between the lives of Hercules and of Christ is so close that orthodox writers admit Hercules to have been a type of that which the Christ was to accomplish and to endure. And the Rev. Mr. Faber identifies the Greek with the Christian Theology in the following passage: "On the sphere he (Hercules) is represented in the act of contending with the serpent, the head of which is placed under his foot: and this serpent, we are told, is that which guarded the tree with golden fruit in the midst of the garden of the Hesperides. But the garden of the Hesperides, as we have already seen, was no other than the garden of Paradise: consequently, the serpent of that garden, the head of which is crushed beneath the heel of Hercules, and which itself is described as incircling with its folds the trunk of the mysterious tree, must necessarily be a transcript of that serpent whose form was assumed by the tempter of our first parents. We may observe the same ancient tradition in the Phenician fable respecting Ophion or Ophioneus." GEORGE STANLEY

FABER, B.D., "THE ORIGIN OF PAGAN IDOLATRY," VOL. i, PAGE 443.

UU.

MASTER DEFINED.

A Master is an evolved being who has perfected a mental body[183] in which he can function consciously while out of his physical vehicle. A Master, through that degree of Divine Force which his rapidly-evolving Solar Body enables him to contact, has power to understand and to apply many of the laws governing the so-called phenomena of Nature.

Dante Alighieri makes mention of his first meeting with his Master in these words, "for there appeared to be in my room a mist of the colour of fire, within the which I discerned the figure of a lord of terrible aspect to such as should gaze upon him, but who seemed therewithal to rejoice inwardly that it was a marvel to see. Speaking he said many things, among the which I could understand but few; and of these, this: *Ego dominus tuus* (I am thy Master)." LA VITA NUOVA. TRANSLATED BY DANTE GABRIEL ROSSETTI.

---

[183] *Air Body*

Portrait of a Master. Painted by R. Owned by the Brothers

VV.

ROMAN WORSHIP OF A SUPREME DEITY WITHOUT IMAGE OR STATUE.

"Numa forbade the Romans to represent the Deity in the form either of man or beast. Nor was there among them formerly any image or statue of the Divine Being; during the first hundred and seventy years they built temples, indeed, and other sacred domes, but placed in them no figure of any kind: persuaded that it is impious to represent things divine by what is perishable, and that we can have no conception of God but by the understanding." PLUTARCH, LIFE OF NUMA.

WW.

RECENT TIDINGS OF THE ELEMENTARY PEOPLES?

The following document is "278 of 1912" in the records of the British Government Observatory at Bombay, India.

"At 7.30 p.m. on the 17th February, 1912, in Lat. 23° 37′ 01, Long. 67° 20′, E., 19 miles off the nearest point of land on the Kutch Coast, also 127 miles N.W. of the town of Dwarka, on the Kahiawar Coast, the weather at the time being very fine with a clear and cloudless sky, full of stars, sea smooth, wind moderate, breeze from N.W., the ship steaming 9 knots and perfectly steady: we steamed into the most curious and weird atmospheric phenomena it has been my lot to see in all my forty years' experience of a sea life.

As we approached it, it had the appearance of breakers on a low beach, but when we got into it, at first it looked like flashes of light (not bright) coming from all directions in quick time. After some few minutes of this, the flashes assumed a lengthened shape, following quickly one after the other from the North, and these continued for some minutes, steadily veering to the East and South and to S.W. into N.W. All the time this was going on, the surface of the sea appeared to be violently agitated, at times very high seas as if they would completely engulf the ship; *the imagined waves always going in the same direction as the waves of light*, and, at the time, the waves of light were from opposite directions. At the same time *the sea appeared like a boiling pot*, giving one a most curious feeling, *the ship being perfectly still*, and expecting her to lurch and roll every instant.

It turned me dizzy watching the moving flashes of light, so that I had to close my eyes from time to time. We were steaming in this for twenty minutes and then passed out of it, the same appearance on leaving it as we saw approaching it, as of breakers on a low beach, and for twenty minutes everything around assumed its normal condition, a beautiful fine, clear and cloudless night.

At the end of this time we again saw the same thing ahead of the ship, and in a few minutes were fairly amongst it again, but if anything slightly worse, the waves of light acting in precisely a similar manner, this second lot lasting about fifteen minutes; when we again steamed out of it and saw nothing any more all the night until our arrival off Karachi at 2.30 a.m. on the 18th. When the flashes of light passed over, the sea appeared just for that instant of time to be full of jelly fish, but I do not think there were any about. I have seen the white water many times in this Arabian Sea, but this did not appear like that in any way. It gave one the idea of the cinematograph without the brightness, the flashes being so quick in their movements."

(Signed) H. BRADLEY,

Master of S.S. "Ariosto," Wilson Line.

In a letter addressed to the Dire6tor of the Astronomical Department of the Government Observatory at Bombay, Captain Bradley affirms that the above is "certainly as plain a statement of what occurred as I am able to give, the barometer 30.154, thermometer attached 76 in ship's saloon. Thermometers on bridge in wood case, dry bulb 75 and wet bulb 71. At noon ship's barometer in chart room 29.81, thermometer attached 76. When before mentioned barometer 30.142 att., ther. 78. These instruments belong to the Meteorological Office, LONDON, for whom I have the honour of keeping a log on my voyage, and to whom I am sending a copy of this paper. The ship's barometer is an aneroid, the office barometer a Mercurial one. The ship's is 33 feet above the waterline, and the other 20 feet."

XX.

TYRESIAS,

A native of Thebes, was the most celebrated prophet of all antiquity, and during his lifetime honoured as a God. His daughter Manto instituted the famous Oracle of the Clarian Apollo which foretold the untimely death of Germanicus.

YY.

MERLIN'S PROPHECY OF THE CONQUEST OF THE AIR AND OF AERIAL AND SUBMARINE WARFARE.

THE CONQUEST OF THE AIR. "Nitentur, posteri transvolare superna." Posterity shall endeavour to fly above the highest places.

AERIAL WARFARE.

In tempore illo loquentur lapides & mare quo ad Galliam navigatur, infra breve spacium contrahetur. In utraque ripa audietur homo ab homme, & solidum insulæ dilatabitur. Revelabuntur occulta submarinorum & Gallia præ timore tremebit.

Post hac ex Colaterio nemore procedet ardea, quæ insulam per biennium circumvolabit. Nocturno clamore convocabit volatilia & omne genus volucrum associabit sibi. In culturas mortalium irruent, & omnia grana messium devocabunt (devocabunt) [184] Sequetur fames populum, atque dira mortalitas famen.

TRANSLATION.

At that. time stones shall speak, and th, sea where crossing is made to go to Gaul shall be abridged to a short distance. A man upon one shore shall be

---

[184] *Usual reading.*

heard by a man upon the other, and the territory of the island shall be enlarged. Hidden things under the sea shall be discovered, and Gaul shall tremble for fear. After this a heron shall come forth from the Colaterian Grove which shall fly about the island for two years. With noturnal clamour she shall assemble the winged nations and shall ally with herself all manner of flying things. They shall attack agriculture and charm away (devour) all the grain of the harvests. Famine shall result among the people and dire mortality from the famine.

SUBMARINE WARFARE.

Favillæ rogi mutabuntur in cygnos, qui in sicco, quasi in flumine natabunt. Devorabunt pisces in piscibus & homines in hominibus deglutient. Superveniente vero senetute efficientur submarinæ luces atque submarinas insidias machinabuntur. Submergent navalia & argentum non minimum congregabunt.

The sparks of destruction shall be changed into swans which shall sail upon dry ground as upon a river. They shall devour fishes among the fishes and shall swallow up men among men. Indeed when the age grows old[185]submarine lights shall be

---

[185] *Superveniente vero Senectute.* These words are usually taken to mean "But when old age comes upon them." Senectus, however, has the meaning when used metonymically of "the old skin, slough of serpents." (*Smith, Latin-English Dictionary, page* 1014.) And since the inventions described have been made in the present period when the Sun behind the Sun is coming into conjunction with the Sun of our Solar system and regenerating its Force,

skilfully contrived and they shall plot submarine ambushes. They shall submerge naval arsenals and collect not a little money.

Senectute appears to be an allusion to the skin of the World Serpent--Solar Force--which presses upon it (*Superveniente*) as the age grows old, and prior to the advent of that new epoch in evolution on this planet which the closer approach of the Parent Sun ever initiates. LATIN TEXTS TAKEN FROM MERLIN AMBROSII BRITTANI, ETC. FRANCOFURTI TYPIS JOACHIMI BRATHERINGIJ, MDCIII.

AAA.

CHERUBIM,

Signifies in Hebrew fulness of knowledge. This name is used by Cabalists to denote Beings of that Heavenly Hierarchy ranking below the Seraphim, and charged with the duty of adjudging and of answering prayers according to the Law. Ezekiel thus describes them, "their appearance was like burning coals of fire, and like the appearance of lamps: it went up and down among the living creatures; and the fire was bright, and out of the fire went forth lightenings." EZEKIEL i, 13.

AAA. Part 2.

THE BIRTH OF JESUS AS RELATED IN THE KORAN

The Moslem world acknowledges and reverences the divine mission of Jesus, "And to Jesus, son of Mary, gave we clear proofs *of his mission*, and strengthened him by the Holy Spirit," (Koran Sura 2,) and holds that he was miraculously born. A statement of this belief is to he found in the Koran Sura 19.

"And make mention in the Book, of Mary, when she went apart from her family, eastward,

And took a veil to shroud herself from them: and we sent our spirit to her, and he took before her the form of a perfect man.

She said: 'I fly for refuge from thee to the God of Mercy I If thou fearest Him, begone from me.'

He said: 'I am only a messenger of thy Lord, that I may bestow on thee a holy son.'

She said: 'How shall I have a son, when man bath never touched me? and I am not unchaste.'

He said: 'So shall it be. Thy Lord path said 'Easy is this with me;' and we will make him a sign to mankind, and a mercy from us. For if is a thing decreed.'

And she conceived him, and retired with him to a far-off place.

This is Jesus, the son of Mary; this is a statement of the truth concerning which they doubt

It beseemeth not God to beget a son. Glory he to Him! When he decreeth a thing, He only saith to it,

Be, and it IS."

BBB.

PROCLUS ON PRAYER.

"To a perfect and true prayer however, there is required a conformation of our life with that which is divine; and this accompanied with all purity, chastity, discipline, and order, through which our concerns being introduced to the Gods, we shall attract their benificence, and our souls will become subject to them. In the third place, contact is necessary, according to which we touch the divine essence with the summit of our soul, and verge to a union with it. But there is yet farther required, an approximating adhesion: for thus the oracle calls it, when it says, *the mortal approximating to fire will possess a light from the Gods*.[186] For this imparts to us a greater communion with, and a more manifest participation of the light of the Gods.

In the last place, union succeeds establishing *the one* of the soul in *the one* of the Gods, and causing our energy to become one with divine energy; according to which we are no longer ourselves, but are absorbed as it were in the Gods, *abiding in divine light, and circularly comprehended by it.* And this is the best end of true prayer, in order that the conversion of the soul may be conjoined with its permanency, and that everything which proceeds from *the one* of the Gods, may again be established in *the one*, and the light which is in us may be comprehended in the light of the Gods.

---

[186] "*For [according to the oracle] the rapid Gods perfect the mortal constantly employed in prayer.*" PROCLUS.

Prayer therefore, is no small part of the whole ascent of souls. Nor is he who possesses virtue superior to the want of the good which proceeds from prayer. The perfedion however of prayer, beginning from more common goods, ends in divine union, and gradually accustoms the soul to divine light.

All nations likewise, that have excelled in wisdom, have diligently applied themselves to prayer."

PROCLUS ON THE TIMAEUS OF PLATO. EXTRACTS, BOOK II, PAGES 176, 175, 179.

CCC.

LORD OF BAVARIA.

"Sabine in his comment on the I oth of Ovid's Metamorphoses, at the tale of Orpheus, telleth us of a gentleman of Bavaria, that for many months together bewailed the loss of his dear wife; at length the Devil in her habit came and comforted him, and told him, because he was so importunate for her, that she would come and live with him again, on that condition he would be new married, never swear and blaspheme as he used formerly to do; for if he did, she should be gone: he vowed it, married, and lived with her, she brought him children, and governed his house, but was still pale and sad, and so continued, till one day falling out with him, he fell a swearing; she vanished thereupon, and was never after seen. This I have heard, saith Sabine, from persons of good credit, which told me that the Duke of Bavaria did tell it for a certainty to the Duke of Saxony."

ROBERT BURTON, "THE ANATOMY OF MELANCHOLY."
YORK LIBRARY EDITION, VOL. iii, PAGE 51.

DDD.

THE SABBAT.

The following definition of the Sabbat is translated from the "Dictionnaire Infernal" by Collins de Plancy, and is cited as a typical example of those imbecilities which the Comte deprecates.

"The Sabbat is the assembly of devils, sorcerers and witches in their nocturnal orgies. Usually they are there engaged in doing or in plotting evil, in causing fear or terror, in preparing witchcraft and abominable mysteries. The Sabbat is held at a place where several roads cross, or in some deserted and wild spot near a lake, pool, or marsh, because hailstorms are there made and tempests manufactured."

EEE.

ZEDEKIAS.

A Jewish physician who lived in the ninth century. He was greatly in favour with the Emperor Charles the Bald, whose medical attendant he had been. He is said, further more, to have been so great a wizard that once in the presence of the court he ate a whole load of hay, together with the driver and the horses; that at other times he flew around in the air and played other such juggling tricks.
TRANSLATED FROM ZEDLER, UNIVERSAL LEXICON.

FFF.

KAROLI MAGNI ET LUDOVICI PII CHRISTIONISS:--CAPITULA.

There are assuredly some who perform diverse evil FFF deeds, whom the divine law also frowns upon and condemns, and for whose diverse ill deeds and crimes the people are grievously punished with famine and pestilence, while the state of the Church is weakened and the kingdom endangered. Against these we, taking a most serious view of their wickedness (sternly anathematized though it is in Holy. Scripture) have thought it meet by admonition and exhortation to take all possible precautions. For they claim that by their evil ads they can confound the air and send down showers of hail, foretell the future, rob a man of his fruit and milk and give them to others, and numberless ads are said to be performed by such men. When men or women of this sort are discovered, the more openly they fear not to serve the devil with their rash and heinous daring, the more severely must they be punished by the unsparing rigour of the prince. Concerning these it is also written in the Ancyritan Council, chapter xxiii: "those who seek out divinations and follow after them after the manner of the Gentiles, or bring men of such sort into their houses in order by mischievous ads to seek out anything or atone for anything, are to be imprisoned for five years according to the degrees of punishment appointed. This must be done in all places, and especially so in those where many men trust that can do deeds of this sort lawfully and with impunity, to the end that may be admonished with the greater zeal and diligence and punished the more severely. TRANSLATED FROM "KAROLI MAGNI ET LUDOVICI PII CHRISTIONISS:--CAPITULA SIVE LEGES ECCLESIASTICÆ ET CIVILES." PARIS, 1603. EXTRACT ADDITIO ii, C. 18. " Of the diverse crimes of evil-doers."

GGG.

MAGICIANS SENT BY GRIMALDUS, DUKE OF BENEVENTUM.

A few years ago a certain folly was spread abroad. There had been a great mortality among cattle; and it was said that Grimaldus, Duke of Beneventum, had sent men with powders to scatter over fields, mountains, meadows and springs, for the reason that he was an enemy to the most Christian Emperor Charles, and that the cattle had died by this same powder. For this cause many were arrested, as we heard and indeed saw; some were killed, most fastened to boards, thrown into the river, and so sent to death. And what is highly astonishing, the persons arrested testified against themselves, stating that they had had such a powder and had scattered it. AGOBARDUS, LIBER DE GRANDINE ET TONITRUIS, CAP. xvi.

HHH.

779 A.D. AGOBARD, 840 A.D.

BISHOP OF LYONS.

The record of the date of the birth inscribed by his own hand is extant in Bede's Martyrology, which is preserved at Rome. This book states that Agobard was born in Spain and came to France when three years of age. At thirty-seven he became Archbishop of Lyons, and was one of the most celebrated and learned prelates of the ninth century.

COMMENTARY CONCLUDED

SEVEN ANCIENT PROPHECIES

OF

WORLD PEACE.

TRUTH IS JUSTICE

AND THE

MESSENGER OF PEACE

TO

MANKIND.

"The paternal self-begotten intellect disseminated in all things the bond of love, heavy with fire, that all things might remain loving for an infinite time ; that the connected series of things might intellectually remain in all the light of the Father ; and that the elements of the world might continue running in love." PROCLUS.

FIRST PROPHECY.

THE MAGI'S PROPHECY OF WORLD PEACE AND A UNIVERSAL LANGUAGE.

It is the opinion and belief of the majority of the most ancient sages . . . that there will come a fated and predestined time when the earth will be completely leveled, united and equal, there will be but one mode of life and but one form of government among mankind who will all speak one language and will live happily. TRANSLATED FROM PLUTARCH, "ISIS AND OSIRIS," §47.

SECOND PROPHECY.

THE SIBYLLINE PROPHECY OF WORLD PEACE AND THE REIGN OF JUSTICE.

The Kingdom of God shall come upon good Men; for the Earth, which is the producer of all things, shall yield to Men the best, and infinite Fruits; . . . and the Cities shall be full of good Men, and the Fields shall be fruitful, and there shall be no War in the Earth, nor Tumult, nor shall the Earth groan by an Earthquake; no Wars, nor Drought, or Famine; nor Hail to waste the Fruits; but there shall be great Peace in all the Earth, and one King shall live in Friendship with the other, to the End of the Age; and the Immortal, who lives in the Heavens adorned with Stars, shall give a common Law to all Men in all the Earth, and instruct miserable Men what things must be done; for he is the only God, and there is no other; and *he shall burn the great Strength of Men by Fire.*

Then he shall raise a Kingdom for ever over all Men, when he hath given a Holy Law to the Righteous, to all whom he promised to open the Earth; and the World of the blessed, and all Joys, and an immortal Mind, and Eternal chearfulness. Out of every Country they shall bring Frankincense, and Gifts to the Houses of the Great God, and there shall be no other House to be enquired for by the Generations of Men that are to come, but the faithful Man whom God has given to be worshiped, for Mortals call him the Son of the

310

Great God; and all the Paths of the Fields, and rough Shores, and high Mountains, and the raging Waves of the Sea, shall be easily passed, or sailed through in those Days for all Peace shall happen to the Good, through all their Land, the Prophets of the Great God shall take away all Slaughter, for they are the Judges of Mortals, and the righteous Kings. And there shall be just Riches for Men, for the Government of the Great God shall be just Judgement. [187]

Now no longer shall gold and silver be full of guile, nor shall there be possessing of land nor toilsome slavery; but one love and one ordering of life in kindness of soul. All things shall be common and light equal in the lives of men. Vice shall leave the earth and be sunk in the divine ocean. Then is the summer of mortal men nigh at hand. Strong necessity will be laid upon (the world) that these things be accomplished. No wayfarer meeting another will then say: "The race of mortal men, though now they perish, shall some day have rest." And then a holy people shall wield the sceptre of the whole world through all the ages, along with their mighty offspring. TRANSLATED FROM THE GREEK "SIBYLLAE," BOOK xiv, CONCLUSION.

---

[187] *Sir John Ployer, "The Sibylline Oracles," Book iii, Extracts pages 80-2.*

THIRD PROPHECY.

ENOCH'S PROPHECY OF WORLD PEACE AND THE GIVING FORTH OF BOOKS.

"And now I know this mystery, that sinners will alter and pervert the words of righteousness in many ways, and will speak wicked words, and lie, and practise great deceits, [188] and write books concerning their words. [189]

But when they write down truthfully all my words in their languages, and do not change or minish ought from my words but write them all down truthfully--all that I first testified concerning them,

Then, I know another mystery, that books shall be given to the righteous and the wise to become a cause of joy and uprightness and much wisdom.

And to them shall the books be given, and they shall believe in them and rejoice over them, and then shall all the righteous who have learnt therefrom all the paths of righteousness be recompensed.

In those days the Lord bade (them) to.summon and testify to the children of earth concerning their wisdom: Show (it) unto them; for ye are their guides, and a recompense over the whole earth.

---

[188] *"Create a great creation."*
[189] *"And compose books in their own words."*

312

For I and My Son will be united with them for ever in the paths of uprightness in their lives; and ye shall have peace: rejoice, ye children of uprightness. [190] Amen." R. H. CHARLES, D.LITT., D.D., TRANSLATION OF THE BOOK OF ENOCH, CHAPTERS civ, 10-13, cv.

---

[190] *"Rejoice, children of integrity, in the truth."*

FOURTH PROPHECY.

MICAH'S PROPHECY OF WORLD PEACE AND FREEDOM OF RELIGION.

But in the last days it shall come to pass, that the mountain of the house of the Lord shall be established in the top of the mountains, and it shall be exalted above the hills; and people shall flow unto it.

And many nations shall come, and say, Come, and let us go up to the mountain of the Lord, and to the house of the God of Jacob; and he will teach us of his ways, and we will walk in his paths: for the law shall go forth of Zion, and the word of the Lord from Jerusalem.

And he shall judge among many people, and rebuke strong nations afar off; and they shall beat their swords into plowshares, and their spears into pruning hooks: nation shall not lift up a sword against nation, neither shall they learn war any more.

But they shall sit every man under his vine and under his fig tree; and none shall make them afraid: for the mouth of the Lord of hosts hath spoken it.

For all people will walk every one in the name of his god, and we walk in the name of the Lord our God for ever and ever. MICAH, CHAPTER iv, VERSES 1-5.

FIFTH PROPHECY.

ELDER EDDA

PROPHECY OF WORLD PEACE AND RETURN OF THE ANCIENT WISDOM.

"The bond shall be broken, the Wolf [191] run free; hidden things I know; still onward I see the great Doom of the Powers, the gods of war.

I see uprising a second time earth from the ocean, green anew; the waters fall, on high the eagle flies o'er the fell and catches fish.

The gods are gathered on the Fields of Labour; they speak concerning the great World Serpent, [192] and

---

[191] **INTERPRETATION ELDER EDDA PROPHECY.**
THE WOLF.--"Fenrir or Fenrisúlfer. The monster-wolf. The gods put him in chains, where he remains until Ragnarok (the last day). In Ragnarok he gets loose, *and* swallows the sun . . . "(Norse Mythology. R. V. Anderson, A.M.) The Fenris Wolf symbolises the Super Solar Force operative for the regeneration of mankind when the Sun behind the Sun is in conjunction at the end of the age with the Sun of our own Solar system. Hence the Wolf is said to run free in the last day, and to swallow the Sun.
[192] THE GREAT WORLD SERPENT.--All-Father "threw the serpent into that deep ocean by which the earth is encircled. But the monster has grown to such an enormous size, that holding his tail in his mouth he engirdles the whole earth." The serpent is the Solar Force (Thomas Carlyle, "Heroes and Hero Worship.") manifesting ungoverned in the unpurified lower nature of man during the present cycle of evolution.

remember there things of former fame and the Mightiest God's old mysteries. [193]

Then shall be found the wondrous-seeming golden tables hid in the grass, those they had used in days of yore. [194]

And there unsown shall the fields bring forth; all harm shall be healed; Baldr [195] (the Saviour) will come--Höd (the Adversary) and Baldr shall dwell in Val-hall, at peace the war gods.--Would ye know further, and what? . . . Comes from on high to the great Assembly the Mighty Ruler [196] who orders all. Fares from beneath a dim dragon flying, a glistening snake from the Moonless Fells.

EXTRACTS FROM "THE SOOTH SAYING OF THE VALA." OLIVE BRAY'S TRANSLATION, THE ELDER OR POETIC EDDA, PAGES 295-7.

---

[193] THE MIGHTIEST GOD'S OLD MYSTERIES.--The ancient Wisdom shall be given anew to the world by those who guide its evolution.

[194] GOLDEN TABLES HID IN THE GRASS.--The Solar Flame or Spirit evolving in man shall bring back to his consciousness the books of his lost remembrance.

[195] BALDR.--"Balder, again, the White God, the beautiful, the just and benignant (whom the early Christian Missionaries found to resemble Christ)."

[196] THE MIGHTY RULER.--The Christ Ray or Paraclete of which Baldr is the supreme manifestation on earth, and the Fenris Wolf or regenerative force its cosmic expression. This is a ray of the Divine Consciousness operative on this planet when the Sun behind the Sun is in conjunction with the Sun of our Solar System. At this time the vital energy or Solar Force tends to be balanced by Spiritual energy or Super Solar Force, and the spirit of man seeks anew its Divine Source.

SIXTH PROPHECY.

BIBLE PROPHECY OF WORLD PEACE DECLARING THE MANNER OF ITS ACCOMPLISHMENT.

How beautiful upon the mountains are the feet of him that bringeth good tidings, that publisheth peace; that bringeth good tidings of good, that publisheth salvation; that saith unto Zion, Thy God reigneth!

Thy watchmen shall lift up the voice; with the voice together shall they sing: for they shall see eye to eye, when the Lord shall bring again Zion.

The Lord hath made bare his holy arm in the eyes of all the nations; and all the ends of the earth shall see the salvation of our God.

Behold, my servant shall deal prudently, he shall be exalted and extolled, and be very high.

So shall he sprinkle many nations; the kings shall shut their mouths at him: *for that which had not been told them shall they see; and that which they had not heard shall they consider.* ISAIAH, CHAPTER lii., VERSES 7, 8, 10, 13, 15.

INTERPRETATION.

Proof that this prophecy has not been as yet fulfilled lies in the fad that no Saviour has arisen whom the Jews have recognised as such; whereas they were promised a messenger from God whom they should know, "Therefore my people shall know my name: therefore they shall know in that day that I am he that doth speak:" ISAIAH lii, 6. Their prophets of old foretold the coming of a Giver of the Law to the Nations whom Israel should acknowledge and follow. The covenant of the Most High is sure, and the fulfillment of His promise shall not fail.

MOUNTAINS.

The word mountains is often used in the Old Testament to signify those higher levels of consciousness wherein the Law of God is understood and obeyed. The prophet is able to ascend into these states of consciousness and descending, retains and makes known to his fellowmen a knowledge of divine concerns. Man in the flesh is encompassed by illusion, a wanderer in the valley of the shadow. Let him lift up his eyes unto the hills whence cometh his help, seeking "for the precious things of the lasting hills," hearkening for "the sounding again of the mountains." DEUTERONOMY xxxiii, 15. EZEKIEL. vii, 7.

The feet upon the mountains are that manifestation of the Messenger which is nearest to earth. Upon the higher levels of consciousness the prophet is conscious of this Divine Influence to which the generality of mankind are not at the period, consciously subject.

WATCHMEN.

The meaning of the word watchmen is indicated by *Ezekiel iii, 17.* "Son of man, I have made thee a watchman unto the house of Israel: therefore hear the word at my mouth, and give them warning from me." In this sense of the word, the watchmen are the witnesses of the Lord whose advent Muhammed foretells in his Prophecy of Truth.

The word "watchmen" has also an inner meaning which is revealed in *Ecclesiasticus xxxvii, 14,* where, after exhorting the disciple to heed the counsel of his own heart (higher nature), the Sage warns him against the danger of being led astray by the mind ever the prey of illusion when not governed by the soul. "For a man's mind is sometime wont to tell him more than seven watchmen, that sit above in an high tower." Used in this sense, the word watchmen signifies the seven principal ganglia of the sympathetic system[197] which when awakened and energised by the inflowing Solar Force establish in man superphysical states of consciousness, and endow him with knowledge of the Law of Nature, God, which wills obedience from all things. The answer given by the Oracle at Delphi when questioned regarding Proclus sheds light upon the mystical meaning of this verse, "Oft when the bolts. of thy mind willed of their own impulse to follow crooked ways, the deathless ones set them aright to move in their fixed curves and eternal path and gave to thine eyes the frequent

---

[197] Compare The Inmates of the Cave or the Story of the Seven Sleepers

gleam of lights that from their night-shrouded watch-tower they might clearly see." TRANSLATED FROM THE GREEK, PORPHYRIUS,, DE VITA PLOTINI §22.

FOR THEY SHALL SEE EYE TO EYE.

That this inner meaning of the word watchmen is also intended is shown by the explanatory phrase, "for they shall see eye to eye." The word eye is not infrequently employed in the sacred writings of Israel to denote these ganglia or focussing centres of the Divine Force, "Those seven; they are the eyes of the Lord," *Zechariah iv, 10.* To say that the watchmen shall see "eye to eye," is to say that these ganglia shall be energised, and joined "eye to eye," by the currents of the Solar Force, and that man shall become God-enlightened.

To arrive at a just estimate of Hebrew word values in the Old Testament, it is necessary to bear in mind that the language and religion of Egypt exercised an appreciable influence upon the Jews during their captivity. The word "eye," used in the sense here noted, is an instance of this influence. To the Egyptians, the "Sun behind the Sun" was known as Osiris, [198] whose name was written by the hieroglyph of the eye, and also by that of the scarabeus. Of this species of beetle, no female is known to exist. The male scarabeus pro- duces the element of life, rolls it in a ball of earth, and leaves it to be brought to birth by the warmth and life-giving force of the Sun. Hence the scarabeus

---

[198] *Compare The Principle of All Things*

became the fitting symbol of the Divine or Solar Spark in man, placed in the earth sphere that it may be regenerated and brought to "the birth from above" by the rays of the Solar Force. "The so-called scarabeus, the great cockchafer of southern countries, was considered an especially mysterious and sacred animal, and the figure of this insect was almost as symbolic to the followers of the Egyptian religion as the cross is to the[199]Christian." [200] Under the New Empire, the Egyptians replaced the heart of the dead by a stone scarabeus, emblem of Osiris, [201] and, as it were, a finite symbol of the Omnipotent Eye of the Sun behind the Sun, and an enduring expression of their prayer that the departed soul might receive that Creative Light which would perfect its immortal evolution and bring it to the Everlasting Land. This use of the scarabeus bears mute witness to the fad that there existed in Ancient Egypt, knowledge concerning that centre in the human heart whose awakening or 'lifting up' to a higher plane of evolution or consciousness reveals to man the vista of his immortal destiny. A proof that Israel also had this knowledge is found in *Ecclesiaticus xvii, 8.* " He set his eye upon their hearts, that he might shew them the greatness of his works."

Primarily applied to the manifestation of the force of the Sun behind the Sun in the human heart, the

---

[199] *Christ is called "The Sun-rising from on high," Luke i, 78.*
[200] *Adolf Erman "Life in Ancient Egypt." Page 315.*
[201] *"Homage to thee, O Governor of those who are in Amentel, who dost make men and women to be born again."* PAPYRUS OF HU-NEFER.

word eye came in course of time to denote the centres of the cerebro-spinal [202] and sympathetic nervous systems, and especially the seven principal centres of the latter, whose perfecting brings man into greater knowledge and love of God. "For the eyes of the Lord are upon them that love him, he is their mighty protection and strong stay, a defence from heat, and a cover from the Sun at noon, a preservation from stumbling, and an help from falling. He raiseth up the soul, and lighteneth the eyes: he giveth health, life, and blessing." *Ecclesiasticus xxxiv, 16, 17.* "The statutes of the Lord are right, rejoicing the heart: the commandment of the Lord is pure, enlightening the eyes." *PSALM XIX, 8.*

THE LORD HATH LAID BARE HIS HOLY ARM.

The word here translated Lord is "YHWH, the (ineffable) name of God." "These substitutions of 'Adonay' and Elohim' for YHWH were devised to avoid the profanation of the Ineffable Name." [203] But Elohim, exoteric name of YHWH (Jehovah), is the Sun behind the Sun. The holy arm of the Lord is therefore seen to be a ray of its Divine Force. This Force is more or less potent on earth according to cyclic law. At the beginning and end of the age, the Sun behind the Sun is in conjunction with the .Sun of our Solar System, and its energy, descending deep into matter, brings to birth God-enlightened men; which the prophet states

---

[202] *The back-bone was sacred to Osiris.*
[203] *Jewish Encyclopedia, Vol. vii Pages 87, 88.*

figuratively when he says that this Divine or Super-Solar Force shall manifest "in the eyes of all the nations." "Awake, awake, pat on strength, O arm of the Lord; awake, as in the ancient days, in the generations of old. Art thou not it that hath cut Rahab, and wounded the dragon. ?" *Isaiah li, 9.*

SO SHALL HE SPRINKLE MANY NATIONS.

And thus shalt thou do unto them, to cleanse them: Sprinkle water of purifying upon them, *Numbers viii, 7.* Then will I sprinkle clean water upon you, and ye shall be clean. . . A new heart also will I give you, and a new spirit will I put within you. . . . And I will put my spirit within you, and cause you to walk in my statutes, and ye shall keep my judgments, and do them. EZEKIEL xxxvi, EXTRACTS VERSES 25-27.

CONCLUSION.

This prophecy foretells the cyclic return of that Force, subtle in character but positive in demand, which proceeds from the Lord and Giver of Life, the Great Architect of the Universe, the Supreme Source. This Divine Ray liberates the souls of its servants in every nation that they may labour as one for the establishment of Truth, Justice and Peace.

SEVENTH PROPHECY.

MERLIN'S PROPHECY OF WORLD PEACE AND ENLIGHTENMENT.

A man shall grasp the lion within the earth, and the brightness of gold shall blind the eyes of those who behold it. Silver shall be of brilliant whiteness upon the circumference and shall disturb the different wine-presses. Mortals shall be drunk with the wine set forth for them and from a deferred heaven shall look back upon the earth. Their stern faces shall turn the stars from them and shall confound their usual course. They shall plow fields for those who are unworthy and for those to whom the moisture of heaven shall be denied. Roots and branches shall change places and the newness of the world shall be a miracle. The brilliance of the Sun shall be tarnished by Mercury's alloy of gold and silver and there shall be dread among those who investigate. Stilbon of Arcadia shall change the disk of the Sun. The helmet of Mars shall call for Venus. The helmet of Mars shall cast a shadow. Iron Orion shall unsheathe his sword. The Phoebus of the sea shall trouble the clouds. The madness of Mercury shall pass all bounds. Jupiter shall. forsake his lawful paths, and Venus shall desert the lines appointed for her. The ill will of the star Saturn shall subside, and it shall hinder mortals with a crooked sickle. The twelve houses of the stars shall deplore the transition of their guests. Gemini shall forego their accustomed embraces and shall call the urn to the fountains. The scales of Libra shall hang obliquely until Aries shall put his curved horns under them. The tail of Scorpio shall produce lightnings and Cancer shall quarrel with the Sun. Virgo shall mount the back of Sagittarius and shall dim the flower of her virginity. The chariot of the Moon shall disturb the Zodiac and the Pleiades break forth into weeping. Hereafter the offices of Janus shàll never return but his gates shall lie hid in the interstices of Ariadne's crown. The waters shall rise at the stroke of a wand and the labour of the ancients shall be recreated. The winds shall strive together with an awful blast and shall make their sound among the stars.

LATIN TEXT OF MERLIN'S PROPHECY.

Amplexabitur homo leonem in humo, & fulgor auri oculos intuentium excæcabit. Candebit argentum in circuitu, & diversa torcularia vexabit. Imposito vino inebriabuntur mortales, postpositoque coelo in terram respicient. [Postpositoque e coelo in terram respicient]. Ab eis vultus avertent sidera, & solitum cursum confundent. Arebunt segetes his indignantibus & humor convexi negabitur [Arabunt segetes hi indignis quibus humor convexi negabitur]. Radices & rami vices mutabunt, novitasque rei erit miraculo. Splendor Solis electro Mercurij languebit, & erit horror inspicientibus. Mutabit clypeum Stilbon Arcadiæ. Vocabit Venerem Galea Martis. Galea Martis umbram conficiet. Nudabit ensem Orion ferreus, vexabit nubes Phoebus æquoreus. Transibit terminos furor Mercurij. Exibit Jupiter semitas licitas & Venus deseret statutas lineas. Saturni sideris livido corruet & falce recurva mortales perimet. Bissenus numerus domorum syderum deflebit hospites ita transcurrere. Omittent Gemini complexus solitos, & urnam in fontes provocabunt. Pensa libræ obliquæ pendebunt, donec aries recurva cornua sua supponat. Cauda scorpionis procreabit fulgura, & cancer cum sole litigabit. Ascendet virgo dorsum sagittarij & flores virgineos obfuscabit. Currus Lunæ turbabit Zodiacum, & in fletum prorumpent Pleiades. Officia Jani mina redibunt, sed clausa Janua in crepidinibus Ariadnæ delitebit. In ictu radij exurgent æquora & pulvis veterum renovabitur. Confligent venti diro suffiamine& sonitum inter sidera conficient.

The Latin texts used are taken from Prophetia Anglicana, Merlini Ambrosii Britanni, ex incubo olim (ut hominum fama est) ante annos mille ducentos circiter in Anglia nati, Vaticinia & praedictiones: à Galfredo Monumetensi Latinè conversæ: una cum septem libris explanationum in eandem prophetiam, excellentissimi sui temporis Oratoris, Polyhistoris & Theologi, Alani de Insulis, Germani, Dotoris (ob admirabilem & omnigenam eruditionem, cognomento), Universalis & Parisiensis Academiæ, ante annos 300, Rectoris Amplissimi.

Opus nunc primum publici juris factum, & lectoribus ad historiarum, præcipue vero Britannicæ, cognitionem, non parum lucis allaturum. Francofurti Typis Joachimi Bratheringij, MDCIII.

NOTE ON TEXT.

The various rescensions of the text of Merlin's Prophecy exhibit marked differences. The fad that a single word, the fifth in line one, is read in four different ways [204] is but one proof out of many which might he adduced as evidence that the original manuscript has been much corrupted in transcription. Since certain passages of the text as it now stands bear no relation to the general tenor of the Prophecy they have been emended, these emendations being inserted in brackets and followed in the translation.

INTERPRETATION OF MERLIN'S PROPHECY.

A man shall grasp the lion within the earth, and the brightness of gold shall blind the eyes of those who behold it..

The first lines of this Prophecy describe the coming of the World-Saviour and its results. He is the man who shall grasp or understand and govern the lion, Solar Force and its action in the earth, the physical body. The brightness of gold, that is of the Saviour's golden or Solar Body [205], I shall blind the eyes of those who behold it.

Silver shall be of brilliant whiteness upon the circumference,

---

[204] *Humo, uno, auro, vino.*
[205] The Solar Body is the Spiritual Body.

As gold is used mystically to signify that which is Solar or spiritual, so silver is employed to symbolise that which is intellectual. To say that silver shall be of brilliant whiteness upon the circumference of the gold is equivalent to saying that brilliant minds shall gather about the Manifested Spiritual Light.

and shall disturb the different wine-presses.

Wine is the symbol of the blood of Christ or spiritual life of the church. Hence the wine-presses (the instruments through which spiritual life should flow into the world) are the churches. Brilliant minds inspired by the Manifested Light shall radiate the truth which they are receiving and shall trouble and disturb the different churches and their theological concepts of truth.

Mortals shall he drunk with the wine set forth for them and from a deferred heaven shall look back upon the earth.

Mortals shall be intoxicated with the spiritual truth given out to them, and from a state of felicity long deferred shall look back upon their earthly or former conditions.

Their stern faces shall turn the stars from them and shall confound their usual course.

Through knowledge of the Law governing Solar Force man shall gain power to awaken those ganglia corresponding to the planets[206] and thereby controlling the planetary forces manifesting in him, shall unfold the immortality of his own being and become the master of his destiny.

"It is said that a wise man rules over the stars; but this does not mean that he rules over the stars in the sky, but over the powers that are active in his own mental constitution." PARACELSUS, PHILOSOPHIA OCCULTA.

They shall plow fields for those who are unworthy and for those to whom the moisture of heaven shall be denied.

The more evolved will work for the lesser evolved hitherto enslaved by religions of men's own thought creation, and will seek to bring them into a realisation of God's truth and omnipotence.

Roots and branches shall change places and the newness of the world shall be as a miracle.

The spinal cord is "just like a tree with its innumerable branches covering the whole of the human body, the roots being upwards-- and the branches downwards." [207] The spinal cord is the tree whose roots and branches are here mentioned, and connects those minor brain centres which are seats of the higher consciousness in man and which when energised enable him to draw spiritual nourishment and illumination

---

[206] *Compare Interior Stars*
[207] *Uttara Gila. D. K. Laheri's Translation, page 28.*

from the heaven-world". "As trees by their extremities are rooted in the earth, and through this are earthly in every part, in the same manner divine natures are rooted by their summits in the One." PROCLUS. To-day man is rooted in the earth. To-morrow, awakening to a consciousness of his divine nature, he shall be rooted in the One, and such radiation of Spiritual Light will result that the newness of the world will be a miracle.

Here ends the prophecy of the coming of the World Saviour, and some lines are now devoted to a description of the era in which these events will occur.

The brilliance of the Sun shall be tarnished by Mercury's alloy of gold and silver and there shall be dread among those who investigate.

Spiritual knowledge and truth shall be tarnished and obscured by teachings which are intellectual rather than spiritual.

Stilbon of Arcadia shall change the disk of the Sun.

Stilbon is a Latinised form of the Greek ὁ Στίλβων, the Shining One, a name given in antiquity to the planet Mercury;while Arcadia is a district in Greece which latterly became so identified . with the cult of Hermes (Mercury) that Statius terms the caduceus of the Messenger of the Gods *virga Arcadia,* [208] the Arcadian rod. Stilbon of Arcadia would therefore appear to be a reference to the Messenger of the Gods or World

---

[208] *Thebais ii, 70.*

Teacher who shall change the disk of the Sun, cause men to regard the Sun in its true light. Aristotle in the De Mundo [c. 2] says, But the multitude of the planets being collected into seven parts, is distributed into as many circles. . . . Stilbon is the next (circle) in order, which some say is sacred to Hermes, but others to Apollo." Hermes is the God of Intellect, Apollo the Sun God and radiator of spiritual light and life. Hence it is not improbable that by the beautiful title Stilbon of Arcadia, Merlin obscurely signifies the tenor of the coming ministry to mankind which is destined to inspire an intelledtualism vivified by spiritual realisation.

The helmet of Mars shall call for Venus.

Mars "was worshipped at Rome as the god of war, and war itself was frequently designated by the name of Mars." * Similarly Venus signifies love. The armour of war shall call for love. The armament of war will become Aso terrible as to compel love among the nations.

The helmet of Mars shall cast a shadow.

There shall be war.

Iron Orion shall unsheathe his sword.

"Orion, a handsome giant and hunter. Having come to Chios, he fell in love with Merope, the daughter of Oenopion; his treatment of the maiden so exasperated her father, that, with the assistance of Dionysus, he deprived the giant of his sight. Being informed that he should recover his sight if he exposed his eye-balls to the rays of the rising sun, Orion found his way to the island of Lemnos, where Hephaestus (God of Fire) gave him Cedalion as his guide, who led him to the East. After the recovery of his sight he lived as a hunter along with Artemis. After his death, Orion was placed among the stars, where he appears as a giant with a girdle, sword, a lion's skin and a club."[209] Orion typifies the enlightened soul descended deep into matter who, through giving way to his lower nature, loses his spiritual vision and after many tests and trials regains his divine birthright through the healing power of the Solar Force or Sun manifesting in man, being at last clothed with Light. The girdle, sword, lion's skin and club are symbols of Initiation; the sword being emblem of Justice and the Divine Law; the lion's skin of the lower nature slain for the clothing of the God in man. Orion symbolises the Initiate and his story recounts the progress of his Initiation. The meaning is that an Initiate or God-enlightened man shall unsheathe that sword which is the emblem of Divine Justice and God's Great Law,--shall reveal the Law of Nature, God, which wills obedience in all things.

The Phoebus of the sea shall trouble the clouds.

The Phoebus of the sea is the Moon which symbolises the soul of man, and the clouds are the illusion which encompasses it when incarnate. The soul of man again awakening into a realisation of its true purpose shall endeavour to penetrate and dispel the

---

[209] *Smith's Smaller Classical Dictionary.*

illusion which enthralls it and prevents its mastery of the mind.

The madness of Mercury shall pass all bounds.

"Mercury presides over every species of erudition."[210] The folly of man-made theories about Nature shall exceed all limits. Dominating intellects will struggle for supremacy over that which is divine.

Jupiter (Justice) shall forsake his lawful paths, and Venus (Love) shall desert the lines appointed for her. The ill-will of the star Saturn shall subside, and it shall hinder mortals with a crooked sickle.

The crooked sickle is the Moon. A favourable aspect of Saturn to the Moon makes operative the sterling qualities of Saturn, restraint and a true sense of justice. Under such an aspect, the ill will of Saturn would subside. The word perimet (hinder) is used in this sense only when governing an abstract object. Mortales (mortals) must therefore stand for an abstrat idea, signifying the trend of mortal evolution which shall be hindered or restrained in its present course by a manifestation of Divine Justice. Saturn is said to bridge the gap between the mortal and the immortal natures of man, and similarly that which separates the mortal from the immortal evolution of the race. It is the property of this planet to crystalise events, or bring them to a crisis, in order that their lesson may be learned, and their experience garnered and transmuted into

_____

[210] *Thomas Taylor.*

that truth which is justice, and which brings divine realisation and spiritual progress.

Merlin appropriately places Saturn after a prophecy of war and the confusion of mortal concerns, and before his concluding words which shadow forth the immortal destiny of the race.

The twelve houses of the stars (the twelve signs of the Zodiac) shall deplore the transition. of their guests. Gemini shall forego their accustomed embraces and shall call the urn to the fountains,

Gemini, "the well-known heroes Castor and Pollux. Although they were buried, says Homer, yet they came to life every other day, and they enjoyed divine honours. Castor, the mortal, fell by the hands of Idas, but Pollux slew Lynceus. At the request of Pollux, Zeus allowed him to share his brother's fate, and to live alternately one day under the earth, and the other in the heavenly abodes of the gods."[211] In this ancient myth the divine and mortal natures of man are represented by the brothers Castor and Pollux. To say that they shall cease their embraces is to imply that the divine, when understood by man, will be differentiated from the human, and that both will call the urn to the fountains of living waters, or consciously partake of the same essence. " He (the Sun) enters into Gemini at the time when the Pleiades rise." VITRUVIUS.

The scales of Libra shall hang obliquely until Aries shall put his curved horns under them.

---

[211] *Smith's Smaller Classical Dictionary.*

Libra is the sign of the Balance, while Aries "the ram is the principle of generation." [212] Balance cannot be achieved by man until the principle of generation is understood and applied for the awakening and lifting up of that Regenerative Force which is the instrument the soul uses to build up its Solar or Spiritual Body. The spiritual equilibrium of the world will be upset until the generative force in man is transmuted into Regenerative Power. [213]

The tail of Scorpio shall produce lightnings,

Scorpio represents the negative side of manifestation and here symbolises opposition. There shall be fiery opposition to the coming Spiritual Light.

and Cancer shall quarrel with the Sun.

Cancer represents power. Those in authority will quarrel with the Sun, oppose the coming of Spiritual Light, because it illu minates the ignorant and dethrones segregated forces.

Virgo shall mount the back of Sagittarius and shall dim the flower of her virginity.

Virgo is the virgin or woman, while Sagittarius is the house of Jupiter, the giver of the law or holder of authority. It is possible to interpret this as an allusion to the present feminist movement.

---

[212] *Compare Dual Aspect of Solar Force*
[213] *Proclus.*

"Astrea in the mythology of the ancients, was the goddess of Justice, who resided on earth during the reign of Saturn, or the golden age. Being shocked by the impiety of mankind, she returned to heaven, and became one of the twelve signs of the Zodiac, under the name of Virgo."

The chariot of the Moon shall disorder the Zodiac,

The Moon or soul of humanity is here represented as progressing and thereby upsetting and disturbing existing conditions.

and the Pleiades break forth into weeping.

The Pleiades were seven in number, six of whom are described as visible and the seventh as invisible. The Pleiades were virgin companions of Artemis and, together with their mother, were pursued by the hunter Orion in Boeotia; their prayer to be rescued from him was heard by the gods, and they were metamorphosed into doves, and placed among the stars." [214]

The Pleiades represent the seven principal ganglia of the sympathetic nervous system, pursued by the Initiate Orion who seeks to energise them. When energised (when the Divine Force flows through them) they are said to weep[215] and through prayer are changed into doves. The dove has been in marry ages the symbol of the Super Solar Force. To say

[214] *Smith's Smaller Classical Dictionary.*
[215] *"Theologists also signify the extension of the Solar Providence to mortal natures through tears." Proclus on the Timaeus of Plato. T Taylor's Translation, page 95.*

that the Pleiades become doves is to say that they become vehicles of the Super Solar Force, and energised by it appear as stars. Thus "the Pleiades break forth into weeping" means that at a certain period of evolution the ganglia of the sympathetic nervous system shall be highly energised, and men shall become God-enlightened and no longer subject to illusion.

Hereafter the offices of Janus shall never return,

There shall be no more war. "Janus occupied an important place in the Roman religion. He was the porter of heaven. On earth also he was the guardian deity of gates. At Rome, Numa is said to have dedicated to Janus the covered passage bearing his name, which was opened in times of war and closed in times of peace." [216] "He has also a temple at Rome with two gates, which they call the gates of war." PLUTARCH but his gates shall lie hid in the interstices of Ariadne's crown.

"Ariadne's crown, which is one of the celestial constellations, who left the world in Saturn's reign, called the golden age." THE LIFE OF MERLIN. LONDON, .1813. PAGE 275. Ariadne's crown here symbolises the advent of the golden age which shall cause wars to cease.

The waters shall rise at the stroke of a wand,

The waters are influenced by the Moon, and symbolically represent feeling or soul expression which

---

[216] *Smith's Classical Dictionary.*

shall flood the world when the magician, World Saviour, shall come. The wand of the magician is the spinal column energised by the power the Paraclete can give to man. This is the power Moses had, and which before Moses built up ancient Egypt.

and the labour of the ancients shall be recreated.

Thus translated this passage may be taken to signify the return of the Ancient Wisdom brought back by old souls incarnate for this purpose; or literally rendered means "the dust of the ancients shall be restored." When the generality of mankind become enlightened, and understand the profound spiritual purpose which inspired the Egyptians to preserve their dead, they will return the sacred relics which they have in their ignorance desecrated.

The winds shall strive together with an awful blast, and shall make their sound among the stars.

These are the "winds" of the Apocalypse (anemoi) or differentiations of the Solar Force manifesting in the cerebro-spinal system, and when man is able to sustain their inflow, they shall make their sound among the stars, energise the cerebro-spinal centres. These centres when energised are visible to the seer as rapidly revolving stars of great luminosity and restore to man super-physical states of consciousness. For the purpose of clear statement we have refrained from differentiating Lunar from Solar and Super Solar Force in this book. The Pleiades[217] are the ganglia of the sympathetic nervous system energised by Lunar Force, while the stars here referred to, are the centres of the cerebro-spinal system, vehicles of Solar Force. The sympathetic and cerebro-spinal systems are thus prepared to sustain the inflow of the Super Solar Force, the Redeemer and Regenerator of mankind and the world.

"And He hath subjected to you the night and the day; the sun and the moon and the stars too are subjeeted to you by his behest; verily, in this are signs for those who understand: KORAN SURA xvi. THE BEE. EVERYMAN'S LIBRARY EDITION, PAGE 201.

Wherefore let God be exalted, the King, the Truth! There is no god but He! Lord of the stately throne!" KORAN SURA xxiii. THE BELIEVERS, PAGE 150.

TRUTH.

---

[217] *"Companions of Artemis,"* (*Diana the Moon Goddess.*)

MUHAMMED'S PROPHECY OF TRUTH.

"TO ITS OWN BOOK SHALL EVERY NATION BE SUMMONED."

1. "Men have rent their great concern, one among another, into seéts; every party rejoicing in that which is their own;

Wherefore leave them till a certain time, in their depths of error.

2. One day God will call to them and say, 'Where are my companions as ye supposed them?'

And we will bring up a witness out of every nation and say, 'Bring your proofs.' And they shall know that the truth is with God alone, and the gods of their own devising shall desert them.

3. And thou shalt see every nation KNEELING *to its own book shall every nation be summoned:*"

THE KORAN. I, SURA xxiii, THE BELIEVERS; 2, SURA xxviii, THE STORY; 3, SURA xlv, THE KNEELING. EVERYMAN'S LIBRARY EDITION.

JUSTICE.

ISRAELS' PROPHECY OF JUSTICE.

Behold, I will send my messenger, and he shall prepare the way before me: and the Lord, whom ye seek, shall suddenly come to his temple, even the messenger of the covenant, whom ye delight in: behold, he shall come, saith the Lord of hosts.

But who may abide the day of his coming? and who shall stand when he appeareth? for *he is like a refiner's fire*, and like fullers' soap:

And he shall sit as a refiner and purifier of silver: and he shall purify the sons of Levi,[218] and purge them as gold and silver, that they may offer unto the Lord an offering in justice. [219]

Then shall the offerings of Judah and Jerusalem be pleasant unto the Lord, as in the days of old, and as in ancient years.

And I will come near to you to judgement; . . . .

But unto you that fear my name shall the Sun of Justice t arise with healing in his wings;-MALACHI iii, 1-5, iv, 2.

---

[218] Priests.
[219] Literal translation.

THE MESSENGER.

PROPHECY OF THE MESSENGER AND OF THE STONE THAT SHALL BE SET UP IN EGYPT.

In that day shall five cities in the land of Egypt speak the language of Canaan, and swear to the Lord of Hosts; one shall be called "The City of the Sun."

In that day shall there be an altar [220]to the Lord in the midst of the land of Egypt, and a pillar at the border thereof to the Lord.

And it shall be for a Sign and for a Witness unto the Lord of Hosts in the land of Egypt: for they shall cry unto the Lord because of the oppressors, and He shall send them a Saviour, and a great one, and he shall deliver them.

And the Lord shall be known to Egypt, and the Egyptians shall know the Lord in that day, and shall do sacrifice and oblation; yea, they shall vow a vow unto the Lord, and perform it.

And the Lord shall smite Egypt: He shall smite and heal it[221]: and they shall return even to the Lord, and He shall be intreated of them, and shall heal them.

---

[220] *Literally a sacred stone shall be set up.*
[221] *Restore it.*

In that day shall there be a highway out of Egypt to Assyria, [222] and the Assyrian shall come into Egypt, and the Egyptian into Assyria, and the Egyptians shall serve with the Assyrians.

In that day shall Israel be the third with Egypt and with Assyria, even a blessing in the midst of the land: whom the Lord of Hosts shall bless, saying, "Blessed be Egypt, my people, and Assyria the work of my hands, and Israel mine inheritance." ISAIAH, CHAPTER xix, VERSES 18-25.

---

[222] *The Bagdad Railway is the beginning of this highway.*

"MY PORT PATERNAL IN THE COURTS OF LIGHT."

HYMN TO THE SOVEREIGN SUN.

'Tis thine by heat apparent to exalt
Corporeal natures from the sluggish earth,
Inspiring vivid, vegetative power;
And by a nature secretly divine,
And from the base alloy of matter free,
Inherent in thy all-productive rays,
Thou draw'st to union with thy wond'rous form,
Exalted souls, that in dark Hyle's realms
Indignant struggle for the courts of light:
All beauteous, seven-rayed, supermundane god!
Whose mystic essence secretly emits
The splendid fountains of celestial light.

All-bounteous god, by whom the soul is freed
From Generation's dark corporeal bands,

Assist THY OFFSPRING borne on mental wings,
Beyond the reach of guileful Nature's hands
Swift to ascend, and gain thy beauteous world.
The subtle vestment of my soul refine,
Etherial, firm, and full of sacred light,
Her ancient vehicle by thee assign'd
In which invelop'd, thro' the starry orbs,
Urg'd by the impulse of insane desire,
She fail'd precipitate, till Lethe's shore,
Involv'd in night, unhappily she touch'd,
And lost all knowledge of her pristine state.

'Tis thine, from multitude exempt, t' inspire
In forms subordinate, prophetic truth;
For truth and pure simplicity are one:
And of preserving unpolluted power,
Thy *liberated essence* is the source."

EXTRACTS FROM THE EMPEROR JULIAN'S ORATION
TO THE SOVEREIGN SUN.

19149581R00184

Made in the USA
Lexington, KY
08 December 2012